Domestic policy and ideology

Presidents and the American state 1964–1987

T0371457

Domestic policy and ideology

Presidents and the
American state 1964–1987

David McKay
Reader in Government, University of Essex

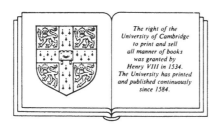

The right of the
University of Cambridge
to print and sell
all manner of books
was granted by
Henry VIII in 1534.
The University has printed
and published continuously
since 1584.

Cambridge University Press

Cambridge
New York   Port Chester
Melbourne   Sydney

CAMBRIDGE UNIVERSITY PRESS
Cambridge, New York, Melbourne, Madrid, Cape Town, Singapore, São Paulo, Delhi

Cambridge University Press
The Edinburgh Building, Cambridge CB2 8RU, UK

Published in the United States of America by Cambridge University Press, New York

www.cambridge.org
Information on this title: www.cambridge.org/9780521320337

First published 1989
This digitally printed version 2008

A catalogue record for this publication is available from the British Library

Library of Congress Cataloguing in Publication data
McKay, David H.
Domestic policy and ideology: presidents and the American state,
1964–1987/David McKay.
       p.   cm.
Includes bibliographies and index.
ISBN 0-521-32033-X
1. United States – Politics and government – 1945–   2. Federal
government – United States – History – 20th century.   3. United States –
Social policy.   4. Presidents – United States – History – 20th
century.   I. Title.
E839.5.M34   1989
320.973—dc19   89-518   CIP

ISBN 978-0-521-32033-7 hardback
ISBN 978-0-521-10220-9 paperback

Contents

Preface and acknowledgements

The briefest review of the major scholarly works in American politics over the last thirty years would reveal quite radical shifts in perceptions of which issues are important at any one time and how the major political institutions have dealt with them. Even over the last ten years perceptions have changed considerably. By 1980 the loose coalition which had held the Democratic Party together for so long seemed at last to be in terminal decline. At the same time, an incumbent Democratic President looked like confirming the critics' worst fears that the presidency was indeed a 'no-win' institution destined always to be the victim of a capricious Congress, a fickle public, predatory interest groups and an ever more complex international environment. Just one year later, however, a popular Republican President had won a famous victory by persuading Congress to accept a substantial reduction in federal taxes and expenditures. Claims of a 'Reagan Revolution' were premature, however, for although by 1988 the political agenda owed something to the Reagan experience, neither candidate for the presidency in that year was a Reagan-style ideologue. The Democrats failed to win the presidency but they were able to return some traditional Democratic issues such as child care and education to the centre of political debate.

These shifting perceptions tell us a great deal about the importance of leadership and especially presidential leadership in the American political system. Individual Presidents and candidates for the office can and do make a great deal of difference to what is debated and eventually legislated. At the same time Presidents are obviously constrained by what is always a complex and difficult political environment. This book is about the interaction between presidential policy preferences and this political environment. A major motivation for writing it was the conviction that contemporary scholarship has become so concerned with the constraints on the office that it has consistently underestimated the capacity of Presidents to shape the policy agenda.

The particular policies chosen for analysis – welfare and intergovernmental relations – reflect the author's longstanding interest in these subjects. Fortunately, these issues have also been a prominent part of the federal policy agenda over the last forty years. During the 1930s a new political regime was established which transformed the role of the American state in social policy provision. This New Deal regime is still with us, but the political forces accounting for its creation have declined, or at least have been transformed into new, less stable political coalitions. A new environment has emerged which I have characterized as regime fragmentation. In this new political context, presidents can enjoy enhanced opportunities to choose and formulate public policies, and to do so in ways which are relatively insulated from societal and Congressional pressures. These remain formidable obstacles at the legislative and implementation stages, of course, but the capacity to determine the agenda is a crucial one, and Presidents and their staffs can do more in this area than any other actor or institution in the system.

These agenda-setting powers are important in another sense: they give to the executive branch the potential for producing intellectually coherent and consistent policies. Congress, so we are told, cannot be expected to do this, because legislation is the product of trade-offs and compromises which are rarely in the public interest.

I owe a debt of thanks to a number of individuals and institutions. The British Economic and Social Research Council provided me with a Personal Research Grant during 1982–3 which enabled me to spend a prolonged period studying

American politics in general and American federalism in particular. During 1985 I was able to visit the Lyndon Baines Johnson Library in Austin Texas, thanks to a grant from the Johnson Foundation; I am grateful to Nancy Smith, one of the archivists at the library, for all the help she provided. I am equally grateful to Joan Lee Roberts of the Richard Nixon Archive in Arlington, Virginia, which proved to be an intriguing source of information into the ever more fascinating Nixon presidency.

The final stages of the book were completed while I was a Visiting Professor at the University of California, San Diego. I am grateful to the Political Science Department there for providing such an undisturbed environment for writing. A number of individuals have provided comments on the manuscript or parts of it, including Richard Champagne of the University of Wisconsin, Madison; Samuel Kernell of the University of California, San Diego; Richard Neustadt of Harvard University; Jon Tucker of the University of Essex, and Graham Wilson of the University of Wisconsin, Madison. I am particularly grateful to the anonymous reader provided by Cambridge University Press who gave me by far the most comprehensive critique not only of the analysis, but also of my sometimes infelicitous – and increasingly Americanized – English. All of the faults that remain are, of course, my own.

Finally, thanks to Kathy Klingenberg of the University of California, San Diego, who typed two of the chapters, and to Anne Slowgrove of the European Consortium for Political Research who struggled long and hard typing and retyping various chapters to produce acceptable final versions.

Abbreviations

ABA	American Bar Association
ACIR	Advisory Commission on Intergovernmental Relations
AFDC	Aid for Families with Dependent Children
AFL–CIO	American Federation of Labor – Congress of Industrial Organization
BJIP	Better Jobs and Incomes Plan
BOB	Bureau of the Budget
CBS	Central Broadcasting System
CCEA	Cabinet Council for Economic Affairs
CEA	Council of Economic Advisers
CEQ	Council on Environmental Quality
CETA	Comprehensive Employment and Training Act
DOT	Department of Transport
EITC	Earned Income Tax Credit
EOA	Economic Opportunity Act
EOP	Executive Office of the President
EPA	Environmental Protection Agency
ESEA	Elementary and Secondary Education Act
FAP	Family Assistance Plan
FR	Federal Register
FSS	Family Security System
GRS	General Revenue Sharing
HEW	Health, Education and Welfare
HHFA	Housing and Home Finance Agency
HHS	Health and Human Services
HUD	Housing and Urban Development, Department of
IGR	Intergovernmental relations

ISP	Income Security Plan
MSPB	Merit System Protection Board
NAPA	National Academy of Public Administration
NASA	National Aeronautics and Space Administration
OEO	Office of Economic Opportunity
OIRA	Office of Information and Regulatory Affairs
OMB	Office of Management and Budget
OPD	Office of Policy Development
OPE	Office of Planning and Evaluation
OPM	Office of Personnel Management
SES	Senior Executive Service
SRS	Social and Rehabilitation Service
SSI	Supplementary Security Income
UDAG	Urban Development Action Grants
URPG	Urban and Regional Policy Group
WHCF	White House Central Files
WHPO	White House Personnel Office
WHSF	White House Special Files
WIN	Work Incentive Program

1 The presidency, public policy and American political development

Introduction

This book is about the evolution of presidential domestic policy strategies and how these relate to American political development. It has become almost axiomatic that since the 1960s American political institutions have been in some sort of crisis. It is also accepted that while the moral basis of the crisis – concern about equality, economic efficiency, the US role overseas – has changed over time, the continuing problem centres on questions of governmental accountability. Whatever the institution involved, it is the abuse of power, the failure to forge policies in the public rather than the people's interest, and excessive bureaucratic and judicial discretion which have dominated the normative concerns of both scholars and public alike.

The political-science community has been assiduous in its efforts to catalogue the reasons for this crisis of public authority. Put simply, they relate to the interaction between an essentially unchanging constitutional framework – most notably the separation of powers, and important structural changes in American society and economy – most notably those which have contributed to a breakdown in traditional class, ethnic and regional allegiances. These changes have in turn contributed both to the erosion of political parties' classic role as coalition builders and to the rise of a new politics based on constellations of special or single-interest pressure-group power.[1]

While almost all democratic states have shared these problems in one variant or another, few countries have been obliged to endure an institutional structure which almost seems designed to inhibit effective policy-making. As an unusually fragmented collegial body, Congress is rarely able to formulate policy or order priorities in any coherent manner. Presidents are in turn constrained by Congress and by public opinion, organized interests and a hydra-like federal bureaucracy. Federalism and independent courts add further complexity to this problematic policy process. By the late 1980s, events (the budget and trade deficits, the Iran-Contra Affair) seemed to confirm the critics' worst fear: that American political institutions were incapable of resolving vital policy problems. Much of the criticism was focussed on the presidency, for in the absence of strong political parties and given the inherent fragmentation characteristic of Congress, the presidency is the only institution in the American system with the potential for national policy leadership. But, as almost every book and essay on the presidency tells us, recent incumbents in the office have almost always failed to realize this potential.

Underpinning this critique is a theoretical perspective on the institution which is shared by almost all modern scholars of the executive branch. This I will call the *bargaining model* of the presidency. So dominant is this model, not only in the study of the American presidency but in American political science generally, that it has almost assumed the status of normal science. Perhaps this is not surprising, given its theoretical simplicity and undoubted empirical application. Its origins lie in the work of Richard Neustadt and such pioneers of pluralist political science as Robert Dahl, Charles Lindblom and Aaron Wildavsky.[2] In essence, these scholars established that constitutional boundaries provided only a very rudimentary framework for political relations. Beyond the legal imperatives lay the reality of an American politics based on politics – negotiation, bargaining, persuasion, logrolling and compromise. As Neustadt so persuasively argued, Presidents were no less subject to this reality than other actors in the political firmament.[3] Perhaps the greatest strength of this model was its extraordinary adaptiveness. In both epistemological and empirical terms its resilience became increasingly apparent through time. Epistemologically it had an obvious appeal to an increasingly liberal, individualistic social science community. It made no *a priori* assumptions about equality and distributive justice. Who got what was determined by the interaction between self-interested political actors, groups and voters and a highly accessible and neutral political system. When, during the 1960s and 1970s, the system appeared to become more pluralistic as parties declined and a new politics of single- and special-interest politics evolved, the model appeared more rather than less relevant. In a startling act of intellectual metamorphosis, it was even able to reject its long-held assumption that institutional processes were value neutral and instead condemn them either for overproviding or distorting the pattern of public-goods provision. Such was the basis of the public-choice critique.[4] Throughout, however, it was rationally motivated actors and interests engaged in negotiations and bargaining who were the basic units of analysis.

As far as the presidency was concerned, further theoretical development within this paradigm has been largely absent. With one or two exceptions, students of public choice have ignored the presidency, their major interest in the executive being confined to analysing the behaviour of what is claimed are budget-maximizing bureaucrats.[5] Presidential scholarship remains firmly rooted in the earlier Neustadtian notion of president as bargainer.

Yet, while for most purposes undoubtedly convincing, the bargaining model tends to lead scholars away from asking certain questions about the institution and in particular how it has adapted over time to changes in the political environment. As always in social science, the established theoretical approach has moulded perception of the facts. In particular, the bargaining model can be faulted on the following grounds:

(1) By stressing the role of the President as a strategic actor in a complex political process, the model tends to be asymmetrically dynamic. Presidents tend to be judged by how well they react to this environment, rather than how they are able to change it. Of course, presidential style/leadership are considered important by almost all observers, but the central question for most students is how *appropriate* an incumbent's style or character is, given the prevailing political climate. Successful Presidents are those whose personalities and capacities are compatible with the needs of the system. Most scholars conclude that the increasing demands placed on the office by recent changes in turn require an exceptional personality type to fill the job. No such person has emerged from the nomination process for many years. Hence the present crisis. While all this is no doubt true, such a highly functional approach leads enquiry away from treating presidential ideology as an independent influence. A review of the leading texts on the institution reveals almost no reference to ideology in the indexes.[6] Ronald Reagan's unusual ideological commitments did produce some acceptance that ideology could be important,[7] but the established model seemed reconfirmed by the serious political difficulties characteristic of his second term.

More specifically, presidential preferences may have altered the political environment over recent years not only by changing the political agenda, but also by altering the strategy space available to presidents. Ideological coherence and determination may make some strategies more important than others. Right-wing ideology may create strategic opportunities not available to liberals and *vice versa*. Subsequent chapters will provide evidence of just such opportunities, drawn from the domestic presidencies of Johnson, Nixon, Carter and Reagan.

None of this is to suggest that presidential scholarship has ignored the independent influence of Presidents. Clearly historians have been absorbed almost exclusively with just this. Nor is it to suggest that the pioneers of the bargaining model were insensitive to presidential leadership. On the contrary, Richard Neustadt was writing at a time (the 1950s) when Presidents were obliged very much to operate 'in the shadow of FDR', whose impact on policy and on the office is unquestioned.[8] The claim is, rather, that recent changes in American society have led scholars to use versions of the bargaining model at the expense of other approaches.

(2) In particular, agenda studies of the presidency have tended to be neglected by the academic community. Few political scientists dispute the importance of agenda setting. More than twenty-five years ago E. E. Schattsneider noted that:

Political conflict is not like an intercollegiate debate in which opponents agree in advance on a definition of the issues. As a matter of fact, *the definition of the alternatives is the supreme instrument of power*, the antagonists can rarely agree on what the issues are because power is involved in the definition. He who determines what politics is about runs the country, because the definition of alternatives is the choice of conflicts, and the choice of conflicts allocates power.[9] (emphasis in the original)

Since then a number of impressive agenda studies have been produced, but most have addressed the subject very much in the context of the bargaining model of American politics. So Paul Light's *The President's Agenda* concludes that recent changes in American politics have converted the office into a 'no-win' institution. According to Light, Presidents now find it much more difficult to order priorities, compete with Congress, and build the coalitions necessary successfully to create and implement new agendas.[10] To be fair, the book was published before the full impact of the Reagan experience was apparent, but even so the clear impression is that the presidential agenda is determined more by uncontrollable external forces than by the preferences of Presidents themselves. This conclusion in part follows from the author's method. By searching for quantifiable patterns of behaviour drawn from interviews and the Office of Management and Budget's

(OMB) legislative clearance records, Light has difficulty distinguishing between important and less important innovations and he is not concerned with the development of policy in broader historical perspective. A more recent study by John Kingdon partly overcomes these problems by concentrating on how the agenda is created in just two policy areas (health care and the deregulation of transportation).[11] But Kingdon is concerned with the whole universe of agenda setting. He rightly asserts that new policies emerge as a result of a complex mix of inputs from Congress, groups, academia, the public, courts and the executive branch.[12] Kingdon is also right to identify the President and his staff as the single most important policy innovators in the system.[13] But the volume concentrates on the process of agenda setting during just one presidency (the Carter administration). We are told little about the development of policy over time, or about the relative importance of the selected policy areas in relation to others.

A developmental approach to the policy agenda

Within presidential scholarship, there is a natural tendency to divide the experience of the office into two broad historical periods: the modern presidency – post 1933 or possibly post 1939 – and the pre-modern presidency. As Fred Greenstein puts it: 'the transformation of the office has been so profound that the modern presidencies have more in common with one another in the opportunities they provide and the demands they place on their incumbents than they have with the entire sweep of traditional presidencies from Washington's to Hoover's'.[14] Again, emphasis on a common experience in the modern era – and especially the post-1968 presidency – puts great premium on the capacity of incumbents to react to essentially similar problems. This in turn has led many scholars to study the capacity of different presidencies to manage this complex environment – in other words, to provide the appropriate political leadership. Leadership skills are *ipso facto* crucial to the effective functioning of the institution and an impressive range of leadership studies have been produced in recent years.[15]

Certainly the present volume must be concerned with presidential leadership capacity, but it attempts to place such skills in the context of American political development. With Greenstein and others, the utility of dividing the presidency into the post- and pre- New Deal eras is acknowledged. But unlike many studies of the modern era – and by definition those that place the study of the institution in a longer historical perspective[16] – this book concentrates on political development *within* the modern era.

There is no question that the New Deal represented a major departure from the past, not only for the presidency but also for the role of political parties, Congress, the Supreme Court, and the integration of state and local governments into a national system. Since the 1960s, however, scholars seem broadly agreed that this regime is decaying or degenerating. The major indicators here are party identification, party organization and the fortunes of the Democratic Party.[17] Decline in all three is indisputable, but few observers have gone so far as to claim that some new regime has emerged to replace the old.[18] There are, of course, a number of ways in which the resilience of the New Deal regime can be measured. As suggested, those social and political forces responsible for its creation have declined. But in institutional and policy terms the situation is much more ambiguous. At the most basic level, the separation of powers does of course persist, as does the associated conflict between an essentially centralizing president and decentralist (if not always decentralizing) Congress. As far as policy is concerned it is true that Keynesian economics is less influential than it used to be. But as Herbert Stein has perceptively pointed out, it is not that Keynesianism had been replaced with some other doctrine – in spite of vigorous attempts. It is more accurate, in the context of a persistently large public sector and numerous, if less than complete, full-employment policies, to talk of a synthesis of Keynesianism with other economic philosophies.[19]

In social policy and intergovernmental relations, possibly the areas most strongly associated with the New Deal, it could be argued that the pattern of federal intervention is broadly similar to that established in the 1930s. To be sure, there have been major changes in magnitude and degree, but, as later chapters will catalogue, the basic framework of intervention has been remarkably resilient through time. This book is concerned both with the changes that have occurred within the New Deal framework, and with challenges to that framework. Very generally this pattern of intervention can be characterized in the following terms:

(a) An acceptance that distributive social security provision involving contributions through payroll taxes should be administered by the federal government with most benefits going directly to recipients. Generally, social security came to assume the status of a necessary and socially progressive programme.

(b) Re-distributive welfare payments should be administered through the states on a matching basis, benefits should be limited, selective and considered in some cases as temporary, emergency measures. Welfare came to assume the status of a widely unpopular but largely unavoidable group of measures necessary to provide minimal benefits for poorer citizens (mainly female-headed families).

(c) Housing and Community Development programmes (public housing and, from 1949, urban renewal) were administered largely via grants direct to local governments. Later, new grant programmes were organized on an *ad hoc* basis. Some went to local governments, some to the states. Some had extensive strings attached, others almost resembled block grants. In other words, no clear conception of the federal role underpinned federal aid.

This series of social-policy measures was the product of a highly political process whereby conservative (mainly southern and western) members of Congress compromised the more comprehensive plans of the New Deal liberals and their successors.[20] Social policy in the New Deal regime, therefore, developed as a result of a complex mix of ideological and institutional forces. It clearly lacked coherence. Unlike the British welfare state, it was not the almost exclusive product of a powerful social movement married to a dominant, ideologically united political party of the left. Instead it evolved on an *ad hoc* basis almost as a series of unrelated measures designed to meet what was perceived as a national emergency.

That it was improvised and inadequate in meeting the needs of large sections of American society is evidenced by the numerous efforts to reform the system ever since. While literally hundreds of bills have been introduced into Congress with this aim in mind, relatively few have been successful and those which have, have usually been the product of, or certainly endorsed by, a major presidential initiative. Indeed, if we examine the domestic agendas of the four Presidents under discussion in this volume, major social-policy reforms challenging the New Deal regime were initiated by all of them. And, with the exception of Jimmy Carter, these reforms dominated their early domestic agendas.

The reforms in question were:

JOHNSON: The early Great Society – most notably the War on Poverty and Model Cities legislation

NIXON: Welfare Reform [The Family Assistance Plan] and General Revenue Sharing

CARTER: Welfare Reform [The Better Jobs and Incomes Plan] and a National Urban Policy

REAGAN: The New Federalism [in part a major Welfare Reform] with the associated budget cuts of the 1981 Budget Reconciliation Act

These initiatives represent a remarkably consistent theme over a twenty-year period (the Ford experience is excluded because his tenure in office was so short and because he largely inherited the Nixon agenda). Each President dealt with these problems in very different ways, however, and in every case the new President exercised great discretion over the actual content of the reforms. Even so, the policy achievements or failures of each President to some extent influenced the choices of subsequent incumbents. In fact, a relatively clear developmental pattern is discernible through time which is intimately related to the ideological preferences and substantive policy content of successive Presidents' reforms. Naturally Presidents have been constrained, thwarted or otherwise influenced by Congress, the courts, organized interests, public opinion, the federal bureaucracy and all those other forces which have led so many commentators to characterize the office as a 'no-win' institution. But how the Presidents have presented and promoted their reforms is also of obvious import, as is the actual content of the reforms. Finally, in terms of the development of policy over time, the capacity of Presidents to adapt their strategies, given the legislative and administrative experience of the reform attempts, can be crucial.

Such a sequence – origins, content, adaptation – may seem obvious in any study of presidential policy-making. Where this study differs from others, however, is in its concentration on a related set of policies over time. The main objective, therefore, is not, as with Barbara Kellerman's study of presidential leadership, to compare the capacities of successive incumbents to deal with different policy problems.[21] It is, rather, to analyse the contribution of the presidency to development of a major policy area given existing institutional and political constraints. Let us look at this design in more detail.

Policy origins

It is now established in the literature that the first two years of first-term Presidents provide more scope for presidential innovation than later years.[22] Indeed, presidencies seem to age adversely in terms of potential for domestic achievements, not only during the second terms but even during the second half of first terms. Hence Roosevelt's major legislative triumphs came between 1933 and 1935, Johnson's between 1964 and 1966 and Reagan's between 1981 and 1982. This is no scientific theory – of course there are exceptions – but new Presidents do enjoy some element of a honeymoon period with Congress, they often enjoy a high level of popular approval and they are normally determined during this early period to establish an imprint on the office. These tendencies apply *tout force* to domestic policy. With foreign policy, uncontrollable external events occurring later in presidencies may enhance presidential success or popularity (World War II, the Camp David Accords) or damage it (Korea, Vietnam, the Iranian Hostage Crisis).

If we are to establish that Presidents do have some independent influence on policy during these earlier periods of office, we have to analyse the origins of policy initiatives in some detail. In particular, it is necessary to:

(a) Assess whether or not the initiatives derive from a response to outside pressure, manifest in the form of a social movement, mandated party platform or the activities of highly organized special interests. While methodological problems are potentially legion here, if no such movements exist the party hold on Presidents is weak and no single powerful and relevant special interest dominates the election of the successful candidate, then we can confidently conclude that White House autonomy is relatively high in relation at least to these indicators of societal influence. It is not being claimed here that Presidents can exercise anything approaching total discretion over which policies to promote or inhibit. Rather, the claim is that they can exercise relative autonomy over the policy agenda and act relatively independently of outside forces.

Recent work on political development suggests that the greatest opportunities for the successful exercise of presidential leadership are provided when new regimes are established following a re-alignment of political forces and elite values. Hence, after 1932 Roosevelt was able to exploit a highly favourable regime environment.[23] Subsequent Presidents were less fortunate, either because they were out of tune with the New Deal regime (Eisenhower, Nixon) or because they found themselves facing serious regime deterioration (Carter). Johnson's legislative agenda was broadly compatible with the existing regime, but he always faced the danger of advancing his policies in ways which eventually would fall out of line with prevailing social and political forces.[24] While useful, such an approach makes it difficult to distinguish between the contribution made by individual Presidents and the (implicitly) rigid constraints imposed by the regime environment. More problematic is the experience of the Reagan administration. As we will see, Reagan was able to change domestic policies in a number of important ways, but evidence of the emergence of the sort of re-alignment indicative of a new regime is scant. Reagan seemed able to shift the policy agenda to the right independently of any social or political movement, or of a discernible shift in elite or mass attitudes towards the role of the state in American society.

(b)   Presidential policy autonomy may be limited internally by the constraints imposed by the federal bureaucracy. What role Presidents themselves and their immediate political appointees play in relation to the bureaucracy is therefore central to our concerns. This is a familiar issue in presidential scholarship and one which also relates to two of the most influential schools of thought in the general area of bureaucracy and public policy. The bargaining model addresses this problem via such concepts as policy networks, iron triangles, or more generally, interest-group liberalism.

Clearly the implication is that presidents and other centrally placed policy-makers are constrained by a bureaucracy infused with societal influence. Most state-centred theorists also attribute much importance to the bureaucracy, but more as an independent source of power than as a societally based constraint on the presidency. This is particularly true of studies in domestic policy where, for example, Department of Agriculture officials (Skocpol and Finegold)[25] or, more broadly, a new intellectual elite (Skowronek)[26] were responsible for major innovations or even transformations in policy. State theorists of the foreign-policy process usually give a more prominent role to the President. Hence, Krasner asserts that 'the American state: the president and those bureaus relatively insulated from societal pressures, which are the only institutions capable of formulating the national interest . . . must always struggle against an inherent tendency for power and control to be dissipated and dispersed'.[27] Even so, Krasner has difficulty in the subsequent empirical analysis distinguishing between presidential and officials' policy preferences. The reader is left with the impression that the central decision-maker's adherence to general goals (his definition of the national or public interest) is essentially a collective exercise, rather than a mix between bureaucratic values and the preferences of individuals. In the light of the breakdown of foreign policy consensus and the events surrounding the conduct of policy towards Vietnam, Iran and Central America, distinguishing between the personal preferences of actors and more general bureaucratic values is especially important.

In this book an attempt will, therefore, be made to distinguish between policies which originate specifically from presidential initiatives and those whose origins lie in the values and preferences of officials in the federal bureaucracy. While the methodological problems inherent in such a scheme are acknowledged, a careful analysis of the policy process can throw light on this distinction. Perhaps more difficult is establishing the extent to which the detailed content of policies reflects presidential as opposed to White House staff priorities and preferences. But even if this distinction cannot always be drawn, it is important to establish that reforms originate in the White House – however defined – as opposed to elsewhere.

Policy content and coherence

The bargaining model of American politics discourages scholars from examining the coherence or consistency of public policies. If, as the model suggests, government activities are always the result of a complex bargaining game, then public policy is likely to be some sort of compromise between competing groups, institutions and interests. As such, policy packages are unlikely to be internally coherent or consistent. Trade-offs produce untidy, compromised and often con-tradictory policies. Public-choice theorists agree that this policy process produces a level of public welfare below the optimal.[28] And the less formal approaches of such students of the American system as Theodore Lowi, Samuel Huntington and James McGregor Burns come to similar conclusions.[29]

If, however, Presidents exercise considerable discretion over the content of policies, then the potential for coherence should be much higher. Policies may subsequently be com-promised by Congress and during implementation, but at their inception a small number of policy actors operating in one institution should have the potential for producing more coherent or 'rational' reforms. Again, this claim is relative. Naturally, White House policy-makers have to be alive to the political environment and to the political feasibility of reforms. Compromise is always necessary given these political realities. But even so, a unitary, internalized policy process should result in more coherent policies than a fragmented, open-policy process which is highly amenable to the representation of conflicting values and interests.

Measuring coherence is also difficult. Broadly speaking, this book judges the coherence of policies in terms of their own objectives and standards. In other words, the presidential initiatives under examination have, by definition, all attemp-ted to modify or challenge the social-policy New Deal regime. In so doing they invoked a range of economic and political theories as justification of the need for reform. Moreover, as time has gone by, so the amount and quality of social science scholarship relating to the general areas of welfare and intergovernmental relations has improved. We do now have measures of coherence in these areas which were largely absent thirty or forty years ago. What is involved here is an intellectual rather than a technocratic exercise. The aim is not so much to judge whether policies will work in political terms, as to judge whether their detailed content is compatible with stated objectives.

Crucially, this can relate to how programmes have been designed. If programme designs are poorly thought out or internally inconsistent it can damage their legislative and/or implementation experience. Moreover, the intellectual debates inspired by such problems constitute a learning process for future administrations. Future reforms may take past design problems into account. Or, as was the case with the Reagan administration and welfare, the perceived design problems of earlier reforms may help to lead the President to pursue a completely different approach to the problem.

There is no inherent incompatibility between coherent policies and presidential ideology. A President deeply committed to (say) equality or improved economic efficiency may produce programmes and policies which directly advance these values in a highly coherent manner. Equally, there may be a serious disjunction between ideological preferences and programme content and design. As suggested, if the latter prevails, the potential for successful enactment and/or implementation of the measures is likely to be reduced. Very generally, such was the case with the implementation of many Great Society measures and with the legislative fortunes of Reagan's New Federalism. Clearly presidential leadership qualities and ideological determination can represent an influence independent of intellectual coherence. As a result, the agenda can change in sometimes crucial ways even if the reforms are partial failures.

Policy adaptation

All the reform initiatives under discussion in this book were either subject to serious amendment or modification by Congress, or failed to win Congressional approval, or experienced grave implementation problems. But in every case the policy agenda was changed as a result of presidential initiatives. As earlier noted, this had important implications for subsequent Presidents' agendas. However, it also affected the development of policy-making within administrations. Hence each of the Presidents made attempts to adapt following legislative or implementation failures or, in the case of Reagan, concurrent with them. With the latest three presidencies studied, this meant changing the decision-making process within the White House and/or opting to adapt policies in ways which avoided legislation and the Congressional contest. While these administrative strategies have had important policy consequences, this book argues that they are no substitute for the legislative initiatives which, early in the presidential career, have the greatest potential for changing the policy agenda.

The role of Congress

All of the above acknowledges the central importance of Congress in the making of public policy. This accepted, presidential/Congressional relations are not the main focus of this book. Numerous studies of this political dynamic exist, including many specifically concerned with welfare and intergovernmental relations. Later chapters will cite these when appropriate, but the objective is not to catalogue the legislative fortunes of Presidents' programmes. As later chapters will show, Presidents can adopt a number of strategies when dealing with Congress, and no President is pre-ordained to meet with legislative success or failure. Recent changes in Congress and in the broader society have produced a more difficult legislative/executive environment, but Presidents retain considerable discretion over the choice, content and presentation of public policies. To repeat the point, scholars have tended to underestimate this facet of presidential power in part because of their *a priori* assumption that the White House is bound to encounter effective Congressional and societal resistance to its plans. As will be shown, the initial choice of policies, the process whereby they are forged and the presentation of policies to Congress and the public can be crucial in deciding whether such policies eventually become law or not.

The theme of the book

Chapter 2 provides further justification for the choice of welfare reform and intergovernmental relations as the theme of this book by examining currently influential theories of how and why policy has changed in these areas over recent years. Chapters 3 to 7 deal respectively with the major reform initiatives of the Johnson, Nixon, Carter and Reagan presidencies, with two chapters devoted to the Reagan experience. For each President the origins and coherence of reforms are analysed with a final section – or in the case of Reagan, a chapter – devoted to how policy had been adapted via administrative and other devices. Various methods and sources have been mined to achieve these objectives. In three cases (Johnson, Nixon and Carter) original documents were examined. For all Presidents, secondary sources and contemporary comments have been utilized to supplement original sources. In one case (the Carter Urban Policy) some of the findings rely on elite interviews. The picture is not always complete – especially with respect to the Reagan experience. But enough information exists on all four Presidents for general, if sometimes qualified, conclusions to be drawn.

NOTES

1 Perhaps the most eloquent, and one of the earliest, statements of this position is Theodore Lowi's *The End of Liberalism: The Second Republic of the United States*, New York: Norton, 1969, 2nd edn 1979. For more recent critiques see James McGregor Burns, *The Power to Lead: The Crisis of the American Presidency*, New York: Simon and Schuster, 1984, and James L. Sundquist, *Constitutional Reform and Effective Government*, Washington, DC: The Brookings Institution, 1936.

2 Richard E. Neustadt, *Presidential Power: The Politics of Leadership From FDR to Carter*, New York: Wiley, 1980; Robert A. Dahl and Charles E. Lindblom, *Politics, Economics and Welfare*, New York: Harper and Row, 1960; Aaron Wildavsky, *The Politics of the Budgetary Process*, Boston: Little, Brown, 1964.

3 Neustadt, *Presidential Power*, chapter 3.

4 See, *inter alia*, James Buchanan and Richard Wagner, *Democracy in Deficit*, New York: Academic Press, 1977; Morris P. Fiorina, *Congress: Keystone of the Washington Establishment*, New Haven, CT: Yale University Press, 1977; Kenneth Shepsle and Barry R. Weingast, 'Legislative Politics and Budget Outcomes', in Gregory B. Mills and John L. Palmer (eds.), *Federal Budget Policy in the 1980s*, Washington, DC: Urban Institute, 1984.

5 For a full discussion see Patrick Dunleavy, 'Bureaucrats, Budgets and the Growth of the State: Reconstructing an Instrumental Model', *British Journal of Political Science*, 15 (1986), 299–328.

6 See, for example, Thomas E. Cronin, *The State of the Presidency*, Boston: Little, Brown, 1975; Louis W. Koenig, *The Chief Executive*, 5th edn, New York: Harcourt Brace Jovanovich, 1986; Richard E. Neustadt, *Presidential Power: The Politics of Leadership From FDR to Carter*, New York: Wiley, 1980 edn; Raymond Tatalovich and Byron W. Daynes, *Presidential Power in the United States*, Monterey, CA: Brooks/Cole, 1984.

7 See in particular the collection of essays edited by Fred I. Greenstein, *The Reagan Presidency: An Early Assessment*, Baltimore: Johns Hopkins Press, 1983, and that edited by John E. Chubb and Paul E. Peterson, *The New Direction in American Politics*, Washington, DC: The Brookings Institution, 1985.

8 For a discussion of the impact of the Roosevelt years on subsequent administrations, see William E. Leuchtenburg, *In the Shadow of FDR: From Harry Truman to Ronald Reagan*, Ithaca, NY: Cornell University Press, 1983.

9 E. E. Schattsneider, *The Semi Sovereign People*, quoted by Jack Walker, 'Setting the Agenda in the U.S. Senate: A Theory of Problem Selection', *British Journal of Political Science*, 7: 4 (1977), 423.

10 Paul C. Light, *The President's Agenda: Domestic Policy Choice From Kennedy to Carter (With Notes on Ronald Reagan)*, Baltimore: The Johns Hopkins Press, 1982, chapter 9.

11 John W. Kingdon, *Agendas, Alternatives and Public Policies*, Boston: Little, Brown, 1984.

12 Kingdon, *Agendas*, chapter 9.

13 Ibid., p. 33.

14 Fred I. Greenstein, 'The Need for an Early Appraisal of the Reagan Presidency', in Greenstein, *The Reagan Presidency*, p. 3.

15 See Barbara Kellerman, *The Political Presidency: Practice of Leadership from Kennedy through Reagan*, New York: Oxford University Press, 1984; Fred I. Greenstein, *The Hidden Hand Presidency: Eisenhower as Leader*, New York: Basic Books, 1982; James McGregor Burns, *Leadership*, New York: Harper and Row, 1978; Bert A. Rockman, *The Leadership Question: The Presidency and the American System*, New York: Praeger, 1985.

16 See Stephen Skowronek, 'Presidential Leadership in Political Time', in Michael Nelson (ed.), *The Presidency and the Political System*, Washington, DC: Congressional Quarterly Press, 2nd edn, 1988, pp. 115–59; James David Barber, *The Pulse of Politics: Electing Presidents in the Media Age*, New York: Norton, 1980.

17 There is an enormous literature on this subject. For a review and discussion, see John E. Chubb and Paul E. Peterson, 'Realignment and Institutionalization', in Chubb and Peterson (eds.), *The New Direction*.

18 But for an interesting polemic claiming such a re-alignment led by corporate interests, see Thomas Ferguson and Joel Rogers, *The Decline of the Democrats and the Future of American Politics*, New York: Hill and Wang, 1986.

19 Herbert Stein, *Presidential Economics: The Making of Economic Policy From Roosevelt to Reagan and Beyond*, New York: Simon and Schuster, 1984, chapter 9.

20 Numerous accounts of this dynamic exist. But see Theda Skocpol, 'Political Response to Capitalist Crisis: Neo-Marxist Theories of the State and the Case of the New Deal', *Politics and Society*, 10 (1980), 155–201; Theodore Lowi, *The Personal Presidency: Power Invested, Promise Unfulfilled*, Ithaca, NY: Cornell University Press, 1985, chapter 3, 'The Legacies of FDR'.

21 Kellerman, *The Political Presidency*.

22 See in particular Michael B. Grossman, Martha Joynt Kumar and Francis E. Rourke, 'Second Term Presidencies: The Aging of Administrations', in Nelson (ed.), *The Presidency*, pp. 207–25.

23 See Skowronek, 'Presidential Leadership', also his 'Notes on the Presidency in the Political Order', in Karen Orren and Stephen Skowronek (eds.), *Studies in American Political Development, Volume 1*, New Haven, CT: Yale University Press, 1986, pp. 294–6.

24 Skowronek, 'Notes on the Presidency', pp. 291–301.

25 Theda Skocpol and Kenneth Finegold, 'State Capacity and Economic Intervention in the Early New Deal', *Political Science Quarterly*, 97 (1982), 255–78.

26 Stephen Skowronek, *Building a New American State: The Expansion of National Administrative Capacities, 1877–1920*, Cambridge: Cambridge University Press, 1982.

27 Stephen D. Krasner, *Defending the National Interest: Raw Materials, Investments and US Foreign Policy*, Princeton, NJ: Princeton University Press, 1978, p. 62.

28 See note 4.

29 Samuel Huntington, 'The Democratic Distemper', in *The Public Interest*, 10 (1975), 1–38; Burns, *The Power to Lead*; Lowi, *The End of Liberalism* and *The Personal Presidency*.

2 Explaining federal spending

Until the 1970s, one of the more established truths in American political science was that government expenditure – especially at the federal level – was destined either to change only incrementally over the years or was likely to drift upwards. Since 1970, however, the distribution of spending between different categories has fluctuated quite wildly. As can be seen from table 1, only payments for individuals (mainly social security and Medicare) have risen consistently, and even these have levelled off over the last few years. In contrast, defence spending first fell sharply and more recently has risen sharply. Grants to state and local governments have fallen steadily since the late 1970s. As table 2 shows, this followed a dramatic increase in this spending category between 1955 and 1978.

Between 1955 and 1978, federal aid to state and local governments increased from $5.6 billion to $49.4 billion (in 1972 dollars, table 2). Put another way, intergovernmental grants increased from 4.7% of all federal outlays to 17% of federal outlays. However, by 1987 grants in aid had declined to an estimated $37.7 billion, representing just 10.1% of federal expenditure. While few scholars have attempted to explain these changes in any systematic fashion, by the late 1970s three fairly distinct explanations of the increases in spending to that point had emerged, the two most influential of which predicted, explicitly or by implication, that spending would continue to increase – or at least not fall – during the 1980s. These we will call the neo-pluralist and technocratic critiques, to which we will add a third, radical, interpretation. Many of these arguments apply not only to social spending but also to other areas of expenditure.

Table 1. *Percentage distribution of federal budget outlays, 1959–87*

Year	% distribution					
	Defence	Total non-defence	Payments for individuals	Grants[a]	Other	Net interest
1959	49.1	50.9	20.6		19.7[b]	10.7
1960	48.9	51.1	21.9		18.3	10.8
1965	40.1	59.9	24.6		25.7	9.7
1969	43.9	56.1	28.6		20.6	6.9
1971	39.8	61.2	35.5	8.4	14.9	6.7
1975	27.3	72.7	45.4	10.0	14.5	6.9
1979	24.1	75.9	45.7	10.9	14.5	8.3
1980	23.5	76.5	46.5	9.8	14.8	8.9
1982	24.9	75.1	47.8	6.7	12.7	11.4
1984	26.8	73.2	46.7	6.2	11.2	13.0
1985	27.0	73.0	44.7	6.0	12.2	13.6
1986	28.0	72.0	45.0	6.0	10.9	13.6
1987[c]	28.1	71.9	45.4	5.3	11.4	13.4

[a] Grants to state and local governments.
[b] Grants included in 'Other' category pre 1970.
[c] Estimated.

Source: U.S. Budget in Brief 1982 and 1988, Washington DC, US Government Printing Office, Table 2, p. 77 (1982) and p. 99 (1988).

Table 2. *Federal grants in aid in relation to state/local receipts, total federal outlays and gross national product, selected years, 1955–1987*

	Federal grants in aid				Number of grant programmes (selected years)
	Amount (1972 $ billions)	As a percentage of			
		state/local receipts from own source	total federal outlays	GNP	
1955	5.6	11.8	4.7	0.8	n.a.
1960	10.8	16.8	7.6	1.4	132
1965	15.5	17.7	9.2	1.7	n.a.
1970	27.0	22.9	12.3	2.5	379[a]
1972	34.4	26.1	14.9	3.0	n.a.
1975	39.2	29.1	15.0	3.4	442
1978	49.4	31.7	17.0	3.7	492
1979	48.1	31.3	16.5	3.5	n.a.
1980	48.2	31.7	15.5	3.6	n.a.
1981	46.1	30.1	14.0	3.3	539
1982	40.4	25.6	11.8	2.9	441
1983	40.7	24.7	11.4	2.9	n.a.
1984	41.3	23.7	11.5	2.7	405
1985	43.1	23.7	11.2	2.8	n.a.
1986[b]	40.1	21.4	10.7	2.5	n.a.
1987[b]	37.7	19.5	10.1	2.2	n.a.

[a] 1969–
[b] Estimated

Source: Advisory Commission on Intergovernmental Relations, *Significant Features of Fiscal Federalism, 1985/86 Edition,* Washington DC: US Government Printing Office 1986, adapted from table 8.

At first sight, the neo-pluralist perspective is simple and familiar. Myriad groups and interests helped create and in turn were strengthened by the Great Society programmes of the 1960s. They increasingly focussed their attention on Washington because national institutions, and especially Congress, were most amenable to the increased spending and distributive policies which they favoured. At the same time the institutional dynamics of the New Deal regime resulted in many of these new programmes being organized on some sort of intergovernmental basis. Usually the money came from Washington, while the administration of programmes was left to state and local governments. Neo-pluralists disliked these developments for three rather different reasons. One school, which we could aptly name the populists, were outraged at the unequal distributional consequences.[1] Producer groups – programme administrators and clients' leaders – benefited in relation to the broader client or consumer population. Hence, with new housing or welfare programmes, the real beneficiaries were the builders, welfare-rights organizations and bureaucrats, rather than the poor.[2] A second school, the public-choice theorists, were aroused not so much by matters of equity, as by the conviction that the interaction of interest groups, with the particular institutional structure of American government – notably an independent Congress – had led to levels of public spending that were either too high,[3] or were distorted in ways which damaged the public welfare.[4]

This is not the place to review these critiques, but neither the populists not the public-choice theorists look carefully at the origins of programmes. The assumption is that programmes have emerged as a result of some sort of societal pressure manifest through organized interests and strengthened by self-serving bureaucrats and politicians. Systematic research in support of this specific point was not forthcoming. That institutional factors distort to some extent the provision of public goods seems incontrovertible. But this is true in every political system. And, as earlier indicated, grants increased rapidly to 1978, but have declined considerably since. The rules of the legislative and bureaucratic bargaining game were not somehow transformed from within after 1978. Clearly some exogeneous influence (or influences) were at work to produce this dramatic drop in spending.

A third group of neo-pluralists (usually labelled neo-conservatives) were concerned not so much with the distributional consequences of the increased federal role, as with the overloading of the system which the growth of government represented. A crisis of public authority resulted, which held all sorts of dangers for the legitimacy and even for the viability of the American state.[5] These critics are in no doubt that an excess of democracy or 'The Democratic Distemper', as Samuel Huntington put it, was the root cause of the problem.[6] In essence, the increasing openness of the system placed far too many demands on the government. It was the resulting gap between promise and performance that constituted the real threat to public authority. But as with the other neo-pluralists, excessive democracy as a source of government activity is assumed rather than demonstrated. Furthermore, decline in both the funding and the number of federal programmes after 1978 was not accompanied by any discernible move away from democracy, whether measured in terms of institutional reform or political behaviour. Indeed, by some measures (the use of direct democratic devices such as referenda and initiatives) democracy actually increased after 1978.

The technocratic thesis takes two distinctive forms. Samuel Beer, noting the rapid rise of intergovernmental spending, attributes much of it to the emergence of a bureaucratic state. Officials and experts are therefore largely responsible for the new and enlarged programmes. As he puts it:

I would remark how rarely additions to the public sector have been *initiated* by the demands of voters or the advocacy of pressure groups or the platforms of political parties. On the contrary, in the fields of health, housing, urban renewal, transportation, welfare, education, poverty and energy, it has been, in the very great measure, people in government service, or closely associated with it, acting on the basis of their specialized and technical knowledge, who first perceived the problem, conceived the program, initially urged it on the president and Congress, went to help lobby it through to enactment, and then saw to its administration.[7]

To be fair, Beer does acknowledge that Presidents can make a difference,[8] but the major source of new policy lies not with Presidents so much as with experts and officials. Beer refines this claim by adding another group of policy initiators to his scheme. 'Topocrats', or the intergovernmental lobby have, he suggests, developed a sort of symbiotic relationship with the technocrats. In sum: 'I am saying that over the past generation, and especially since the early 1960s, the technocratic tendencies of the new professionalism have called forth the topocratic tendencies of the intergovernmental lobby.'[9] Organizations representing state, county and local officials encourage new programmes (and increased spending) along with the technocrats in Washington. So powerful is this tendency that Beer labels it 'government by place' or 'topocracy'.

But, as with the neo-pluralists, little systematic work on the policy-initiating role of this intergovernmental lobby was conducted.[10] Even so, the clear implication was that a new dimension had been added to the American representational system which would encourage further growth in the public sector.[11] While the activities of the intergovernmental lobby are undoubtedly important, it seems unlikely that they play a major policy-initiating role. Again, the data in table 2 are apposite. For exactly contemporary with Beer's interesting polemic came first the levelling off of intergovernmental aid, followed in the 1980s by sizeable reductions. Lower-level governments do play some independent policy role and their organizations certainly work hard to maintain and increase federal grants. But their role seems much more one of *reacting* to federal initiatives than helping to initiate them. By 1987, one student of federalism was able to conclude that: 'Another factor in the failure of the re-authorization effort [for revenue sharing] was the disarray among state and local lobbying groups that had appeared to be so powerful in the late 1960s and early 1970s.'[12]

As for the technocrats, if, as Beer suggests, they do play an independent role, the interesting questions are: under whose direction and on whose behalf? The reversal of policy after 1978 implies that a different set of officials were at work whose objectives must have been to reduce spending and the size of federal programmes. If this is so, some higher political authority must have been able (somewhat miraculously) to replace budget maximizers with budget cutters, or, more feasibly, the basic premise of the technocratic school – that experts and officials play a genuinely initiatory role – needs to be heavily qualified.

Another approach which could also be categorized as a critique of technocracy, is taken by some students of implementation. Here the assumption is that federal officials armed with myriad and sometimes contradictory rules and regulations dominate the implementation process, which leads to a high degree of policy confusion – and policy failure.[13] While it is not altogether clear whether this tendency leads to increased spending, the literature does suggest that the public interest is ill served by what is a messy and complex policy process. But as Paul Peterson *et al.* have noted, the implementationists fail to specify how policy goals might be advanced by an alternative system.[14] Most of the implementation studies were a product of the early and mid 1970s when the programmes under scrutiny were relatively new and when a general antipathy to the federal bureaucracy – often reinforced by political leaders – was rapidly gaining currency. But many federal programmes have been in operation for thirty or forty years and are subject to constant Congressional and public scrutiny. Why should these programmes have succeeded while others of more recent vintage have failed? The implementationists may claim credit for having helped to inspire the review of federal programmes undertaken by the Reagan administration. But some of the programmes which suffered the most Draconian cuts had no greater implementation

problems than those remaining intact.[15] Taking the whole
Reagan experience, some programmes which failed to survive
– most notably revenue sharing – simply did not involve
federal officials at the implementation level.

Both the neo-pluralist and technocratic critiques can be
nicely accommodated by the bargaining model of American
politics outlined in chapter 1. In marked contrast, the radical
critique utilizes a power/control model of the system. So for
Piven and Cloward, federal aid is a response to actual or
potential revolt on the part of the poor, which, once the
rebellion is past or bought off, is then systematically cut back
to re-instil the work ethic in the population.[16] Although
variants on this theme have appeared since the publication of
Regulating the Poor in 1971, it remains the single most complete
radical explanation of the changing pattern of welfare policy.
Unfortunately, however, the thesis constitutes a poor explanation of data presented in table 2 – even acknowledging that
the analysis applies only to income maintenance and related
work-relief benefits, rather than to the whole universe of
intergovernmental aid. As chapter 3 will show, most of the
Great Society programmes were conceived before the urban
riots of that decade broke out. And new programmes appeared
and benefit levels continued to increase long after protest had
subsided. Most commentators agree that programme benefits
peaked in 1977 or 1978.[17] While few would dispute that the
Reagan cuts were in part designed to reinforce the work ethic,
they came at a time (1981–2) when the objective condition of
the urban poor (unemployment and benefit levels) was
considerably worse than during the mid and late 1960s.[18]
According to the thesis, the cutbacks should have occurred in
the early 1970s rather than ten years later. Whichever way you
look at it, the radical critique, at least in its power/control
variant, has little explanatory power. While the same cannot
be said of the neo-pluralists or technocratic perspectives – both
have validity and application in some context or other – they
are, as was argued, less than adequate as explanations of the
fluctuating pattern of federal aid characteristic of the 1955–87

period. As was indicated in chapter 1, to understand and explain this pattern fully it is necessary to complement these perspectives with a different approach which focusses on executive power, and in particular on the role which Presidents and their advisors play in shaping the policy agenda. This leadership role can challenge existing values and political alignments whether in Congress, the bureaucracy, among interest groups or in the mass public.

We will begin this analysis with the Johnson administration, which it is generally accepted was the first to produce an ambitious series of policies designed to modify and challenge the nature of the New Deal regime.

NOTES

1 See in particular Grant McConnell, *Private Power and American Democracy*, New York: Knopf, 1966; Theodore J. Lowi, *The End of Liberalism: The Second Republic of the United States*, New York: Norton, 2nd edn, 1979.

2 Lowi, *The End of Liberalism*, chapters 8 and 9.

3 See Morris P. Fiorina, *Congress: Keystone of the Washington Establishment*, New Haven, CT: Yale University Press, 1977; James M. Buchanan and Richard Wagner, *Democracy in Deficit*, New York: Academic Press, 1977.

4 For a general discussion of whether the institutional dynamics of Congress distort spending towards particular interests or simply increase spending, see David R. Mayhew, *Congress: The Electoral Connection*, New Haven, CT: Yale University Press, 1974, pp. 139–41; and Barry Weingast, 'A Rational Choice Perspective on Congressional Norms', in Matthew D. McCubbins and Terry Sullivan (eds.), *Congress: Structure and Policy*, New York and Cambridge: Cambridge University Press, 1987, pp. 131–46.

5 See in particular the collection of essays celebrating the tenth anniversary of *The Public Interest*, published as *The New American Commonwealth 1976*, New York: Basic Books, 1976.

6 Samuel P. Huntington, 'The Democratic Distemper', in *The New American Commonwealth*, pp. 9–38.

7 Samuel H. Beer, 'Federalism, Nationalism, and Democracy in America', *American Political Science Review*, 72 (1978), 17.

8 Beer, 'Federalism', p. 17.

9 Ibid., p. 18.
10 But see Donald H. Haider, *When Governments Come to Washington: Governors, Mayors and Intergovernmental Lobbying*, New York: Free Press, 1974. Beer's own work in this area is confined to revenue sharing, where he concentrates on the legislative rather than executive process: 'The Adoption of General Revenue Sharing: A Case Study in Public Sector Politics', *Public Policy*, 24 (1976), 127–95.
11 Samuel H. Beer, 'Political Overload and Federalism', *Polity*, 10 (Fall, 1977), 5–17. See also the present author's own piece, making similar claims, David H. McKay, 'The Rise of the Topocratic State: US Intergovernmental Relations in the 1970s', in Douglas E. Ashford (ed.), *Financing Urban Government in the Welfare State*, London: Croom Helm, 1980, pp. 50–70.
12 Robert W. Rafuse, Jr, 'Fiscal Federalism in 1986: The Spotlight Continues to Swing Toward the States and Local Governments', *Publius, The Journal of Federalism*, 17 (1987), 37.
13 See, *inter alia*, Eugene Bardach, *The Implementation Game*, Cambridge, MA: MIT Press, 4th edn, 1982; Richard E. Neustadt and Harvey V. Fineberg, *The Swine Flu Affair: Decision-Making on a Slippery Slope*, Washington, DC: Department of Health, Education and Welfare, 1978; Martha Derthick, *New Towns in Town: Why a Federal Program Failed*, Washington, DC: The Brookings Institution, 1982; Jeffrey L. Pressman and Aaron Wildavsky, *Implementation*, Berkeley and Los Angeles: University of California Press, 3rd edn, 1984. The general assumption that federal officials complicate – and ultimately undermine – the implementation of policy is implicit in much of the work produced by the *Advisory Commission on Intergovernmental Relations* (ACIR). See, in particular, their bi-monthly *Intergovernmental Perspective*.
14 Paul E. Peterson, Barry G. Rabe and Kenneth K. Wong, *When Federalism Works*, Washington, DC: The Brookings Institution, 1986, pp. 8–10.
15 For example, Supplementary Security Income was cut by 11%, food stamps by 14% and the child nutrition programme by 28%. It is unlikely that these programmes suffered from greater implementation problems than a range of protected defence-related programmes.
16 Frances Fox Piven and Richard A. Cloward, *Regulating the Poor: The Functions of Public Welfare*, New York: Pantheon, 1971; see also their *Poor People's Movements: Why They Succeed, How They Fail*, New York: Pantheon, 1977.
17 Aid for Families with Dependent Children (AFDC) benefits peaked as early as 1970 and have been declining in real terms ever since. Once other benefits are included, however, and in particular food stamps, the benefit decline is gentler and dates from around 1978. See Paul E. Peterson and Mark C. Rom, 'Federal Welfare Performance: The

Determinants of Interstate Differences in Poverty Rules and Benefit Levels', paper before the Annual Conference of the American Political Science Association, The Palmer House, Chicago, 3–6 September 1987, pp. 19–22 and figure 1. Both the officially defined poverty rate and the unemployment rate rose substantially between 1978 and 1983 from, respectively, 11.5% to 15% and 5.8% to 9%. For a full discussion, see Tom Joe and Cheryl Rogers, *By the Few For the Few: The Reagan Welfare Legacy*, Lexington, MA: D. C. Heath, 1985, chapters 1 and 2.

18 Unemployment remained below 5% from 1965 to 1969, but was between 7% and 9% in the early 1980s. Poverty rates were generally similar to the early 1980s, in the 1965–9 period, but were declining fast in the 1960s and increasing steadily in the 1980s. Poverty rates for the urban population of older cities were increasing particularly rapidly in the 1980s. See Joe and Rogers, *By the Few For the Few*, chapter 1, and Judith Feder and Jack Hadley, 'Cutbacks, Recession and Hospitals' Care for the Urban Poor', in George E. Peterson and Carol W. Lewis (eds.), *Reagan and the Cities*, Washington, DC: The Urban Institute, 1986, table 13.

3 Lyndon Johnson: executive-led ideology

Origins

There are few doubts about the specific origins of the Great Society. They lie in two initiatives: a Johnson follow-up to a Kennedy administration proposal to attack poverty in the US, and the preliminary findings of the Johnson 'outside' task forces created in 1964. Close examination of these initiatives reveals that the policy package that came to be known as the Great Society was: (a) the result of a highly internalized policy process – individuals, not interests, dominated decision-making; (b) that Johnson himself should play the central role in elevating the policies to the top of the political agenda and selling them to the American people; (c) that he should do this almost independently of any social movement in, or pressure from, the broader society. In this sense the Great Society was fundamentally different from the Progressive era and from the New Deal.

On 1 May 1963 Walter Heller, Chairman of the Council of Economic Advisers (CEA), sent a memo to Kennedy outlining how a CEA study showed a marked slowdown in 'the rate at which the economy is taking people out of poverty'.[1] Later in June 1963 memos were exchanged between Heller and his staff which, with Kennedy's approval, led to a long memo from Heller to all relevant Secretaries (Agriculture; Commerce; Labor; Health, Education and Welfare) plus the Budget Director and Administrator of the Housing and Home Finance Agency (HHFA), announcing a 1964 Legislative Programme for

'Widening Participation in Prosperity – An Attack on Poverty'.[2] Almost all of the subsequent War on Poverty legislation
was contained in embryonic form in this memo, namely:
maximum feasible participation by the poor in proposals
designed to alleviate poverty; targeting poverty aid on the
most needy, defined spatially and by individual charac-
teristics; the coordination and upgrading of existing programmes, including AFDC and social security; and the acceptance
that because poverty was multi-faceted its elimination had to
proceed along a broad front involving everything from health
to pre-school education.[3] Costs, at least initially, would be kept
low, the main effort being devoted to consciousness raising
and administrative coordination.

Although Heller discussed the matter just three days before
the assassination (19 November 1963) and Kennedy approved a
'go ahead' on the programme,[4] there is no evidence that
Kennedy was planning to make the 'Attack on Poverty' the
centrepiece of his 1964 State of the Union Message.

Johnson, however, immediately picked up the idea. As he
reports in his autobiography, Walter Heller came to see him at
7.40 p.m. on the very first full day of his presidency and
presented him with 'research recently conducted on the
problem of poverty'.[5] Over the next few weeks Heller and staff
members in the CEA prepared a further memo (dated 20
December 1963) which would become the basis for a declaration of a 'War on Poverty' in the 1964 State of the Union
Message.[6] The final decision to proceed on this basis was made
over Christmas at the LBJ ranch in discussions with Ted
Sorensen (who was in receipt of the CEA memo on 20
December) and Bill Moyers.[7]

The declaration itself was lengthy (over one-third of the
State of the Union Message), strong on rhetoric, but short on
how, precisely, poverty would be 'prevented' and eventually
'cured'. In subsequent months he made, according to Doris
Kearns, dozens of speeches on the subject to groups 'ranging
from the "Daughters of the American Revolution" to the
Socialist Party, from the Business Council to the AFL–CIO'

[American Federation of Labor – Congress of Industrial Organization].[8] Johnson's 'Unconditional War on Poverty' (the actual words of the Message) were very quickly translated into a first legislative draft of the Economic Opportunity Act (EOA – 24 February), Senate approval (23 July), House approval (8 August) and signing into law (20 August).

Perhaps the most remarkable thing about this whole initiative was how it was snatched almost from nowhere and translated into a major national issue. In 1963 there was very little consciousness of a poverty problem in the US, either among academics, politicians or the mass public. Concern with civil rights and Appalachia not withstanding, Kennedy's priorities lay in foreign rather than domestic policy, and although Walter Heller's 1 May memo was later to become of crucial importance, it provoked little in the way of positive action in the Kennedy administration. Outside the White House the public were largely unaware of any problem. Indeed, Almond and Verba's famous five nations' study, *The Civic Culture*, was almost contemporary with the period and it reinforced the image of Americans as distrustful of government and infused with notions of individualism and self-reliance.[9] And, as Henry J. Aaron notes, 'If poverty was not a problem in the eyes of the public, it was equally ignored by scholars. A complete bibliography of studies relating to poverty compiled in the early 1960s ran to less than two pages.'[10] What is true is that Michael Harrington's book, *The Other America*, had been published in 1962, had received quite wide publicity and had been given by Heller to Kennedy to read – although whether Kennedy read it is not known.[11] Some consciousness of the issue existed, therefore, but it was hardly of national import. Finally, except in the sense that racial discrimination was often related to poverty, no social movement on the part of the poor existed, which may have prompted the administration into action. Civil rights were perceived at the time primarily as a battle to achieve legal rights for blacks rather than as a struggle for economic advancement. Evidence of strong support for the War on

Poverty from the AFL-CIO and particularly its President, George Meany, and Executive Committee member, Walter Reuther, exists.[12] But there is no evidence either (a) that this support was important in changing the content or nature of the programme; or (b) that the support among labour leaders was in response to any sort of mass-membership pressure.

What is established is the close connection made by Walter Heller (a University of Minnesota Professor) and other economists between anti-poverty programmes and the state of the economy. Heller's 5 November 1963 memo itemized how prosperity by-passes 'certain individuals, groups and areas' and stressed how (a) new and existing programmes could help bring these people and areas back into the labour force; and (b) this would in turn produce benefits 'in the form of such things as additional national product from investment in people and reduction of market barriers, reduced crime and delinquency, and wider sharing of selective service obligations'.[13] Heller, along with Galbraith, Samuelson, Charles Schultze and other Keynesian economists, represented something of a consensus of opinion in the profession that government efforts to achieve full employment could legitimately include a broad range of macro- and micro-economic tools. As far as poverty was concerned, it was assumed that programme costs could be kept quite low if the macro-economic environment was appropriate. In fact a major tax reduction to stimulate the economy – a policy inherited from the Kennedy years – was another major domestic initiative of Johnson's first year. As will be discussed later, this faith in government action resembled a simple economism – the relationship between government action and a complex political and social system was not appreciated. Indeed, professional social science except for economics had little interest in poverty as such and tended to view government action or intervention as essentially neutral. The behavioural revolution in political science and sociology was premised on the belief that in order to remain scientific, social science must remain value free and confine itself to measurement and analysis.[14]

Given the times (a bereaved nation intent on maintaining the missionary zeal of the Kennedy administration), the apparent simplicity and low cost of the poverty programme and Johnson's personal style, it is not surprising that he decided to elevate the issue to centre-stage. Johnson's rhetoric was extravagant, his appeal to the populist impulse in the American people extensive and his success in moulding a new political agenda unquestioned. By late 1964, the War on Poverty was established as a major part of domestic policy. Johnson himself characterized 1963 as a special year in American history, when major social change was realizable:

Before me now was a call for action, a call for a revolutionary new program to attack one of the most stubbornly entrenched social ills in America. Like most social change, such a revolution would not come without a struggle. My perceptions of America persuaded me that three separate conditions were required before social change could take root and flourish in our national life – a recognition of need, a willingness to act, and someone to lead the effort. In 1963 I saw those three conditions coming together in historic harmony.[15]

The EOA and the War on Poverty heralded a much wider programme of social reform, which was to become the Great Society. As with the War on Poverty the process whereby these reforms were forged was remarkably internalized. Johnson announced his plan to build a Great Society in a speech at Michigan on 22 May 1964. Again, the rhetoric was extravagant, as Johnson promised that: 'the Great Society rests on abundance and liberty for all. It demands an end to poverty and social injustice, to which we are totally committed in our time. But that is just the beginning.'[16] The President then proceeded to identify three broad areas where action was needed: the improvement of urban conditions, the preservation of the countryside and the improvement of educational opportunities – especially for minorities and the disadvantaged.[17] In addition, Johnson promised other programmes to meet the 'emerging challenges'. For all these initiatives working groups would be established to identify priorities and recommend legislation. Within five weeks, Johnson had assigned newly appointed Press Secretary Bill Moyers to convene what were to be known as task forces on (initially) fifteen policy issues: transportation, natural resources, education, health, urban problems, government cooperation, pollution of the environment, preservation of natural beauty, intergovernmental fiscal cooperation, efficiency and economy, anti-recession policy, agriculture, civil rights, foreign economic policy and income maintenance policy.[18]

Kennedy had also used the task-force device, but of his seven task forces all but one concerned foreign policy. All but one of Johnson's concerned domestic policy. Also the work of Kennedy's groups were publicized – even advertised. Johnson's were very specifically to operate in secret, so as to avoid destructive press coverage which might affect the task-force recommendations before their work was completed.[19] Membership of the task forces was decided by Moyers, Budget Director Kermit Gordon, Walter Heller, speechwriter Richard Goodwin, Presidential Assistant Douglass Cater and other senior White House staffmembers.[20] Johnson approved the final names and objected only on the grounds of geographic imbalance.[21] Most of the members were establishment figures – academics, corporate and public leaders – and relatively few were drawn from within the administration. The idea was to create in what were to be known as 'outside task forces' sources of policy intelligence for the 1965 legislative agenda. Task-force members were encouraged to innovate, criticize existing programmes and policies and be as broad as possible in scope.[22]

All the task forces had reported by late 1964 and their recommendations bore fruit in the form of major legislative achievements in 1965. In particular, the Education Task Force, chaired by John Gardner, led directly to the 1965 Elementary and Secondary Education Act, and the Task Force on Metropolitan and Urban Problems, chaired by Robert Wood, led to the 1965 Housing Act and indirectly to the creation of the Department of Housing and Urban Development.[23] Some observers have even gone so far as to say that the task force recommendations were the major influence on the 89th Congress. Philip S. Hughes of the Bureau of the Budget (BOB) notes:

The Task Force was the basic tool which made much of the success of the Eighty-ninth Congress. The routine way to develop a legislative program has been to ask the Departments to generate proposals. Each agency sends its ideas through channels, which means that the ideas are limited by the imagination of the old-line agencies. They tend to be repetitive – the same proposals year after year. When the ideas of the different agencies reach the departmental level, all kinds of objections are raised, especially objections that new notions may somehow infringe on the rights of some other agency in the department. By the time a legislative proposal from a department reaches the President, it's a pretty well-compromised product.[24]

This assessment seems right – at least for the 1965 legislative programme. Indeed a summary of the task-force reports almost reads like a list of the messages sent by Johnson to Congress in early 1965 – even before his inauguration.[25] After 1965, however, the structure and functioning of the task forces changed in three crucial ways. First, under the direction of newly appointed Special Assistant, Joe Califano, they came to be called Inter-Agency Task Forces. Outside advice was sought, but only at the behest of internal task-force members. With over a hundred task forces reporting by the end of Johnson's presidency, they obviously became more specialized. More important – and this is the second difference – they were required to provide 'detailed pricing out of all proposals'.[26] The original outside task forces operated under no such constraints. For example, the Task Force on Income Maintenance estimated that its recommendations would lead to an additional $4 billion per year commitment by the federal government over ten years.[27] As will be discussed later, this almost certainly encouraged a number of open-ended commitments by the federal government. Third, after 1964, the external policy environment became increasingly conflictual and complex. The simplicity of the 1965 agenda was not to be repeated in 1966, 1967 or 1968. Many task-force recommendations were not translated into legislative action, and some important measures were proposed and/or enacted in response to outside pressures.

Of the policies considered central to the Great Society,

Medicare (and to a lesser extent Medicaid) are generally acknowledged as having origins dating back to 1935.[28] Medicare was not so much a Johnson bill as a bill with established Congressional and societal support, whose passage was greatly aided by Johnson's endorsement and by the spirit of the age. Civil Rights legislation, too, had origins in an earlier era. Indeed the omnibus 1964 Civil Rights Act was already proceeding through Congress before the Great Society had been declared. Johnson gave strong support both to the 1964 and to the 1965 Civil Rights Act (voting rights) which almost certainly assured their passage,[29] but both were very much part of an ongoing policy process.[30]

Of the remaining Great Society measures, the 1966 Model Cities Act and possibly the 1968 Housing Act are particularly important for our purposes, because both could have resulted from reaction to outside pressure rather than from the essentially internal policy process characteristic of 1964 and 1965. It should not be forgotten that, even though there had been minor outbreaks in 1964, urban rioting did not become a major issue until 1965, with the outbreak in Watts on 11 August. It was not until 1967 (Newark, 12 July and Detroit, 23 July) that the worst riots occurred. None of the 1964 or 1965 Great Society measures can be considered in any sense a response to riots or to the other protests which became commonplace after 1966. Moreover, it is hard to relate the Model Cities legislation to outside pressures – although its origins are somewhat different from those of policies already discussed.

The original 1964 outside Task Force on Metropolitan and Urban Problems dealt mainly with housing and recommended below-market-interest-rate loans for the construction of low-income rental housing – a measure which was eventually, and after much discussion and modification, to be incorporated into the 1968 Housing Act. The idea of 'Demonstration' or 'Model Cities' came, surprisingly, not from a task force, or from Congress, but from Walter Reuther, the President of United Auto Workers and Vice-President of the AFL–CIO. For although the 1964 task force had made brief reference to the notion of rebuilding selected city sections,[31] it was Walter Reuther who developed and promoted the suggestion — probably taking the demonstration concept from the Office of Economic Opportunity (OEO) and War on Poverty where it had first been developed. Reuther, a nationally prominent liberal with a membership concentrated in the Detroit area, sent a long memo to the President on 13 May 1965 outlining in some detail the Demonstration Cities idea.[32] He proposed a 'crash program' totally to rebuild neighbourhoods of 50,000 people each in six of the nation's largest cities. Johnson liked the idea, later met with Reuther personally to discuss it, and with Johnson's go-ahead Demonstration Cities became a major part of the 1965 Inter-Agency Task Force on Urban Problems chaired by Robert C. Wood.[33] All these initiatives occurred before the outbreak of rioting in Watts in August 1965.

What is clear is that the subsequent bill met with rather more opposition in Congress than had earlier Great Society measures. The President sent the housing message to Congress on 25 January 1966, but it was not finally signed into law until 3 November. By 1966, opposition to what looked to many like open-ended federal government commitments had increased, and the fiscal version of the bill reduced appropriations from an original $2.3 billion to $1.2 billion over three years.[34] As is well documented, urban disorders rather than accelerating Congressional action often produced a backlash against what were considered ill-thought-out new programmes.[35] Johnson staffmembers were obliged to work hard on Congressional liaison. On 10 October, for example, Joe Califano drafted a statement of support for the bill, signed by seventeen of the country's top corporate leaders, which was sent to all members of the House, where the measure was still pending.[36] The statement concluded:

As businessmen, we are especially mindful of the need to hold down federal expenditures until the immediate threat of inflation is contained. The proposal is a fiscally responsible measure. The funds proposed will move this humane program forward, consistent both with the nation's economic well-being and with our highest hopes for the future of our cities. In our business judgement, it deserves to be ranked as high on any list of national priorities as any domestic program we know. America needs the Demonstration Cities Act.[37]

This and other contemporary comment confirms that the Administration considered the Demonstration Cities – later Model Cities – Bill a central part of the Great Society programme.[38]

The Model Cities initiative was, therefore, still the result of a predominantly internal policy process. For while Reuther was an outsider representing a clear constituency based in Michigan, he was not acting under pressure from the big cities or his mass membership, but as an ambitious individual with extensive political contacts who saw the opportunity provided by the urban issue to advance his national career.[39]

Given that the 1968 Housing Act was the last major programme enacted under the general heading of the Great Society, it is not surprising that its legislative history was influenced by outside events and by the growing experience of those Great Society programmes already being implemented. Its origins, however, like so many other measures, lie in the early years of the Johnson presidency. As a follow-up to the President's May 1964 Michigan speech, a number of memos on the subject of 'the cities' were circulated within the White House,[40] and during every year thereafter Johnson sent special messages to Congress, each one containing requests for new subsidized housing programmes. These met with limited success via the 1965 Housing Act and the 1966 Model Cities legislation, but in 1967 a more comprehensive measure was introduced in Congress by the Republicans. The specific concept in this legislation was interest subsidies for developers of low- and moderate-income rental and owner-occupied housing. This idea had been floated by the 1965 Task Force on Housing and Urban Affairs, chaired by Robert Weaver.[41] During 1967, with the Republicans apparently sympathetic to the idea, Joe Califano directed the 1968 Task Force on Housing and Urban Development to make a special effort to examine the question of providing more low-income housing, which existing programmes were clearly not doing.[42] Model Cities was seen to be in disarray, in part because funding was unavailable for this purpose. Public housing was discredited as encouraging dependence rather than self-reliance and was widely condemned as a segregated programme catering for a few poor black families rather than the low-income population in general.[43] Interest-subsidy programmes would, it was hoped, remove housing from the control of local housing authorities, stimulate the private sector and encourage self-reliance on the part of poorer tenants and owners.

Johnson accorded the 1968 bill high priority, labelling it 'the most farsighted, the most comprehensive, the most massive housing program in all American history'.[44] In fact, the initial price tag was to be $5.3 billion over three years.[45] That Congress enacted the programme in 1968 amid a backlash against urban disorders says a great deal about the authority which Lyndon Johnson had established over the legislative agenda.

For example, on 31 August 1967, Republican Congressman Melvin Laird sent an impassioned plea to Johnson calling for increased spending on housing and urban affairs generally. Barefoot Sanders gave the letter high priority, urging the President to take action in view of Laird's leadership position in the House. Johnson referred the letter to Califano and asked Laird to see him personally.[46] But, to put these events in perspective, it should be remembered that the interest-subsidy issue had been on the agenda for some years. Its final approval was significant because it brought the federal government directly into an area previously thought largely to be the responsibility of the private sector or of local governments (who were effectively excluded from the 1968 Act).

Within just a year of the passage of the Economic Opportunity Act (EOA) and the creation of the Community Action Program, social service professionals, social scientists, politicians and other commentators began to attack the new programme for its apparent failures and contradictions. By

1968 the litany of criticism had been extended to include most of the Great Society legislation,[47] although those programmes which turned out to be of the most lasting importance – Medicare, Medicaid, food stamps, the Elementary and Secondary Education Act (ESEA) and numerous environmental, consumer protection and occupational safety and health laws – received much less criticism.[48] This is not the place to review these critiques, most of which dwelt on the yawning gap between Great Society objectives and rhetoric and the economic and political realities of urban America. But it is important to judge the Great Society from a broader theoretical perspective. We will do this by assessing public policy in terms of its coherence in relation to economic and political theory.

Coherence

Economic theory

As earlier suggested, the first Great Society initiatives were based on the ideas of economists rather than other social scientists. Within the Executive Office of the President (EOP), the Council of Economic Advisers (CEA) became the main institutional focus at least for the early Great Society proposals. Indeed, the 1964 programme was largely written by two CEA staff economists, Burton Weisbrod and William Capron.[49] In addition, the several Income Maintenance Task Forces set up during the Johnson years were chaired by CEA staff. In spite of involvement by OEO, HEW and BOB, the CEA remained the lead agency.[50] Although the CEA played a less prominent role in education, housing, and urban affairs, staff economists played some part in all the relevant task forces and were often the source of crucial advice in particular areas. For example, the idea of converting the Model Cities Program into a sort of revenue sharing for cities came from the CEA.[51]

The dominance of economists in anti-poverty programmes is not altogether surprising, given the intellectual consensus within economics at the time. Very generally, American economists believed that:

(a) Full employment (around or just below 4% of the labour force) was not only achievable but necessary for the realization of the good society.

(b) Government action to aid this objective was wholly legitimate.

(c) Social and economic programmes, both macro and micro, which brought individuals, families or social groups out of poverty produced the double benefit of increasing national income and reducing unemployment.

(d) All of the above was achievable without excessive government spending or large tax increases.

A substantial technocratic element exists in this scheme. Problems could be solved through properly designed interventionist policies. As far as poverty was concerned, it seems unlikely that the CEA economists and others involved in formulating the Community Action Program were absorbed with the specific causes of poverty or with the ongoing debate on whether poverty was environmentally induced or part of the culture or life-cycle of hopelessness.[52] Instead, it was assumed that a multi-faceted attack on the problem, including education and retraining programmes, participation in community action and the 'rationalization' of existing welfare provision, would somehow lift people out of poverty.[53] An improved macro-economic environment would also help. Henry Aaron claims in his influential *Politics and the Professors* that the whole scheme was based 'on an ambiguity so profound that it should be called a contradiction'.[54] Put simply, the alleged contradiction was that the programmes failed to appreciate the complex relationship between the working and the non-working poor. Those permanently out of the labour market could not be helped by an improved economic environment, but at the same time the War on Poverty was, according to Aaron, devoted to alleviating the causes not curing the symptoms of poverty. For the unemployable poor only 'cash hand-outs' would help, so alleviating the causes through community action was irrelevant.[55] While this may be true of the actual administration of the programme through OEO, it is not an accurate characterization of War on Poverty during its inception. Analysis of the original documents reveals an approach which in many respects was intellectually coherent. For example, the 20 December memo from Walter Heller to the President, which was to become the basis of the subsequent State of the Union Message and the 1964 legislation, advised the President to:

Emphasize that the major focus of the attack on poverty is on youth: to *prevent* entry into poverty. Indicate that additional purposes will be to encourage *exit* from poverty and to *alleviate* the hardships of those living in poverty.[56] (emphasis in original)

The youth emphasis clearly shows that Heller was sensitive to the fact that barriers to labour market entry, such as poor education, cultural and racial disadvantage, were a major problem. And the references to the alleviation of poverty show that the CEA economists were aware that welfare payments (or 'cash hand-outs') would have to be increased to bring the unemployable poor above the poverty line. This and later documents reinforce the impression that the War on Poverty was conceived as a multi-faceted attack on the problem. The economy – and society generally – would benefit from increased tax revenue, and eventually from reduced transfer payments as the employable poor got jobs. Parallel to this effort, a generally sound economy would ensure that the numbers of poor would not increase via structural unemployment. It is very important to remember that unemployment was, by today's standards, low during the early 1960s. Aaron's excoriation of the War on Poverty for its insensitivity to the relationship between the macro-economic environment and the poor's willingness to work is, in the context of near full employment, unconvincing. Heller, Kermit Gordon and the other Keynesian economists were almost certainly right in assuming that any reductions in unemployment below the 4% level would make little impact on the numbers living in poverty. Some extra special effort focussed on target groups and areas was necessary to help such people.

On the face of it, these early Great Society measures were not irresponsible in fiscal terms. Original estimates for the War on Poverty were for extra spending in the order of $500 million (out of a total price tag of $962.5 million, which included agency requests already filed).[57] Even the Elementary and Secondary Education Act (ESEA) was not a massively funded bill, allocating as it did an extra $1.06 billion in its first year (1966) the lion's share of which ($1.03 billion) went to the states for disbursement to school districts with high proportions of low-income children.[58] As earlier indicated, Model Cities was quite modestly funded as was the 1968 Housing Act, at least in its first year. Funding for Medicare was of a quite different order with some $6.5 billion being appropriated for the first year of the programme.[59] However, $5.1 billion of this was to be financed by increases in payroll taxes and by individual contributions. Only $1.4 billion was to be drawn from general reserves.[60] Eventually the costs of Medicare would spiral, in part because title XIX provided for matching funds for the states up to 83% of the full cost of medical assistance for the poor. Eventually this title would come to be known as Medicaid and would develop into one of the largest items on the federal domestic budget.

Where the Great Society economists failed was in their naive assumptions about the substance and detail of the policy-making environment in the United States. For example, any debate that took place on income-maintenance programmes and whether they should be preventative, ameliorative, corrective, or what, largely ignored the problem of which level of government should be involved in the administration of new programmes. And this was in spite of the well-known inequities and anomalies that the federal system encouraged (of which, much more later). Later, economists in the OEO began to argue in favour of a negative income tax administered directly by the federal government (but still with some involvement by the states).[61] But by 1966–7 the steam had gone out of the anti-poverty drive; OEO's status was low and Johnson himself disliked the idea of the negative income tax.[62]

In sum, although in terms both the prevailing economic orthodoxy (Keynesian economics) and in the context of near full employment and fiscal stability the Great Society was quite coherent, the economists failed to grasp the political realities of policy implementation. Johnson officials had little sense that, once legislated, programmes might become distorted, or grow rapidly as increasing numbers of states, localities, groups and individuals scrambled for inclusion in new grants and subsidies. Put another way, they were unaware that the sheer rhetorical power of the Great Society might change the policy agenda in ways which undermined the autonomy and independence of the executive branch.

Political theory

As earlier mentioned, few public policies have received as much opprobium for poor design as have those associated with the Great Society. The catalogue of criticism is long and this is not the place for anything but a brief summary. But most of the critiques focus on the War on Poverty and the specific activities of OEO. Among the most commonly quoted problems are:

(a) A failure to appreciate the complexities of local politics and how community-action agencies would interact with local power structure.

(b) A failure to appreciate the problems associated with coordinating disparate federal agencies through a central bureaucracy based in the White House.

(c) A failure to elaborate priorities and objectives and in particular to define how the participation of the poor in a range of programmes would help reduce or eliminate poverty.

(d) Related, was OEO's blurred conception of how a limited amount of money would be able to achieve the exalted objectives of preventing entry into, encouraging exit from, and alleviating the hardships of, poverty.[63]

Part of the explanation for the heady optimism implicit in the War on Poverty was the assumption on the part of its authors that they were building something very distinct from the traditional welfare strategy. Established welfare provision – notably Aid for Families with Dependent Children (AFDC) – was held in low public esteem. It conjured up notions of dependence and hopelessness, which were out of harmony with the positive rhetoric of the Great Society.[64] By emphasizing self-reliance through community action and retraining and rehabilitation, the War on Poverty was designed, as Johnson put it, to 'make taxpayers out of taxeaters'.[65] David Zarefsky has further stressed how the military metaphors of the programme came to resemble 'a rhetorical crisis' and after 1964 it was increasingly difficult to match the promises of 'victory' and 'all out war on poverty' with reality.[66] Most commentators have concentrated on these aspects both of the War on Poverty and the Great Society generally. The gap between promise and performance, administrative chaos, insensitivity to the nature of social problems in America and inadequate funding have dominated the critiques.

In fact, most of the Great Society measures – and especially those which were to survive the 1960s as major programmes – ESEA, Civil Rights, Medicare and Medicaid – were very much in the mainstream of what we have called the New Deal regime. If we accept, along with Harold Wilensky and others, that among state-supported social provision in America, education is 'different',[67] then ESEA was hardly revolutionary. The major change involved the principle of *federal* aid for education, rather than government aid as such. But the programme concentrated aid not on individual children or on teachers' qualifications and salaries, but on the physical fabric and equipment of schools. It was selective, focussed on equality of opportunity and administered through the states. Indeed, the Gardner Task Force which wrote the crucial title I of the Act, specifically stated a preference for aid to be channelled through the states, and to be selective rather than general in nature. This is in contrast to the earlier (failed) Kennedy proposals, which involved general aid and the preferences of

BOB Director Kermit Gordon, who wanted aid to go directly to school districts.[68] In sum, the major change involved the admission of the federal government into the funding of elementary and secondary education. Although originally funded wholly out of local sources, elementary and secondary education had long received aid from the governor's mansions in a number of states, so ESEA was merely an extension of this principle. Incursion by the federal government into the domain of the states was, of course, originally part of the New Deal philosophy which Johnson was reinforcing and extending.

The same could be said of Medicare and Medicaid. Both medical programmes were, in fact, officially an extension of the 1935 Social Security Act. Model Cities was more innovative, focussing as it did on direct aid to cities, therefore by-passing the states. The OEO also largely by-passed the states, but both programmes stressed self-reliance, and both were highly selective, focussed as they were on those individuals and areas most in need. In retrospect, it is clear that it is these two programmes, together with a number of housing programmes which were at once the most innovative, the most controversial and, in terms of longevity, the least successful. They were also the result of the most internalized policy formulation process and they were the programmes most intimately associated with the President.

The New Deal regime had established a pattern of social-policy-programme administration which, while not universally accepted, was broadly established as legitimate among political elites at federal, state and local levels. (For a full discussion, see chapter 1, pp. 8–9.)

In total, this New Deal regime hardly amounts to a coherent theory either of the welfare state or of federalism. Instead, as is well documented, it was a result of a combination of American ideology and the institutional complexity of federalism and the separation of powers.[69] As such the New Deal programmes had all the hallmarks of improvisation. If there was a theoretical foundation, it is what might be called re-distributive centralism, or the assumption that only the federal government could act positively to redistribute resources across areas and social groups (see chapter 2, pp. 24–5). In this context it is not surprising that the more successful of the Great Society programmes in terms of longevity and funding were those most compatible with the New Deal regime. The ESEA was selective and administered via the states, its equalizing effects tempered by a formula based on the poverty of parents rather than the prevailing per-student expenditure by school districts. Medicare benefits, which were at least partly paid for by contributory social-security payments went directly to recipients, while Medicaid was to be administered through the states. This was hardly a rational arrangement for, equity problems apart – benefits were to vary considerably from state to state – most economists agree that the most efficient way to administer re-distributive welfare payments is directly from the central government to beneficiaries.[70] Inclusion of the states in the administration of Medicaid made little economic sense, therefore. It was a political expedient.

Indeed, taken as a whole, the Great Society programmes contained no clear conception of federalism. Johnson himself spoke often about the need for 'co-operation' and 'partnership' between the three levels of government.[71] He even launched a new contract between the federal government and the states and localities, which was to be called 'creative federalism', or sometimes 'New Federalism'. On 26 August 1964 Johnson announced that: 'We are entering a new day of relations between government and private institutions and individual citizens. This New Federalism – this new day of co-operation – is not fully understood. But the problems are apparent.'[72] Judging by his legislative programme and its implementation, however, Johnson seemed largely unaware of these problems. Federal grants were to grow like topsy following the Great Society legislation. And while states and localities were often all too willing to accept these grants, little thought was devoted to what the limits to federal aid might be. The Johnson programmes displayed a similar obtuseness towards the state-locality relationship. Model Cities and EOA, indeed, showed considerable insensitivity towards prevailing notions of federalism. Both programmes were originally designed to by-pass existing state bureaucracies and policy professionals. The assumption was that officials were bogged down in a 'welfare mentality' engendered by the inadequate design and implementation of the AFDC programme.[73] By going direct to the local level, community-action agencies could not only mobilize the poor but raise the consciousness and professionalism of local officials. Sometimes they did just this and were relatively successful. In other instances they aroused considerable opposition from local governments by radicalizing local people.[74] But whatever the outcome, the OEO and Model Cities programmes were not built in any sense of what the proper role between federal, state and local governments should be. New networks of interest representation, and dependency on federal aid, were created with little thought for the consequences.

In essence, Johnson's support for the particular policy thrust and administrative arrangements adopted by the War on Poverty was theoretically incoherent. He showed little interest in overhauling the essentials of the existing welfare system and he was downright hostile to the negative income tax concept with its implicit nationalization of welfare benefits.[75] Johnson was personally repelled by the notion of welfare and reportedly often referred to HEW as his 'Department of Health and Education'.[76] Given this, it is perhaps not surprising that the President's undoubted commitment to fighting poverty would take the form of a combination of political expediency, unrealistic optimism and rhetorical flourish.

As far as notions of democracy and equality were concerned, the Great Society was equally obscure. 'Maximum feasible participation', the much-touted slogan of the War on Poverty, was more of a means to an end rather than an objective valued in itself. Once out of poverty, those of the poor who could work would become ordinary tax-paying, voting citizens. Under this assumption there would be no transformation towards participatory democracy in America. Moreover, the anti-poverty programme deliberately underplayed notions of equality which might have led to expensive transfer-payment commitments. Instead, and in the mainstream of American tradition, equality of opportunity was the central value of the programme. Interestingly, the War on Poverty, and many other Great Society measures, were in no sense party-political initiatives. As David Broder and others have noted, Johnson did his best to undermine the Democratic Party as an organizational force independent of the presidency.[77] His ambition to build a Great Society required a concentration of power in the presidency, not in a party system whose strength lay in the states and local governments. Of the Great Society measures, civil rights and Medicare probably owed most to party support, and both had been on the Democratic agenda for many years. But even with civil rights, it was necessary for the administration to build bridges with the Republicans in order to overcome Southern Democratic Congressional opposition.

These programmes apart, it is clear that in origins and design most of the Great Society legislation owed little to anything resembling party government. Instead, the laws came from within the Executive branch and from a President who, more in populist than party-political tradition, saw himself as responsible to the American people, indeed to the whole society. In this sense, Johnson was continuing a trend dating from the beginning of the century involving the gradual usurpation of party power and its replacement with executive power.[78]

We can conclude, then, that while the Great Society extended the functions and responsibilities of the American state, in ideological and legislative terms it did so in ways largely within the framework established by the New Deal regime. As will be elaborated below, the major strains produced by this agenda were political and institutional and resulted from a policy-implementation experience.

Institutional adaptation

In a 3 June 1964 memo to the President, Douglass Cater urged that: 'The most important idea to be communicated during the campaign is that the people need a *Can Do* President during the coming years. This idea is more important than the specific programs you announce.'[79] In many respects this advice sums up the style and spirit of the Johnson presidency. Johnson was obsessed with achieving results and achieving them quickly. For the ex-Senate-majority leader intent on changing the domestic policy agenda, this meant concentrating on a legislative strategy. He was by all accounts remarkably successful in this. Most observers agree he was an able legislative leader,[80] although he was also blessed by the good fortune of a largely pliant, predominantly Democratic Congress, and, at least until 1966, a generally benign political environment. Johnson adopted a similar stance with regard to administrative re-organization. Accomplishment meant creating new departments and agencies (the Department of Housing and Urban Development (HUD), the Department of Transport (DOT) and OEO), and setting up task forces into government organizations (the Price and Heineman Task Forces). Much less thought was devoted to the consequences of creating new departments, and the advice of the task forces was generally ignored.[81]

For example, the Price Task Force concluded pessimistically in June 1967 that: 'Many domestic social programs are under severe attack . . . Some criticism arises because of alleged organizational and managerial weaknesses. After several months of study, we believe the organizational criticism is merited.'[82] But Johnson was largely uninterested in such comment. He was absorbed with the challenge of process rather than substance. As Doris Kearns puts it: 'When Johnson signed a law, he brought to an end a legislative process that had begun with the preparation of a presidential message . . . This process was the center of Johnson's life, and the ceremony of successful completion was also a personal celebration.'[83] In this context, Johnson's lack of interest in the complexity of policy implementation is not surprising. Almost all his organizational innovations and adaptations were geared to legislation. The task force concept was used predominantly in this way and as indicated, it was the *creation* of the HUD, DOT and OEO which sparked the president's enthusiasm, not their activities thereafter.

Appropriately, BOB, which was one of the main institutional devices available for control of the executive branch, did not assume a high status in the Johnson presidency. BOB played a crucial role in the various re-organization plans including the creation of HUD and DOT. But Special Assistant to the President, Joe Califano, rather than Budget Directors Kermit Gordon and Charles Schultze, became the key domestic policy official. Later, information ran from Schultze to the President via Califano and on a number of occasions BOB organizational advice was rejected or ignored.[84] Moreover, while a number of recommendations were raised to modernize BOB, create field offices and generally use the agency as a means of control over rapidly spawning federal departments and programmes, they came to nothing.[85] As Redford and Blisset note, these recommendations came at the height of the Vietnam War when, 'obviously, the opportunity for President Johnson to turn from large policy issues – his primary concern through his total government experience – to structural and operational problems in implementation of policy was not present'.[86]

So, while consciousness of increasing difficulties over the control of the executive branch in general and of the new social programmes in particular was increasing during the last years of the Johnson presidency, it provoked little in the way of presidential action.

Conclusions

Without doubt, the Great Society legislation greatly expanded the role of government in a range of social-policy areas. Whether measured as a percentage of GNP devoted to grants in aid or to transfer payments for the old, unemployed and poor, the increases were impressive. In 1960 grants to state and local governments totalled $19.5 billion or 1.4% of the gross national product (GNP). By 1970 this amount had increased to $51.1 billion or 2.4% of GNP.[87] Grants of all sorts including transfer payments to individuals increased from 6.3% of GNP in 1961 to 8.7% in 1969 and 13.4% in 1976.[88] From our analysis of the origins and coherence of, and institutional adaptation in response to the Great Society, we can conclude the following:

(1)   The major impetus for a general programme of social reform came from Lyndon Johnson personally. His objective was to transform the social agenda in an even more radical fashion than the changes achieved under the New Deal. In this sense he wanted to 'out do' FDR. As William Leuchtenburg observes: 'He was not satisfied to go down in the history books merely as a successful president in the Roosevelt tradition. He aimed instead to be "the greatest of them all, the whole bunch of them". And to be the greatest president in history, he needed not just to match Roosevelt's performance, but to surpass it.'[89] As recorded, the major political device employed to achieve this objective was innovative legislation. And although many of the laws most intimately associated with Johnson (OEO, Model Cities and housing subsidies) were to founder in later years, the drama and rhetoric with which they were launched helped to transform the legislative environment for many other measures. Of course we will never know whether Medicare, Medicaid, food stamps and a number of education bills would have been passed in the absence of Johnson's leadership, but the fact that these programmes too focussed on America's disadvantaged surely helped to assure successful passage. For the fact is that he was *able* to choose his agenda. It was not thrust upon him, nor for the most part, did he inherit it.

(2)   So, with the launch of the War on Poverty in early 1964, Johnson was in the business of creating a new social agenda for

redistributive public policy. A highly internalized policy process guided by Keynesian economists and promoted for public consumption by the President was largely responsible for this agenda. So much is clear. What we cannot answer is the extent to which these new policies inspired what in disparate forms could be called a social movement for change in America after 1964. Urban riots, Vietnam, Democratic domination of Congress and the Civil Rights Movement all undoubtedly played a part. But no matter in which direction the causal lines run, what is established is that no such movement (civil rights apart) existed prior to 1964, to the President's rhetoric and action obviously played a part.

With myriad new laws came new constituents, clients, bureaucracies, media pressures and, as catalogued, very serious problems of executive coordination and control. Such is often the case with innovative legislation. But rarely do such laws come with such comprehensiveness and frequency. Johnson personally appeared indifferent to these problems, and even in his final economic report Johnson claimed that 'the advances in the War on Poverty' were the accomplishments that gave him greatest pride.[90] Perhaps as a result, institutionally little fundamentally changed during the Johnson years. New departments were created, but these were largely collections of established agencies organized under one new name (HUD, DOT). BOB continued to function much as it had during the 1950s. Johnson did not use his appointment power in any overtly political sense, except when nominating to the highest echelons.

But Johnson's apparent indifference to implementation and institutional reform were at least partly in keeping with the intellectual mood of the times. Kennedy too had a primarily legislative focus. Technocracy promised problem solving through action, rather than the arcane business of policy evaluation and the complexity of institutional reform.

(3) Even though the legislation was innovative and potentially wide in scope, most of the Great Society measures

remained broadly within the bounds of the New Deal regime. Those that did not (OEO, Model Cities and subsidized housing) proved short lived. In other words, the institutional, ideological and political pressures accounting for the particular nature of the New Deal agenda remained in place, even if in modified form. Welfare payments should be channelled through the states according to some matching formula, thus greatly aggravating problems of equity and status. Social-security payments could be allocated direct to individuals — although even here major elements of selectivity remained. Education programmes, also administered through the states, strived to permit continued state and local control over curricula and the hiring and firing of faculty.

For the most part, this pattern was not imposed on the Administration by Congress. It was, rather the 'natural' way to administer programmes, given the existing political and institutional traditions and constraints. In the anti-poverty and urban-policy areas the new laws were more innovative, involving as they did citizen participation, the demonstration concept and by-passing state (and even sometimes local) governments. But they were poorly funded and politically unrealistic. The failure of Johnson and the architects of the Great Society – although not, later, OEO officials – to propose a more radical overhaul of the Welfare and federal grant-in-aid system is striking. It is almost as though they viewed the particular arrangements of the War on Poverty as a sort of *Deus ex machina* which, descending from above, would cut through the bothersome complexity of the existing system. Paradoxically it was left to what was widely perceived as a conservative Republican administration to propose a truly radical reform of welfare and federal grants.

NOTES

1 Walter Heller to Kennedy, 1 May 1963, enclosed with Heller to Johnson, 16 November 1964, 'CEA during the Johnson Administration, Vol. 2 Documentary Supplement' (LBJ Library).

2 Walter Heller to the Secretaries of Agriculture, Commerce, Labor, Health, Education and Welfare, Director of the Bureau of the Budget and the Administrator of the Housing and Home Finance Agency, attachment to Heller to Johnson (LBJ Library).
3 Heller to Departmental Secretaries, attachment to Heller to Johnson (LBJ Library).
4 Ibid.
5 Lyndon Baines Johnson, *The Vantage Point: Perspectives on the Presidency, 1963–1969*, New York: Holt Rinehart and Winston, 1971, p. 69.
6 CEA to Ted Sorensen, 20 December 1963, White House Central Files (WHCF), WE25, Container 25 (LBJ Library).
7 Reported in a number of sources, including Louis Heren, *No Hail, No Farewell*, New York: Harper and Row, 1970, p. 27.
8 Doris Kearns, *Lyndon Johnson and the American Dream*, New York: Harper and Row, 1976, p. 188.
9 Gabriel A. Almond and Sidney Verba, *The Civic Culture: Political Attitudes and Democracy in Five Nations*, Princeton, NJ: Princeton University Press 1965.
10 Henry J. Aaron, *Politics and the Professors: The Great Society in Perspective*, Washington, DC: The Brookings Institution, 1978, p. 17.
11 New York, Macmillan, 1962. Almost as important as the book was the 19 January 1963 review of the book in the *New Yorker* by Dwight McDonald. Ted Sorensen apparently encouraged Kennedy to read this piece. Reported in David Zarefsky, *President Johnson's War on Poverty: Rhetoric and History*, Alabama: University of Alabama Press, 1986, p. 25.
12 Letter from Johnson to Meany and Meany to Johnson with attachments, 6 March and 12 March 1964, WHCF, WE9, Container 25, Poverty Program (LBJ Library).
13 Heller to Departmental Secretaries, 16 November 1964, p. 1 (LBJ Library).
14 For a critique and debate on this subject, see Charles A. McCoy and John Playford (eds.), *Apolitical Politics: A Critique of Behaviouralism*, New York: Crowell, 1967.
15 Johnson, *The Vantage Point*, p. 70.
16 Remarks at the University of Michigan, 22 May 1964, *Public Papers of the President, 1964*, Washington, DC: US Government Printing Office, p. 704.
17 *Public Papers*, pp. 704–5.
18 Quoted in William E. Leuchtenberg, 'The Genesis of the Great Society', *The Reporter*, 34 (21 April 1966), 37.
19 Ibid.
20 Ibid.

21 Nancy Kegan Smith, 'Presidential Task Force Operation During the Johnson Administration', *Presidential Studies Quarterly*, 15: 2 (Spring 1985), 322.
22 Leuchtenberg, 'Genesis of the Great Society', p. 38.
23 Smith, 'Presidential Task Force Operation', p. 322.
24 Quoted in Hugh Davis Graham, 'The Transformation of Federal Education Policy', in Robert A. Devine (ed.), *Exploring the Johnson Years*, Austin, TS: University of Texas Press, 1981, p. 158.
25 Memo from Cater to Moyers, 3 November 1964, Files of Bill Moyers, (LBJ Library).
26 Nancy Kegan Smith, 'Presidential Task Force Operation', p. 323.
27 Cater to Moyers, 3 November 1964, Files of Bill Moyers (LBJ Library).
28 See *Congressional Quarterly, Weekly Report*, 30 July 1965, 'Medicare Chronology', p. 1494. Wilbur Cohen to Cater, 'Presidential Statements on Health Legislation', 20 September 1965, WHCF, Ex Health (LBJ Library).
29 *Congressional Quarterly, Almanac, 1965*, vol. 21, Washington, DC, 1966, pp. 538–40.
30 Congress had, of course, first legislated in this area in 1870 and 1871. In the modern era, the issue had been on the agenda since the late 1940s.
31 'Notes on Model Cities', in 'Origins and Deliberations of the Wood-Haar Task Force', *Legislative Background, Model Cities, 1966*, box 1 (LBJ Library).
32 Memo from Walter Reuther to LBJ, 'The Early Origins', *Legislative Background, Model Cities, 1966* (LBJ Library).
33 Letter from Dick Goodwin to Reuther, 28 May 1965 and Reuther's reply, 4 June 1965, Charles Schultze's Agenda for the First Task Force Meeting, *Legislative Background, Model Cities, 1966* (LBJ Library).
34 *Congressional Quarterly, Weekly Report*, 11 November 1966, p. 2817.
35 For example in August 1967 Congress passed a law making it a federal offence to harm or intimidate firemen and others attempting to quell a riot; see the *New York Times*, 17 August 1967, p. 1. It is also generally accepted that Congress only passed a federal open housing law in the wake of the assassination of Martin Luther King, earlier attempts (most notably in 1966) having failed. See David McKay, *Housing and Race in Industrial Society: Civil Rights and Urban Policy in Britain and the United States*, London: Croom Helm, 1977, chapter 2.
36 Copy of statement from Joe Califano to the president, 'The Legislative Struggle', *Legislative Background, Model Cities Act, 1966*, box 2 (LBJ Library).
37 Copy of statement from Joe Califano to the President, *Legislative Background, Model Cities Act, 1966* (LBJ Library).
38 See *Congressional Quarterly, Weekly Report*, 11 November 1966,

pp. 2817–24, see also *Legislative Background, Model Cities Act, 1966* (LBJ Library).

39 Evidence of the individualized nature of Reuther's power is clear from biographies, see Jean Gould and Lorena Hickok, *Walter Reuther: Labor's Rugged Individualist*, New York: Dodd Mead, 1972, chapter 5; Frank Cormier and William J. Eaton, *Reuther*, New Jersey: Prentice Hall, 1970, chapter 28.

40 Paul Southwick to LBJ, 'Fact Sheet: Great Society', 4 June 1964, WHCF (LBJ Library); Kermit Gordon to Task Force on Urban Problems and Harry McPherson 21 March 1965, *Legislative Background, Model Cities, 1966*, box 1 (LBJ Library).

41 Report of the 1965 Task Force on Housing and Urban Affairs, WHCF, box 11 (LBJ Library).

42 Joe Califano to HUD Secretary Robert Weaver, 25 August 1967, File on Housing and Urban Development, 1968, Files of Joe Califano, Container 78 (LBJ Library).

43 For accounts of public housing see Leonard Freedman, *Public Housing: the Politics of Housing*, New York: Holt, Rinehart and Winston, 1969; Lawrence Friedman, *Government and Slum Housing*, Chicago: Rand McNally, 1968; Harold L. Wolman, *Housing and Housing Policy in the US and UK*, Lexington, MA: Lexington Books, 1975.

44 *Congressional Quarterly, Weekly Report*, 9 August 1968, p. 2125.

45 *Congressional Quarterly, Weekly Report*, 2 August 1968, p. 2031.

46 Barefoot Sanders to LBJ, 7 September 1967, with attachments, Files of Joe Califano, Container 47 (LBJ LIbrary).

47 The more trenchant of the critiques include: Kenneth B. Clark and Jeanette Hopkins, *A Relevant War Against Poverty: A Study of Community Action Programs and Observable Social Change*, New York: Harper and Row, 1969; Stephen M. Rose, *The Betrayal of the Poor: The Transformation of Community Action*, Cambridge, MA: Schenkman, 1972; J. David Greenstone and Paul E. Peterson, *Race and Authority in Urban Politics*, New York: Russell Sage Foundation, 1973; Daniel Patrick Moynihan, *Maximum Feasible Misunderstanding*, New York: Free Press, 1969; Sar Levitan, *The Great Society's Poor Law*, Baltimore: The Johns Hopkins Press, 1969; Peter Marris and Martin Rein, *Dilemmas of Social Reform*, 2nd edn, Chicago: Aldine, 1973; David Zarefsky, *President Johnson's War on Poverty: Rhetoric and History*, Alabama: University of Alabama, 1986.

48 It is sometimes forgotten that the Johnson Administration was responsible for such laws as the Federal Pollution Control Act and Water Resources Planning Act 1965, the Air Quality Act 1967, the Fair Packaging and Labelling Act 1966, the Automobile Safety Act 1966, the Coal Mine Safety Act 1968 and the Occupational Health and Safety Act of 1968.

49 'The CEA's Role in Social Programs', undated, *Administrative History of the CEA During the Johnson Administration*, vol. 1 (LBJ Library), p. v3.
50 Ibid., pp. v4–5.
51 Ibid., p. v10.
52 See the discussion in Aaron, *Politics and the Professors*, pp. 20–3.
53 *Congressional Quarterly, Weekly Report*, 29 May 1964, p. 1037.
54 Aaron, *Politics and the Professors*, p. 29.
55 Ibid., pp. 29–30.
56 Quoted in Mark I. Galfand, 'The War on Poverty', in Robert A. Devine (ed.), *Exploring the Johnson Years*, Austin, TS: University of Texas Press, p. 131. See also *Congressional Quarterly, Weekly Report*, 29 May 1964, p. 1037.
57 *Congressional Quarterly, Weekly Report*, 16 April 1965, p. 666.
58 *Congressional Quarterly, Weekly Report*, 30 July 1965, p. 1493.
59 *Congressional Quarterly, Weekly Report*, 30 July 1965, p. 1493.
60 *Congressional Quarterly, Weekly Report*, 30 July 1965, p. 1496.
61 For a full discussion, see Vincent J. and Vee Burke, *Nixon's Good Deed: Welfare Reform*, New York: Columbia University Press, 1974, chapter 2.
62 Burke and *Nixon's Good Deed*, pp. 22–4.
63 See the references in note 44.
64 See Gilbert Steiner, *Social Insecurity: the Politics of Welfare*, Chicago: Rand McNally, 1966. Also the discussion in Zarefsky, *President Johnson's War on Poverty*, pp. 47–49.
65 Quoted in Zarefsky, *President Johnson's War on Poverty*, p. 49.
66 Ibid., chapter 3.
67 See for example, the discussion in Harold L. Wilensky, *The Welfare State and Equality: Structural and Ideological Roots of Public Expenditures*, Berkeley and Los Angeles: University of California Press, 1975, chapter 1.
68 *Administrative History of Federal Aid to Education*, 31 July 1968, pp. 42–55 (LBJ Library).
69 See, *inter alia*, James T. Patterson, *America's Struggle Against Poverty 1900–1985*, Cambridge, MA: Harvard University Press, 1986; Theda Skocpol, 'Political Response to Capitalist Crisis: Neo-Marxist Theories of the State and the Case of the New Deal', *Politics and Society*, 10 (1980): 155–201.
70 For a discussion, see Claude E. Barfield, *Rethinking Federalism: Block Grants and Federal, State, and Local Responsibilities*, Washington, DC: American Enterprise Institute, 1981, chapter 6.
71 For a discussion see Vaughn Davis Bornet, *The Presidency of Lyndon B. Johnson*, Lawrence, Kansas: University of Kansas Press, 1983, pp. 246–7.
72 Quoted in Bornet, *The Presidency of Lyndon B. Johnson*, pp. 246–7. On the idea of creative federalism, see Max Ways, 'Creative Federalism and the Great Society', *Fortune* (January 1966), 120–3.

73 See in particular Patterson, *America's Struggle Against Poverty*, chapter 9.

74 For a summary see Patterson, *America's Struggle Against Poverty*, pp. 148–54, and sources cited.

75 Burke and Burke, *Nixon's Good Deed*, pp. 22–4 and 44, and sources cited.

76 Ibid., p. 44.

77 David S. Broder, *The Party's Over: The Failure of Politics in America*, New York: Harper and Row, 1971, chapter 3; Doris Kearns, *Lyndon Johnson*, pp. 244–5.

78 Stephen J. Skowronek, *Building a New American State, The Expansion of National Administrative Capacities, 1877–1920*. Cambridge: Cambridge University Press, 1982.

79 Cater to LBJ, Files of Douglass Cater, 3 June 1964 (LBJ Library), p. 1.

80 Nigel Bowles, *The White House and Capitol Hill: The Politics of Presidential Persuasion*, Oxford: Oxford University Press, chapter 10; Barbara Kellerman, *The Political Presidency: Practice of Leadership from Kennedy through Reagan*, New York: Oxford University Press, 1984, chapter 7; William S. Livingston, Lawrence C. Dodd and Richard Schott (eds.), *The Presidency and the Congress: A Shifting Balance of Power?*, Austin, TS: Lyndon B. Johnson School of Public Affairs, 1979, chapter 5. A less sanguine view based on quantitative evidence is provided by George C. Edwards, *Presidential Influence in Congress*, San Francisco: Freeman, 1980, chapters 1 and 7.

81 Emmette S. Redford and Martin Blisset, *Organizing the Executive Branch: The Johnson Presidency*, Chicago: University of Chicago Press, 1980, p. 220.

82 Quoted in Richard P. Nathan, *The Administrative Presidency*, New York: Wiley, 1983, p. 5.

83 Kearns, *Lyndon Johnson*, p. 249.

84 Redford and Blisset, *Organizing the Executive Branch*, pp. 221–23.

85 Redford and Blisset, *Organizing the Executive Branch*, chapter 8. See also Harold Seidman and Robert Gilmour, *Politics and Power: From the Positive to the Regulatory State*, New York: Oxford University Press, 1986, pp. 94–5.

86 Redford and Blisset, *Organizing the Executive Branch*, pp. 209–10.

87 *Special Analyses, Budget of the United States, Fiscal Year 1987*, Washington, DC: US Government Printing Office, 1986.

88 *Budget of the United States Government*, and Appendix: 'Fiscal years 1963–1975', Washington, DC: US Government Printing Office.

89 William E. Leuchtenburg, *In the Shadow of FDR: From Harry Truman to Ronald Reagan*, Ithaca, NY: Cornell University Press, 1983, p. 142.

90 Quoted in Zarefsky, *President Johnson's War on Poverty*, p. 189.

4   Richard Nixon: reluctant reformer?

Origins

Richard Nixon was widely distrusted by the Great Society liberals who suspected that a major objective of his presidency would be to dismantle the Johnson programmes and substitute a conservative or even reactionary agenda. With a few relatively minor exceptions, Nixon did not at first do this in part (as with civil rights) because he was unable to, but mainly (as with federal aid and welfare) because he proposed radical and by some standards progressive alternatives to the existing programmes. By most criteria, the federal government's domestic responsibilities were greater at the end of his presidency than at the beginning.

Liberals' fears were fuelled by Nixon's reputation as a Red-baiter, a cold-war warrior and a man who had always been intellectually and emotionally at odds with what he viewed as a liberal east-coast-based media, academic and bureaucratic establishment. Nixon was also elected at a highly ideologically charged time in American history. Vietnam and race divided the country to such an extent that few politicians could escape some ideological label. Nixon was branded as a dyed-in-the-wool conservative because he opposed a further extension of affirmative action in civil rights and supported the American war effort in Vietnam. Yet down to 1968 his policy statements on the substance of mainstream domestic policy were few and far between. Indeed, although it was part of the Nixon 1968 campaign strategy to keep the issue content as low as possible, this was not difficult, given the candidate's apparent lack of interest in a range of domestic policy areas.[1] But most informed commentators considered Nixon a moderate Republican on domestic issues,[2] and following his election he gathered about him a group which it would be difficult to label 'conservative'. In domestic policy, only Arthur Burns as Counsellor to the President and Martin Anderson a (junior) advisor on domestic affairs were clearly on the Republican Right. In contrast Robert Finch (Secretary of HEW) and John Ehrlichman were moderates and David Patrick Moynihan, newly appointed director of a planned Urban Affairs Council, was an (admittedly disillusioned) liberal Democrat. When making key appointments, Nixon's strategy seems to have been to combine reliance on long-established associates (Burns, Finch) with the programmatic advice of leading Republicans such as Representative – and later Defence Secretary – Melvin Laird, who supported Moynihan.[3] The result was an ideological mix obviously to the right of the Johnson team but by no means uniformly conservative.

Where Nixon clearly did differ from Johnson was in the length of his agenda. Nixon himself later commented that there had already been far too much legislation over the previous eight years, especially measures associated with the Great Society.[4] He also claimed, at least initially, to be intent on dismantling these laws. But he was quickly persuaded – almost certainly by Moynihan – that to move too quickly would invite a serious backlash from vested liberal interests. According to Nixon, Moynihan pleaded that: 'All the Great Society activist constituencies are lying out there in wait poised to get you if you try to come after them: the professional welfarists, the urban planners, the day carers, the social workers, the public housers. Frankly, I'm terrified at the thought of cutting back too fast. Just take Model Cities. The urban ghettos would go up in flames if you cut it out.'[5]

Whether this was Nixon's major motive in holding back on programme cutbacks is impossible to say, but the quote and the subsequent policies actively pursued strongly suggest that both the policy agenda and the implementation environment had changed in ways which put much greater limits on Nixon's freedom of action compared with that enjoyed by Johnson during 1964 and 1965. Like most new Presidents, Nixon was intent, however, on making a personal imprint on a major area of domestic policy. Federalism and welfare provided him with the almost ideal opportunity to innovate, appear both compassionate and efficient and advance at least some aspects of a conservative agenda all at the same time.

How was such a combination possible? Because: (a) the existing grant-in-aid system had evolved in an *ad hoc* fashion. It was widely perceived to be inefficient and over-bureaucratized.[6] Any reform, including the abolition of the OEO, that cut through the prevailing complexity by reducing the size and power of the federal welfare and intergovernmental bureaucracy would advance the conservative position. The reform in question was the adoption of what eventually was to be called the Nixon Family Assistance Plan, involving a limited version of the negative income tax. (b) If at the same time the reforms strengthened the position of the states in relation to the federal government, the trend towards dependence on federally funded and administered programmes would be reversed. By 1969, disquiet at what was perceived to be an encroaching federal role was widespread – especially among conservatives.[7] The major reform here was the adoption of General Revenue Sharing (GRS) and the consolidation of numerous categorical programmes into block grants to be distributed to the states and localities. (c) By combining such reforms with little or no reduction in the services provided to citizens – and especially urban citizens – and, in the case of welfare by actually improving welfare provision, the administration could avoid being labelled as uncaring and prevent a politically unpleasant response from Great Society liberals and their clients.

Although taken together this package of reforms covered three-quarters of domestic federal spending. Nixon's motives were not those of a fiscal conservative. For in spite of mounting macro-economic problems in the late 1960s Nixon was never

persuaded that the solution to inflation and the deficit lay in
large cuts in federal spending. On the contrary, he was
haunted by what he saw as the overcautious fiscal stance of the
Eisenhower administration, which he believed contributed to
his deafeat in 1960.[8] Later he was of course to seek solutions in
that most unRepublican and unconservative of panaceas – a
prices and incomes policy.

In essence, the Nixon agenda was both pragmatic and
technocratic. He sought to re-organize federal programmes
according to rational criteria. He was almost certainly more
interested in improving efficiency than in reducing costs; he
thought that he could get the best of both worlds by improving
the efficiency of programmes without electorally damaging
cuts in service provision. The only 'victims' in his scheme were
what he perceived as large numbers of unnecessary bureaucrats who were in any case unpopular with public and
politicians alike.

Nixon's pragmatism is further exposed by an examination of
the specific origins of these reforms. Let us look at each of these
in turn.

Welfare reform

After the election, almost the first action by the new president
was to create a series of task forces to help set out the priorities
of the new administration. As Daniel Moynihan has observed,
the subjects covered read like a list of the liberal or Great
Society programmes – urban affairs, education, manpower,
resources and the environment.[9] As earlier noted, Nixon
inherited this agenda; these were the pressing domestic
priorities in 1968. To break out of this mould would have been
both politically difficult and dangerous.[10] Membership of the
task forces reflected the spirit of the times. Moderate Republicans and Democrats dominated. For Chairman of the Task
Force on Public Welfare, Nixon chose Richard P. Nathan, a
liberal Republican then on the staff of the Brookings Institution. The group also included James L. Sundquist who had

been actively involved in the Johnson anti-poverty programme and Mitchell I. Ginsberg of New York City's Human Resources (Welfare) Administration.[11]

In contrast to the early Johnson task forces, the Nixon task forces were much more intelligence-gathering devices than policy-making bodies. Policy-making Nixon assigned to a new Council for Urban Affairs headed by Moynihan and given an intended status in domestic policy similar to the National Security Council in foreign policy. However, Moynihan did not have complete control of domestic affairs in the White House. He had major rivals in Arthur Burns, a longstanding Nixon supporter and intellectual patron, and a Burns aide, the brilliant young conservative, Martin Anderson. Burns's status in the White House was somewhat obscure. He would eventually be given the job of Chairman of the Board of Governors of the Federal Reserve, but until then accepted the job of Chief Advisor on Domestic Policy. Conflict, both ideological and political, between Burns and Moynihan was inevitable and this was reflected in the ensuing policy debate over welfare. These events have been chronicled elsewhere,[12] but none of the accounts have benefited from access to the Nixon Presidential Materials Project at the National Archive. What follows is an account of the policy process drawing on both primary and secondary sources. It is important to stress that eventually Nixon was able to choose between three welfare reform plans:

(1) The Nathan plan

During the campaign, Nixon specifically disavowed adoption of a guaranteed annual income or a negative income tax,[13] but by early 1969 the idea was gaining currency. In some forms it had excellent conservative credentials, the idea having first come from economist Milton Friedman. Moreover the 'explosion' of the welfare rolls during the 1960s had revealed the gross inequities and irrationalities of the existing system. Payments varied wildly from state to state with benefits going primarily to mothers with dependent children. This helped encourage the break up of nuclear family units and often constituted a disincentive to work. Two related factors helped boost the popularity of a guaranteed income. One was the political pressure from the larger industrial, high-benefit states, often with Republican Governors, to stem the growth of welfare costs and the alleged immigration of blacks and the poor from lower-benefit states.[14] The other was the evolution of an intellectual welfare community and the publication of what had by 1969 become hundreds of books and articles on the subject. This was a direct outgrowth of Johnson's War on Poverty. New institutes, university departments and, not least, experts in the federal bureaucracy were active in exposing the flaws in the existing system and generally raising the political salience of the issue.[15]

In this context it is not surprising that the Nathan team opted for a scheme involving a minimum national standard. The specific device for achieving this would be a guarantee of $40 per person per month, with the federal government paying all of the first $40 and 50% of benefits from $40 to $70. At the time (1968) benefits ranged from $71.75 per person in New York, to $8.50 in Mississippi.[16] Thus the plan would boost the minimum benefits while not imposing additional costs on the higher-benefit states already providing aid on a 50/50 matching basis with the federal government. The estimated additional cost would be between $1 billion and $1.5 billion, but the task force recommended that the eventual aim should be 'complete federal financing of all welfare benefits'.[17]

In some respects the Nathan plan was quite modest, It did little to overcome the biases in the AFDC system against unemployed fathers and there was no work-incentive element in the scheme. Even so, if implemented, it would have constituted the single most important reform of the welfare system since 1935. It was, however, destined to go no further than the Urban Affairs Council Sub-Committee, not so much because it was unacceptable as because the agenda quickly moved on to other competing plans.

(2) The Bateman/Lyday Plan[18]

The major alternative came almost exclusively from a group of Great Society liberals still active within the administration. The first was the brainchild of Worth Bateman, a HEW official who wrote a paper criticizing the Nathan plan for its failure to tackle the bias in the AFDC system against unemployed fathers. Nathan's scheme would, Bateman forcefully argued, provide additional incentives for the breaking-up of nuclear families. Instead, Bateman suggested a negative income tax consisting of benefits for *all* families with children, including the very low paid, with an income test to decide benefit levels. Some mix of income supplement and work earnings was proposed, therefore. Originally, this plan involved retention of an AFDC element. Federal funds would provide the minimum, but above this a mix of federal and state funds would pay the income supplement. Eventually, however, and following crucial advice provided by another Democrat, James Lyday, an economist in OEO, the plan evolved into something even more radical. The final version proposed setting a guaranteed annual income high enough so that beyond that the states alone could provide supplements up to the level of existing payments. $900 was originally considered an acceptable minimum. So, in one stroke, a federally funded guaranteed income with a work incentive would be introduced but no state would be worse off in terms of its welfare commitments. The cost would be high — $2 billion extra per annum. As Vincent and Vee Burke note, the two Democratic economists ingeniously got around this problem, not by decreasing the cost of their own scheme, but by re-packaging the Nathan proposal to make it sound as expensive.[19]

Much to the authors' surprise, Republican appointees in HEW, notably Under-Secretary Jack Veneman and Secretary Finch actually welcomed the plan. Nathan was persuaded to drop his own scheme and Moynihan, who was delighted with the proposal, argued forcefully for its adoption in the Urban Affairs Council.[20] John Mitchell, another Council member, was generally supportive but wanted more work completed on the subject.[21]

(3) The Burns/Anderson alternative

Arthur Burns and Martin Anderson were aghast at the political and economic implications of the Bateman/Lyday plan. It was, they thought, expensive, undermined the states and would eventually lead to a massive increase in welfare dependency. Anderson, as a member of the Urban Affairs Council, was satisfied that when put to Nixon it would be rejected. When presented with the plan by Moynihan, however, Nixon's first reactions were positive. Vincent and Vee Burke, relying on interviews with major participants, record the discussion as follows:

BURNS (protesting): You would add seven million persons to the welfare rolls!

FINCH: What's wrong with Republicans providing income maintenance for seven million people?

NIXON: I understand, Arthur, that you don't like it; I understand your reasons. But I have a problem. If you don't like it, give me another solution.

Back in the White House on Monday morning Moynihan was ebullient.

'A good meeting', he told Price, 'a very good meeting with Nixon. The president asked me, "Will FSS get rid of social workers?" and I promised him it would wipe them out!'[22]

Nixon did not immediately endorse what by then had become known as the Family Security System, or FSS, which gave Arthur Burns and Martin Anderson time to prepare an alternative strategy. Interestingly, the agenda on the subject had advanced so far that Burns could not avoid incorporating increased welfare benefits into his plan. But he did so in ways which left great discretion to the states. In sum, Burns proposed providing states with a new system of revenue-sharing funds, which they would receive only if they raised welfare benefits up to a new – but still quite low – minimum. The scheme would apply to *all* families with children, not just those headed by a single parent. Finally, Burns insisted that those in receipt of welfare should be required to accept work or some sort of job training. Additional funds should be set aside for this purpose.

Burns sold his plan to the Cabinet through the circulation of a paper by Martin Anderson entitled 'A Short History of the FSS'. In one respect, the Burns strategy worked, for of the eight leading Cabinet and Urban Affairs Council members who responded to the memo, no less than five agreed with its criticisms of the FSS.[23]

As John Ehrlichman's 'Notes on Meetings with the President', show, there then followed a period of intense debate on the subject, with Moynihan playing the lead role in favour of a guaranteed income and Burns most active in opposing it.[24] As several accounts confirm, Moynihan won the battle hands down, mainly because he was able to combine charm and intellect with a highly developed political sense.[25] By the early summer, Labor Secretary George Shultz, HEW Secretary Robert Finch and Attorney-General John Mitchell either openly supported or tentatively accepted the Moynihan position. It was not until June that the idea of a work-incentive-related guaranteed income was accepted by Nixon, however, when he instructed John Ehrlichman to work out FSS in more detail. John Ehrlichman, urged on by HEW officials, eventually settled for a $1,600 floor or supplement for a family of four, with the first $720 of earned income above this to be disregarded or allowable without affecting the supplement. Thereafter, the supplement would be reduced as earnings increased to a maximum of $3,920, at which point it would disappear altogether.

The Burns/Anderson insistence on some sort of work-incentive elements in the plan appealed to most of the Nixon Cabinet, however, and in particular to Labor Secretary George Schultz, who also favoured an extensive day-care programme, to enable welfare mothers to work.[26] What was finally accepted in August was a guaranteed income plan with a strong work-incentive element for single people and parents with children over six (the child-care provision was dropped). The only further change was the replacement of the FSS – reminiscent of the Great Society – with the more neutral Family Assistance Plan (FAP).

On 8 August the President addressed the nation on what were pronounced as his major domestic programmes for the next four years. Curiously, in announcing the FAP, Nixon promised that AFDC 'would be done away with completely',[27] but an AFDC element, or a requirement that states presently paying benefits above the FAP minimum continue to do so, remained. Later in the speech, he contradicted himself by admitting that 'in no case would anyone's present level of benefit be lowered'.[28] Further confusion was added when attempts were made to relate the new programme to food-stamps benefits. Earlier, on 6 May, Nixon had announced to Congress a 'Program to End Hunger in America' which evolved into a substantially enlarged food-stamps programme which eventually would be 'complementary to a revised welfare scheme'.[29] Nixon's subsequent statements, however, failed to make it clear whether FAP beneficiaries would lose food stamps or not. If they did, large numbers of poor in the higher-welfare-benefit states would find themselves less well off than before the reform. Eventually, the administration accepted that FAP recipients would continue to receive food stamps up to the level of their total pre-reform benefits.[30] These and other confusions were to do little to enhance the chances of the reform package's legislative fortunes.

Finally, Nixon's 8 August address contained a pledge to provide a national minimum standard ($69) for the so-called 'adult categories' of welfare aid for the disabled, the blind and the old. The federal government would share the costs of this minimum and benefits above it with the states.[31]

Taken together, these reforms were remarkably radical for what was supposed to be a conservative Republican administration. One estimate was that they would add 12.4 million to the welfare rolls and cost an additional $4 billion in federal spending.[32] Why then did Nixon support them? Undoubtedly one reason was the glaring absence of any alternative domestic-policy initiative. Moynihan repeatedly warned the President that he needed to make an impact in some area of domestic policy.[33] Moreover, as earlier noted, he effectively inherited the liberal agenda of the Great Society; his freedom to break from that agenda was limited. Welfare reform also appealed to his technocratic instincts. Perhaps most important of all was the fact that Nixon, along with many of his advisers, was not an ideologue of the right on domestic policy. Indeed, there were three distinct groups involved in some way in the FAP policy-making process: reforming liberals, both Great Society (Bateman, Lyday) and others (Moynihan, Nathan); Republican technocrats, all of whom supported some rationalization of the 'welfare mess' (Shultz, Finch, Defence Secretary Melvin Laird, Ehrlichman, Mitchell and Nixon himself); and conservative Republicans who opposed any extension of welfare (Burns, Vice-President Spiro Agnew, Anderson, Treasury Secretary David Kennedy, Budget Director Robert Mayo and CEA chairman Paul McCracken). Of the conservatives, only Burns and Anderson devoted time and energy to the FAP policy process. Agnew was also interested, but proved poorly briefed and eventually ineffective. Anderson was really quite junior and Burns had an unfortunate, persistent, didactic style which won him few allies.[34] In contrast, the technocrats numbered among their ranks two men who were both closely involved in the policy process and had unusually good access to the president – John Ehrlichman and George Shultz. On the winning side, too, of course, was the ebullient Daniel Moynihan, who also had excellent access to Nixon.

In sum, the FAP policy process was dominated by liberals and technocrats. It was also essentially internal to the White House. Compared with the early Johnson period, Cabinet secretaries – in particular Finch and Shultz – played a more important role, and HEW officials clearly provided a major input into the process. But external influence or pressure was minimal and among the major actors only Moynihan made any attempt to invoke public support.[35] Richard Nixon was intent on introducing a limited form of Cabinet government during his first term.[36] Another difference between the Johnson and Nixon reforms was the marked contrast between the speed with which the Johnson proposals were drawn up and the long-drawn-out process characteristic of the early Nixon White House. As we will see, this was to provide Nixon with a lesson for the future.

The Legislative history of FAP is well known; after a series of ups and downs FAP was effectively abandoned by the administration in December 1972[37] (although the 1974 State of the Union Message promised a resuscitation). For our purposes, the following features of the legislative history are worthy of note:

(1)   The complexity – and sometimes confusion – associated with FAP did little to enhance its future. One of the first reactions to Nixon's August speech was a chorus of protest that because FAP recipients would be ineligible for food stamps, millions would receive lower benefits. As earlier noted, the White House quickly retreated on this point. FAP was, in addition, intrinsically difficult to understand and was to be superimposed on an existing panoply of welfare and social service benefits ranging from medical benefits to free school lunches. Add to this the complexity inherent in the federal system and the potential for misunderstanding and misrepresentation can be appreciated.

(2)   Furthermore, FAP was vulnerable to criticism from both left and right. On the left, claims that existing welfare recipients in the north, who by some counts made up 80% of the total, would be no better off – and possibly worse off – led some critics to assert that this was really no reform at all.[38] George Wiley of the increasingly powerful National Welfare Rights Organization launched a campaign against FAP precisely on these grounds.[39] Moynihan, who remained active in most of the legislative battles, drew further fire from civil

rights organizations. The revelation of his now-famous memo to Nixon to pursue a policy of 'benign neglect' towards civil rights implementation came at a crucial stage of the bill's passage through Congress (March 1970) and added to the fears of blacks that Moynihan was prejudiced against their community.[40]

On the right, the accusations were that FAP would lead to a further explosion of the welfare rolls and would increase dependency. Russell Long, conservative Democratic chairman of the Senate Finance Committee, was implacably opposed to it on these grounds and the administration version of the bill was eventually to die in his committee.

(3) More important than either of these problems was Nixon's own ambivalence. After his 8 August speech, Nixon virtually ignored the proposal for two months. Thereafter he displayed bursts of enthusiasm and effort in support of the bill, interspersed with periods of apparent indifference. He probably assisted the eventual passage by the House in March 1970 by lobbying individual members and appealing to the nation's Governors for support.[41] Documents from the Nixon archive confirm that the President's support was motivated not so much by any substantive interest in the area, but by a desire – even an obsession – to make some sort of an impression on domestic policy. On 27 August 1970, he said to John Ehrlichman: 'Just get something done, this [the FAP] is the only major reform of our administration, therefore, we must be for it, it is not enough to blame the Senate.'[42] A few days later, in a meeting with Senate leaders, the president conceded that 'all wisdom is not in the executive branch: take suggestions and improve the program'.[43] By 1971, Nixon was prepared to make further concessions to get some sort of reform package through Congress. In a series of meetings with Governor Ronald Reagan of California he was much persuaded by the Governor's state-welfare-reform plan.[44] Interestingly, the Reagan reforms were designed to reduce both the number of people on welfare and to reduce the cost to the state.

Eligibility requirements were tightened substantially, although the 'truly needy' would get more.[45] In other words, the President was prepared to accept a more restrictive reform scheme, if only it would get through Congress.

During discussions in late 1972, the President and his advisers found themselves searching around for their first-term achievements in domestic policy. In one November meeting Nixon declares:

What do we stand for?
1. Changes in law enforcement
   Riots
   Permissiveness
All these are better than in 1968
2. Welfare reform
   The quality of life
   Revenue sharing
[all these were] our initiatives[46]

In another meeting, the President seems almost to be searching around for issues and admits that 'we need a mandate to go on the domestic side like on the foreign side'. He then mentions the key issues and again comes up with welfare reform and revenue sharing.[47] Only government reorganization (of which more later) is a genuine addition to the 1968 or 1969 list.

However, by 28 December 1972, the President seems to have given up on the comprehensive version of the FAP. In a memo to Ehrlichman and Ken Cole he admits as much and stresses the need to identify some major domestic issues. As the memo shows, however, the President is quite unsure of what these might be:

I have some observations with regard to your paper on programs for 1973.

Generally, I thought it was an excellent job of summing up the positions we probably would be well advised to take – the positions you set forth on the issues we are likely to confront during the year.

I was surprised and somewhat disappointed, however, to find that two strong convictions I have expressed over and over again during the past few months were not adequately reflected in one case and completely ignored in another . . .

The other area [the first was higher education] which really surprised me was the reference to family assistance. I don't think I could have made it more clear over the past few months that I am convinced that the family assistance program no longer is viable, and that we must move in other directions in attacking the welfare mess. Yet the tired old reference to subsidizing the 'working poor' somehow found its way in the paper which was submitted to me.

In both of these instances I understand and respect the different points of view which obviously are held by those who prepared the paper. In the future, however, I want to be sure that where such papers are sent in to me items like this are heavily flagged so that when I read them hurriedly I will not scan over them and then all of a sudden find that I have approved something with which I have expressed total disagreement in the past.

With regard to the summary of accomplishments and also our projected programs for 1973, I have another observation I would like reflected in the Domestic Council's thinking.

I once recall that Earl Warren told me in 1950 when I was running for the United States Senate that it was vitally important to seize upon two, or at most three, issues and to become known for those issues. He pointed out that he felt he had done a number of good things as Governor of California but that he put his total public relations emphasis on better roads and better schools. The result was that he went down in California's history as a man who did more for education and more for highways than any other Governor.

In our case I think we have done a number of good things at home and abroad. Abroad, of course, we probably will be remembered for going to China, beginning negotiations on arms control with the Soviet Union, hopefully ending the war in Vietnam and totally changing the direction of US foreign policy through the Nixon Doctrine which is based on the very solid premise that in the future America will help others develop the capability to defend their freedom but will not do the fighting for them. In the domestic field we have so many goodies that our whole image is somewhat blurred. What we must do is to seize upon three, or at most four, major programs and put the PR emphasis on them virtually to the exclusion of others so that the Administration will be remembered for at least doing something *very* well rather than being forgotten because we did a number of things *pretty* well.

It is really a question of PR. Actually, we have done a number of things very well but we have had an enormously difficult time

getting it across. We have made some progress on getting across our
story on drugs and crime and, of course, the economic recovery
speaks for itself. But we need some other areas – perhaps it is
women's rights just to take a way out example or legacy for the parks
or something else where the Nation will know the Administration
has done something that has never been done before. Give me your
thoughts on this at a later time.[48] (emphasis in original)

Finally, the President did not elevate the welfare reform
through public speeches and declarations of support. Johnson
made repeated references to his Great Society, Nixon made a
few key speeches but no more. In the *Public Papers of the
President*, for example, FAP and welfare reform are the subject
of few major speeches.[49] On only four occasions was the issue
raised at presidential press conferences.[50]

Nonetheless, Congress did pass some of the measures
announced in the President's 8 August speech. In October
1972, Supplementary Security Income (SSI) or a national
minimum standard for the aged, the blind and disabled, was
enacted into law. As passed, it represented the single most
important advance of the welfare state in the US since the
enactment of Medicare and Medicaid in 1965. It was, indeed,
the first truly major reform of the much-criticized welfare
provisions of the 1935 Social Security Act. From 1973, almost
all SSI benefits would be funded by the federal government.
Moreover, benefit levels ($140 for aged individuals, $210 for
couples) were higher than the old federal/state categorical
programmes applicable in twenty-six states. Mississippi at the
time provided $75 per individual.[51] A small state element did
continue, for above these minimums states could supplement
the federal contribution. While the passage of SSI can no doubt
partly be explained by the ideological/emotional appeal of
helping the old and disabled as opposed to unemployed
fathers, it was in fact one of the original 1969 Nixon pledges.
Intellectually and politically it fitted into the agenda quite
nicely. By federalizing a range of programmes, bureaucratic
complexity was reduced, national standards were established
and the administration was seen to be both compassionate and
efficient. Initial additional costs were estimated to be $1.9

billion in 1973.[52] By 1983 SSI was costing $9.5 billion per annum.[53]

At the very end of his presidency, Nixon supported the introduction of what became a very limited form of a negative income tax. This was the Earned Income Tax Credit (EITC), which Congress enacted in 1974. Under this scheme, poor working families earning under $8,000 a year could receive a tax credit of up to $400 a year. Since its introduction in 1975, however, the value of the credit has been declining steadily.

A further major reform promised in Nixon's 8 August 1969 speech was the adoption of revenue sharing, which eventually became the central reform in the administration's 'New Federalism'.

The New Federalism

Strictly speaking, FAP and welfare reform were part of a package of reforms announced on 8 August 1969, all of which were originally subsumed under the title 'the new Federalism'. The others were: (a) a recorganization of manpower retraining programmes, including those administered by OEO, into a new federal block grant programme; (b) a major review and reorganization of OEO and (c) the adoption of revenue sharing or a new block-grant system for providing states and localities with federal aid.[54]

Of these, revenue sharing was the most important, both in terms of administration priorities and potential for changes in the nature of federalism. Revenue sharing was hardly a new idea – its origins can be traced back as far as 1820.[55] Much more recently, economists Joseph Pechman and Walter Heller and Melvin Laird had become strong advocates of such a reform of the intergovernmental system.[56] As announced on 8 August, revenue sharing would involve an additional $500 million for state and local governments, provided out of federal revenues with few strings attached. This part of the reform package was, originally, relatively uncontroversial within the administration. Burns broadly supported the idea as part of his anti-FAP strategy, as, for very different reasons, did Richard

Nathan, George Schultz and Daniel Moynihan.[57] Nathan and Treasury Secretary Murray Weidenbaum were eventually given the job of drafting a new revenue-sharing programme.[58] Originally a distinction was drawn between Special Revenue Sharing, or the consolidation of categorical programmes for community development, manpower retraining and the like into block grants, and General Revenue Sharing (GRS), or the creation of new general-purpose no-strings-attached grants for states and localities. Eventually Special Revenue Sharing became known simply as 'block grants'.

Within the administration, controversy did surround GRS, mainly because some advocates considered it should constitute *additional* aid to the states, while some thought it should *replace* existing categorical programmes. Nixon opted for the former, in part because his economic advisers (Shultz and McCracken) urged him that some stimulus to the economy was necessary to balance the budget at full employment.[59] As Paul Dommel has recorded, the ensuing bill received relatively little support in Congress,[60] and two years later, in his 1971 State of the Union Message, Nixon increased the size of the programme to $5 billion per annum. In the same Message, Nixon approved a major reform of existing intergovernmental programmes, with the creation of six massive block grants for education, urban development, transportation, job training, rural development and law enforcement. GRS was enacted, and represented a very substantial *additional* source of funds for state and local governments. The block-grant programmes fared slightly less well, although two of the largest (the Comprehensive Education and Training Act in 1973 and the Community Development Act in 1974) were enacted into law before the end of the Nixon presidency.

Interestingly, the administration ensured the passage of GRS by blocking Congressional attempts to link the programme to HR 1, the welfare reform bill. In an August 1972 memo to Elliot Richardson, Nixon commented:

There is speculation that some selected elements of HR 1 might be amended to the revenue sharing bill. I would strongly oppose such a move because it could doom the possibility of real welfare reform in this Congress and could seriously jeopardize the revenue sharing bill. As we proceed on general revenue sharing, I would like you to make known to the Senate leadership my reasons for this position.[61]

A number of points should be noted about these somewhat surprising developments. First, although the general idea of revenue sharing had good Republican credentials – a number of Republican-sponsored revenue-sharing bills were introduced in the 89th and 91st Congresses – the particular form it eventually took was very much the product of the Nixon White House. Ehrlichman, in particular, feared that something of a domestic policy vacuum would open up following the demise of FAP. GRS would enable the administration to move back on to the initiative, to make it appear that it was doing something in domestic policy.[62] George Shultz was also highly supportive of the idea, as was William Safire. Unlike Ehrlichman, however, their support was as much philosophical as political. This was reflected in an extraordinary exchange of papers during late 1969 between speechwriter Safire, a young far-right conservative called Tom Charles Huston, then also working as a speechwriter, and Richard Nathan. Each author took the pseudonym of a famous philosopher of federalism to represent their view (Publius, Cato and Althusius respectively). What emerged was a fascinating intellectual contest between what could be called an egalitarian decentralizer (Publius), an inegalitarian localist (Cato) and a technocrat and political pragmatist (Althusius, whose solutions closely resembled those of Publius).[63] According to Safire (Publius), Nixon was most receptive to his own scheme, which contained the notion of establishing national standards in such areas as welfare, but preserving local administration over programmes. Revenue sharing would be an ideal mechanism for reconciling these two objectives in a range of policy areas. Put another way, the undoubted tension between federal power and local discretion and variety could be eased through block grants and revenue sharing.[64] Huston (Cato) vehemently attacked this philosophy claiming that increasing, or even maintaining,

federal funding would inevitably increase control and undermine the most prized value of all – the moral authority that
comes from the spirit of local community.[65]

Huston further claimed that GRS, FAP and associated
programmes were little more than Great Society measures in
disguise.[66] While this particular charge is unfair, there is no
question that Ehrlichman, Shultz and other key domestic
policy-makers favoured the Safire/Nathan line. Revenue
sharing to them meant: (a) a return of administration to state and
local govenments; (b) a concomitant reduction in the size and
complexity of the federal bureaucracy; and (c) a move towards
national standards.

In sum, although revenue sharing was on the agenda in
1969, it was the Nixon White House that moved it to centre
stage and moulded its particular form. At the same time,
outside influences became increasingly important as the
various items of legislation proceeded through Congress. As
Paul Dommell and others have noted, the intergovernmental
lobby, or the topocracy as Samuel Beer has called it,[67] began
their lobbying after the agenda was set.[68]

In January 1971, Governor of New York Nelson Rockefeller
sent an impassioned telegram to the President warning of the
dangers inherent in not making additional funds available:

I am deeply disturbed by reports which indicate that Clark
MacGregor expects your revenue-sharing program to involve
primarily a reallocation of existing funds and only 'some' new
money; further, that he thinks revenue-sharing is an effort by
governors and mayors to avoid responsibilities; further, that
telegrams and letters from back home do not change congressional
votes. His position, as your new congressional liaison man, does not
seem to reflect the point of view which you expressed in our meeting
the other day. The prospect of an explosion in our cities if we do not
all work together to halt the breakdown of services to the people is a
very real one.[69]

Nixon was eager to ensure that the states and localities
behaved in a fiscally responsible manner. but there is no
evidence that he was concerned with the extra fiscal burden

that revenue sharing might impose on the federal government. Witness Nixon's reaction to the Rockefeller plea:

One concern I have with our Revenue Sharing Program is that it could well be interpreted simply as an escape-hatch whereby local and state government does not have to make hard decisions on more efficiency and cutting down on some of their service and programs which really should be restricted. As far as most voters are concerned, they want tax relief *at the local and state level, particularly where property taxes are concerned.*

I accept your analysis that states and local governments need all the revenue sharing we can provide simply to avoid having to raise taxes and even then they may not be able to achieve that goal. On the other hand, I think that our Revenue Sharing proposal must be sold on the basis that it provides an opportunity for local and state governments to first, stop the rise in property taxes and other local taxes; and second, if they get proper efficiency at the local and state level even provide some tax relief.

I do not want us to get sucked in on the proposition of Rockefeller and the other governors, as well as the county and city officials, are selling us – that the government at the state, local and city level will go bankrupt unless the Federal government bails them out with the Revenue Sharing Proposal. The average person couldn't care less whether his county, city or state government goes bankrupt. He wants relief.[70]

In effect, Nixon was willing to concede that the federal contribution under GRS should constitute extra spending. It was up to lower-level governments to get their houses in order, but the federal government would help pay the bill. This applied both to GRS and to the new block grants, which once legislated, contained the built-in mechanism to maintain funding at least at existing levels.

Members of Congress, too, were very aware of the consequences of reduced federal funding. State and local fiscal crises were commonplace by the early 1970s, and any policy initiative containing pledges to reduce federal aid would have received a hostile reception from the Democratic Congress. As suggested, however, there is little evidence that what amounted to fiscal expansionism deeply offended the White House.

As late as 1972, Nixon was being urged by his economic advisers to increase federal spending. In a meeting with the President in February 1972, Federal Reserve Chairman Arthur Burns expressed serious doubts that the economy had received enough stimulus. His verbatim comment was that 'we must do everything to help the expansion of the economy'.[71]

In spite of the anxieties expressed by the Governors and Mayors, revenue sharing was never a matter of searing national concern. Not once was a question asked of the Presidency on the subject at a press conference. Nixon made frequent references to it in speeches and reports,[72] but mentions revenue sharing not at all in his autobiography – although FAP does feature quite prominently.

Put another way, the ideological issue content of domestic policy was low. Two domestic policy issues did inspire ideological heat – anti-war 'subversion' and further extensions of affirmative action, especially bussing.[73] Neither are addressed in this book, however. What *did* offend the sensibilities of Nixon and what later became a much more tightly knit staff, was the continuing belief in the overweaning power of the federal bureaucracy. But as we will see, this was rooted more in concerns about control and procedures than about the actual content of policy.

At least in his first term Nixon gathered around him a group of men whose intellectual credentials and political experience were unmatched either in the Johnson or in the subsequent Carter and Reagan administrations. It is perhaps not surprising then, that many of the Nixon domestic policy proposals achieved a relatively high level of intellectual coherence.

Coherence

Economic theory

Most economists accept that the most rational method of distributing income maintenance is directly to individuals rather than through intermediate-level governments. There are a number of reasons for this, namely:

(1) If redistribution is left to lower-level jurisdictions, poorer states will be obliged to raise taxes to a level which will put them at a serious disadvantage in relation to others. Capital and labour mobility will be adversely affected.

(2) In richer states, a tendency will exist to aid the relatively poorly off who in other states would not qualify for aid. With a national system of distribution, the chances of 'non-needy' persons receiving welfare benefits are reduced, because national eligibility requirements can be applied.

(3) A related but more esoteric argument is that welfare constitutes a public good and the provision of aid adds to the utility of the non-poor. If welfare benefits vary from state to state, benefits beyond each state (or externalities) also vary. The greater the variations from state to state the greater will be the free-rider problem for the non-poor citizens of those states where the benefits are low.[74]

None of these arguments addresses the question of the most economically appropriate *level* of welfare benefits, of course. Most economists accept the need for welfare, but great controversy surrounds the question of benefit levels.[75]

What we can conclude is that most of the Nixon welfare reforms were, in terms of accepted economic theory, a move in the right direction. A negative income tax with built-in work incentives was precisely what many economists had called for. Eliminating some state and local discretion from AFDC and removing it almost completely in the case of SSI made good economic sense. What made less sense was the failure to make clear the relationship between income maintenance under FAP and all the other benefits (food stamps and medical care in particular) available under the existing system. It was this essentially intellectual failing that exposed FAP to the fiercest criticism during the ensuing legislative process. Even critics on the right could point to instances where the adoption of FAP would lead to lower overall benefits for some families – although the examples were usually misleading;[76] or, as serious, increased overall benefits – some of them very hard to measure – would constitute a disincentive to work.[77]

In contrast to the general policy thrust of FAP, extending the food stamp programme made little economic sense. For while food benefits go direct to individuals, most economists accept that providing cash for the indigent poor is a more rational income maintenance device than providing 'in-kind' benefits. Cash payments provide recipients with greater discretion over consumption patterns. So although their income comes from the state, they can at least make market-type decisions when spending their money. William Safire put this very well in the *New Federalist Papers*:

New Federalism [FAP was subsumed under this general title] puts priority on the distribution of cash rather than services or food and clothing. If the money is squandered on soda pop and floppy hats, the responsibility of government at every level is to educate the person how better to use money to stay healthy rather than to assume control of the welfare recipient's money 'for his own good'.[78]

Food stamps along with housing allowances and other in-kind benefits can 'distort' a rational pattern of spending. Of course these assumptions are hardly non-controversial – especially if, as in the case of housing and medical care, the market itself fails to provide an adequate level of consumer quality and choice. But our discussion should dwell on food benefits. Few would argue that the American economy has failed the consumer in this area, so the Nixon reformers were hardly grounded in good economics. As is well known, his preference for such benefits was at least partly inspired by political considerations, especially deference to the power of the American agricultural lobby.[79]

What does economic theory tell us about the other major innovation of the Nixon first term – the adoption of block grants and General Revenue Sharing? There is, first of all, no question that revenue sharing can be defended on strictly economic grounds. Two major economic rationales for such devices can be identified. First, revenue sharing can, many economists argue, increase the income elasticity of local government revenues. During the 1960s, state and local fiscal crises increased precisely because local revenues were income inelastic. Demands on services were increasing, but property taxes in particular, and also sales taxes, increased at levels proportionately lower than demand; hence the crises and what many economists saw as a serious under-provision of public goods. Federal taxes, based as they are on the income tax, are so elastic that they tend to increase more rapidly than demands on expenditure. Hence the case for intergovernmental grants.[80] Categorical grants were inadequate because they had been politicized in ways which often led to less needy jurisdictions receiving more help than the more needy.[81] While these general points are valid – at least in the context of the late 1960s and early 1970s – the actual formula adopted for distributing money to state and local governments under GRS ensured that *all* jurisdictions, whatever their need or tax capacities, would be in receipt of aid.[82]

The second justification for the New Federalism is based on the 'externalities' or 'spillover' effects dynamic central to public-choice analysis. Put very simply, the argument is that when a local jurisdiction produces an external economy or diseconomy for the rest of society there is an economic case for aid from higher-level governments.[83] Some empirical examples of diseconomies clearly support the reasoning. If epidemic disease breaks out in one area, central- or state-government intervention is clearly justified. However, measuring externalities, positive or negative, in such areas as education, housing and law enforcement is extremely difficult, and some economists have argued that they are in any case low.[84] This aside, is it possible to reconcile GRS and block grants with the externality thesis by arguing that only state governments are sufficiently close to and familiar with the externalities characteristic of local jurisdictions to enable a rational distribution of grants? But GRS was to be allocated to both state *and* local governments in about equal amounts. Moreover, the 'hold harmless' or 'nobody loses' formula implicit in GRS clearly precluded the sort of discrimination and selection necessary to expedite a rational programme of grant distribution. Block grants are more amenable to such a distribution because they can, in theory, be administered according to carefully worked out formulae based on need in specified – if general – areas of public policy such as housing or manpower retraining. However, as Michael Reagan and others have shown, not only were the programmes subject to formulae determined as much by political as economic considerations, they were also, in the longer run, subject to 'creeping categorization'.[85] In other words, the categorical element slowly returned as Congress and lobbies worked hard to protect particular projects and programmes.

We can conclude, then, that while in theory it is possible to establish good economic arguments in favour of GRS and block grants, the particular forms they took were, in strictly economic terms, less than ideal.

Political theory

There is no question that the Nixon administration's motives in reforming welfare and in adopting the New Federalism were in part based on certain notions of bureaucratic efficiency, equality and democracy. As mentioned, the welfare reforms were intended to improve efficiency by reducing or eliminating the welfare bureaucracy or 'social workers' as Nixon often – and misleadingly – called them. As he put in his auto-biography, 'We hoped to cut down on red tape, and before long to eliminate social services, social workers and the stigma of welfare.'[86] Evidence from the Nixon archive further supports this claim. Nixon disliked the whole culture of welfare dependency including the use of government 'snoopers', which he thought undermined human dignity.[87]

In the sense that the reforms involved federalizing the system by applying national minimum standards, bureaucratic complexity would indeed have been reduced. Had near total federalization been proposed – as was the case with SSI – an even more efficient welfare system would have developed.

Few students of bureaucracy would dispute this point. AFDC, with its involvement of city, county, state and federal officials was indeed 'a mess'.

The New Federalism, too, held out the promise of improved bureaucratic efficiency, for had GRS and block grants *replaced* the prevailing system of categorical programmes, large numbers of officials at all levels would have found themselves redundant. But, of course, this was not to be. For reasons of political expediency, and in order to stimulate the economy, GRS constituted *additional* federal spending. And the block grant proposals were only partly adopted and then in compromised versions.

Given its reputation, the Nixon administration's attitude towards equality was somewhat surprising. It did, predictably, eschew those notions of positive discrimination implicit in affirmative action. Indeed, its hostility towards any further extension of civil rights in such areas as housing and education is well documented.[88] However, Nixon himself, together with such advisers as Moynihan, Nathan, Finch and Shultz did accept the need for the federal government to intervene, not only to provide a minimal income but also to reduce the more glaring inequalities between spatially defined areas. Crucially, however, this urge was technocratic rather than egalitarian in nature. They inherited a liberal agenda and were determined to improve it, not because they were concerned for the poor or the cities but because they disliked inefficiency. For the most part, their programmes did advance equality of condition for many millions of Americans. This was no rhetorical gesture on their part, but reflected a conviction that the only way to come to terms with the Great Society progammes was to make them more workable. In other words, Nixon advanced equality in the name of efficiency.

What of the extension of democracy implied in the Nixon reforms? This applied with particular force to the New Federalism. As later with the Reagan administration, Nixon assumed that the decentralization of a range of programmes would bring them closer to the people, and therefore increase governmental accountability. As he put it in a September 1969 speech to the nation's Governors:

The increase of the New Federalism is to help regain control of our national destiny by releasing a greater share of control to state and local governments and to the people.[89]

As earlier documented, disquiet with the rapid but *ad hoc* expansion of the federal role in domestic policy had been increasing throughout the 1960s. Much of the criticism was rooted in the belief that remote (i.e. federal) government was bad government and that the Jeffersonian tradition of local politics and administration was seriously threatened. As eventually adopted, however, it seems unlikely that GRS and block grants would advance the Jeffersonian position. There are two reasons for this:

(1)   As William Safire and Richard Nathan acknowledged in their guises as Publius and Althusius, the New Federalism's primary objective was to return *administration* to the states and localities rather than political control.[90] In the sense that Washington would still hold the purse strings, the distinction was almost certainly spurious. As Tom Charles Huston (Cato) implored, 'The administration must go beyond the decentralization of administration; it must accept the decentralization of power.'[91] The latter could hardly be achieved while GRS constituted an *additional* source of funds, and while the block grant measures suffered from 'creeping categorization'. As I will show in chapter 6, it was the Reagan administration which first recognized that the only way to achieve true decentralization was to eliminate the federal role altogether.

(2)   While decentralization was intellectually appealing to Nixon and was championed by some of his staff (Burns, Huston, Anderson) he showed little personal interest in expediting the notion. As earlier noted, he makes no reference whatsoever to the issue in his autobiography nor was it ever

raised at a press conference. John Ehrlichman claims in his autobiography that Nixon was anything but an active supporter of revenue sharing and even argued for its abandonment when the federal deficit increased in 1971 and 1972.[92] It seems likely, then, that the eventual design of the New Federalism was more a product of political and economic expediency than the result of some ideological commitment to decentralization. The main ideological drive was, in fact, *antibureaucratic* rather than decentralist. But as suggested, it is difficult to see how, FAP apart, either the federal bureaucracy would be reduced or decentralization advanced given the design of the programmes.

What can be concluded is that both welfare reform and the New Federalism constituted the first major challenge to what we have called the New Deal regime. But they did so in very different ways. Welfare reform, had it been accepted in Congress, would have advanced the New Deal agenda beyond the parameters imposed by the institutional constraints of American federalism, and the ideological constraints of American political culture. As it was, the adoption of SSI – and to some extent the EITC – did just these two things. The New Federalism was, at its core, a reatreat from the New Deal agenda. For, judging by the rhetoric of the reforms, at least, it promised a reduction in the federal role and an enhancement of state and local power. As we will see, this modification in the agenda was to have important repercussions later in the decade and during the early 1980s.

The eventual failure of FAP owed something to the programme's design – although not as much as some critics have alleged.[93] As important was the relatively low interest of the President himself. Unlike Johnson, his personal commitment to legislative success was limited. Given this, and the diversions of Watergate, it is remarkable just how much of his domestic agenda was adopted.

Adaptation: the administrative presidency, myth and reality

It is received wisdom among political scientists that, following the legislative failure of his first term, Nixon pursued an administrative strategy during his second term, and did so in a two-stage process. First, there was the downgrading of the Cabinet and a concentration of power in the White House staff – and in particular John Ehrlichman – during 1970. This was the development of what Richard Nathan calls the 'counter bureaucracy'.[94] At the same time, the Urban Affairs Council was replaced by a new Domestic Council and the Bureau of the Budget was renamed the Office of Management and Budget (OMB). The former was to make policy and the latter to implement it. Nixon also hoped greatly to simplify the federal executive branch by a massive re-organization of all cabinet-level domestic departments through the creation of four super-agencies responsible for human resources, community development, natural resources and economic affairs.[95] In spite of the fact that the proposal was a central part of his 1971 State of the Union address, it made no progress in Congress. And predictably so, for such a reform would have challenged numerous established political relationships at all levels from Congress and bureaucracy down to organized interests and state and local governments. Second, after his re-election in 1972 the President pursued a similar strategy, but largely without recourse to legislation. Nathan noted that this strategy took a number of forms:

(a) The *de facto* creation of super-agencies through the elevation of four Cabinet secretaries to the status of 'Counsellors to the President'. In this role, they would chair Domestic Council committees and perform a sort of overseeing role over a range of domestic policies. The four were Early Butz (Agriculture, with a National Resources brief), Caspar Weinberger (HEW, Human Resources) James Lynn (HUD, Community Development) and George Schultz (Treasury, Economic Affairs).

(b) Civil service appointments. Nixon sought to place men and women loyal to the President in key positions through the bureaucracy.

(c) Re-organization, including the regionalization of federal field offices, or devolving power from Washington to regional administrations, and the break-up of the Office of Economic Opportunity by distributing its functions to other agencies.

(d) Regulation, or the issuing of new regulations to further administration objectives. Sometimes this involved new restrictive regulations, as with the administration's plan to reduce federal social service programmes and sometimes fewer regulations as with the decentralization of manpower retraining programmes under the New Federalism.[96]

In addition, Nixon's 1974 budget planned, for the first time, to limit or reduce federal spending in a range of social-policy areas. In total, Nathan and others have interpreted this as an attempt to further the objectives of the New Federalism and the domestic agenda generally through by-passing Congress.[97] Even the budget reductions could in part be achieved in this way through the impoundment of funds. Congressional investigations and hearings into and inspired by Watergate could be invoked to support these claims. Most of the debate has centred on the question of effectiveness. So Nathan suggests, and Aberbach and Rockman (who interviewed a number of senior civil servants active during the Nixon years) demonstrate, that the administrative strategy was attempted, but ultimately failed because the Great Society liberals were too numerous and entrenched for the administration to unseat them in such a short period of time. The diversions of Watergate made the task even more difficult.[98]

Later, in another piece based on interviews, Cole and Caputo found that while attitude changes were detectable between pre- and post-Nixon appointees they were not very significant and in any case: 'The strategy pursued by the Nixon White House was doomed to insignificance from the outset. So few top officials are selected during a single presidency compared with the total number of senior level executives that any numerical impact which those selected can have must be slight.'[99] Finally, a more-focussed study by Ronald Randall concentrating on the Social and Rehabilitation Service (SRS), the main welfare agency within HEW, found that the Nixon strategy *did* work. AFDC eligibility requirements were tightened and rule changes resulted in a levelling off of the increase in the number of AFDC recipients.[100] Evidence from the Nixon archives throws some new light on this debate — although not enough to resolve all the differences between competing claims. From these sources, the following can be concluded:

(1)   As represented by the mix of initial legislation and later administrative devices. the Nixon agenda was highly inconsistent in ideological terms. In 1971–2 he made an apparent shift to the right, but it was not altogether clear how the more conservative policies were supposed to work in practice. They were obviously anti-bureaucratic both in the technocratic sense (the perceived need to streamline the bureaucracy) and the personal sense (liberal Democrats disliked him and he disliked them.) But the substantive policy objectives of the anti-bureaucratic impulse were never clearly spelt out. Reduced government spending was a central objective in just one year (1973 for Fiscal 1974). By early 1974, admittedly in the midst of the Watergate imbroglio, he had returned to an expansionist stance. Eliminating 'social workers' was clearly an objective, but this was to go hand-in-hand with improved benefits under SSI, food stamps and a number of other programmes.

The Final Report on Violations and Abuses of Civil Service Merit Principles in Federal Employment by the House Post Office and Civil Service Committee *does* point to blatant disregarding of merit principles in the General Services Administration, HEW, HUD and OEO.[101] In 1971 Frederick Malek, head of the White House Personnel Office (WHPO), produced what became known as the 'Malek Manual', or a requirement that within the departments those employed had to be 'philosophically compatible with and loyal to the President'.[102] This purportedly appled only to political appointees but career bureaucrats too were screened, transferred, passed over or ignored in ways which were politically motivated.[103] But the House report suggests that 'political loyalty' meant being a Republican or being sympathetic with the administration's policies.[104] In other words, the substantive policy effects of this undoubted politicization, which went far beyond anything previous administrations had attempted, lacked coherence, since the administration's philosophy was itself inconsistent and unclear. It was certainly to the right of the political spectrum, but this often manifested itself as attacks on Great Society liberals *personally* rather than on their programmes.

(2)   One of the assumptions of the Administrative Presidency thesis is that Nixon deliberately replaced Elliot Richardson with Caspar Weinberger at HEW to further his policy objective of moving the agency to the right.[105] Judging by the extensive notes taken by John Ehrlichman during meetings to decide Cabinet appointments for the second term, this seems not to be the case. On 16 November 1972, the President decided that Weinberger would go 'to HEW or HUD depending on ELR [Richardson]'.[106] Richardson was clearly given the choice of staying at HEW or moving to Defense. In turn, Weinberger desperately wanted Defense.[107] Richardson's preference was the primary consideration, coupled with the fact that the President believed that Weinberger would be good at controlling spending and reducing inefficiency at HEW.[108] When, on 17 November, Nixon interviewed Weinberger, Weinberger was keen to impress on the president that he would reduce waste at Defense or at HEW. However, the two areas he identified as in need of the greatest control in HEW were higher education and health care. No mention was made of welfare, except that he favoured 'cashing out' some programmes to the states.[109] Later, in February 1973, the President suggested to Weinberger that he should proceed

slowly in welfare reform. Weinberger, in turn, supported a limited form of the FAP with stronger work incentives and help for working mothers.[110] This hardly looks like a radical shift to the right. Indeed, by March both Weinberger and his deputy Frank Carlucci were the targets of searing criticism by the WHPO for their failure to 'clean house' at HEW by replacing Democrats with Republicans and non-politicals. In one memo to John Ehrlichman, Tod Hullin pronounces that:

1. Weinberger and Carlucci clearing too many Democrats for good jobs and very important jobs.
2. Each Democrat has sound substantive credentials; political input being ignored.
3. Malek/Jones told Weinberger early that the President wanted to clean house and Malek/Jones wanted to put one of their guys in HEW to assist in that process. Weinberger and Carlucci resisted; they wanted their own guy. The standoff has given way to a compromise candidate.
4. Clearances by Jones/FBI *et al.* for other HEW spots have been slow. I've hit Jones hard on this and he's trying to move clearances faster; however, Weinberger's Democratic selections are also part of the problem.[111]

Another memo from the personnel office to John Haldeman was just as strong:

In my recent memo to the President about plans to gain control over the bureaucracy, I indicated that the WHPO's first effort would be directed toward HEW. I have growing concern with the recommendations that have been made for some of the most important and more substantive 'key pressure point' positions at HEW.

From the beginning, we have been concerned about the under Secretary's ability to pick people. Unfortunately, the Secretary has found it necessary to delegate the re-staffing to Carlucci and the worst of our fears are being realized. This memo describes the reasons for my concern and what steps I intend to take to bring HEW back on the personnel course I believe the President would have it take. If we lose the battle here, it will be difficult to ever gain control over HEW; and our ability to deal with other Departments will be seriously weakened.[112]

The memo continued with a list of senior officials whom Jerry Jones of the WHPO thought should be replaced. But the key officials (Weinberger, Carlucci and their immediate subordinates) had already been appointed, and Watergate was soon to absorb almost all the energies of the White House. It is not, in any case, obvious what substantive difference the appointments would have made, given that, the elimination of waste and efficiency apart, it was not clear what the administration's policy priorities were.

At the Cabinet appointment level, the President seems to have been more concerned with how efficient appointees would be than how ideologically loyal they were. This is consistent with Steven Hess's finding that Nixon's particular style of leadership involved constant shifts in personnel positions. The median tenure for Cabinet officials between 1933 and 1965 was forty months. For Nixon appointees it was eighteen months.[113] Weinberger's appointment was a compromise between Richardson's preferences and the perceived need to increase efficiency within HEW. Reducing welfare provision was not the motive. In any case, the pool of talent upon which Nixon could draw diminished as his presidency aged. By late 1972 most of the Nixon loyalists remained; they tended to be on the right, but their survival owed more to personal than to ideological considerations.

This general point is further supported by John Kessel's study of the Domestic Council. Its staff was not composed of ideologues of the right, or even the Republican stalwarts, but of moderate conservatives with varying views on domestic and economic policy.[114] In sum, Nixon's White House and Cabinet-level appointments reflected no consistent ideological bias. And of all recent Presidents it was Nixon who relied most on an equally mixed band of professors and intellectuals. The list is long: Kissinger, John Dunlop, Burns, Moynihan, Paul McCracken, James Schlesinger, Herbert Stein, Murray Weidenbaum, Lee Dubridge, Arnold Weber and Richard Nathan.[115]

(3) Nixon's legislative programme was by no means a universal failure. GRS and at least three large block-grant

programmes were eventually approved by Congress. FAP failed, but SSI and EITC were adopted and the food-stamp increases went through. Some of these 'successes' (block-grant increases, GRS) occurred *after* the initial 'legislative' period 1969/70 and in at least one case (the Community Development Block Grant) at the very end of the President's tenure in office. The legislative battles were, however, long and many. The administrative strategy was rooted in the President's dislike of such battles, rather than in an essentially programmatic or instrumental urge to shift public policy to the right.

(4)   While the motivations behind the Nixon administrative strategy are unclear, there is no question that the strategy involved some important institutional changes within the Executive Office of the President. Early in his first term, Nixon had appointed a businessman, Roy Ash, to chair an Advisory Council on Executive Organization. The Ash Commission's recommendations included the ill-fated re-organization of the major departments, but they also led to a new status being accorded to BOB or, as it was known after 1971, the Office of Management and Budget (OMB). A new layer of OMB political appointees was created and, as Hugh Heclo has put it, 'the OMB has become identified more as a member of the President's own political family and less as an institutional supplier of independent analytical resources, regardless of who is President'.[116] Heclo also notes how, from Nixon on, the politicization of the agency undermined the managerial continuity which had been its hallmark in the past.[117] In his determination to centralize power in the White House and win control over the bureaucracy, Nixon transformed the role of the OMB. Although Nixon was largely unable to exploit this new role to the full, subsequent Presidents were to find the agency's new status invaluable when pursuing more programmatic objectives.

Conclusions

Richard Nixon was first elected during an unusually turbulent period in American history. The remarkable implementation experience of Johnson's Great Society laws had shifted the domestic-policy agenda sharply to the left. This undoubtedly limited any desire which a Republican administration may have had to return to the *status quo ante*. But as documented, the first Nixon administration was essentially non-ideological, its major policy thrust being technocratic and pragmatic. In this guise, it proposed a number of major reforms in the domestic-policy arena, at least one of which (welfare) constituted the single most ambitious domestic policy innovation since the 1930s. As with Lyndon Johnson's Great Society, the process whereby these policies were conceived was highly internalized and dominated by a relatively few key White House and departmental officials. While the particular options taken reflected personal preference and prejudices, the major actors were constrained by the prevailing political environment. Dismantling the Great Society was never a realistic option. Making it more workable and cost effective was. Subsequent legislative fortunes were mixed. Specific programme design helped contribute to some of the failures, especially with respect to FAP. As important, the President himself received little gratification from the sort of intense political lobbying necessary to win over a Democratic Congress. But the programme designs and the ensuing legislative record reflected the essentially un-ideological stance of the President himself. George Romney, Nixon's HUD secretary, once said that: 'I don't know what the President believes in, maybe he doesn't believe in anything'[118] – a sentiment that has been echoed by Evans and Novak, William Safire and others.[119]

When, later in 1971 and during his second administration, Nixon made an apparent shift to the right, the associated policies were more anti-bureaucratic and anti-Great Society liberal than part of a coherent programme informed by conservative ideology. Some departments did implement conservative policies but the effects were sometimes as much procedural as substantive. It should not be forgotten that spending on a number of major domestic programmes (food stamps, SSI) increased sharply during the Nixon years and as a direct result of Nixon administration initiatives. Only during 1973 did the President resort to major budget-cut proposals. Put another way, the Nixon administrative strategy, while patently a device for increasing White House autonomy and for centralizing power, was motivated more by a sense that the White House and departmental heads were losing control to the bureaucratic hydra, than by a perceived failure to implement an ideologically coherent domestic-policy agenda.

NOTES

1 For a discussion of this point see A. James Reichley, *Conservatives in an Age of Change: The Nixon and Ford Administrations*, Washington, DC: The Brookings Institution, 1981, chapter 4.
2 Reichley, *Conservatives*, pp. 57–8; Rowland Evans Jr and Robert D. Novak, *Nixon in the White House: The Frustration of Power*, New York: Random House, 1971, chapter 2.
3 Nixon had reportedly read Moynihan's contribution to the *Republican Papers*, a collection of policy papers edited by Melvin Laird, *Republican Papers*, New York: Proeger, 1968; Evans and Novak, *Nixon in the White House*, p. 15.
4 Richard Nixon, *The Memoirs of Richard Nixon*, New York: Grosset and Dunlap, 1978, pp. 424–5.
5 Ibid.
6 See in particular, Laird (ed.), *Republican Papers*, contributions by Daniel Moynihan and Milton Friedman. Vincent J. and Vee Burke, *Nixon's Good Deed: Welfare Reform*, New York: Columbia University Press, 1974, chapter 2.
7 Richard P. Nathan, *The Plot That Failed: Nixon and the Administrative Presidency*, New York: Wiley, 1975, pp. 13–16.
8 Alonzo L. Hamby, *Liberalism and its Challengers: FDR to Reagan*, New York: Oxford University Press, 1985, p. 317.
9 Daniel P. Moynihan, *The Politics of a Guaranteed Income*, New York: Random House, 1973, p. 69.
10 Ibid., pp. 69–70.
11 Ibid., p. 71.
12 The most extensive and well-researched account is Vincent and Vee Burke's *Nixon's Good Deed*.
13 In a Presidential statement one month before the election, quoted in Reichley, *Conservatives*, p. 132.

14 Reichley, *Conservatives*, p. 133.
15 See, in particular, Henry T. Aaron, *Politics and the Professors: The Great Society in Perspective*, Washington, DC, The Brookings Institution, 1978, chapter 2 and sources cited.
16 All figures from Reichley, *Conservatives*, p. 133.
17 Ibid.
18 This section relies partly on the authoritative account of the Family Assistance Plan by Vincent and Vee Burke in *Nixon's Good Deed*. This is the most objective account which relied on interviews with the major participants. Two of the main participants have published their own accounts. Daniel Moynihan's *The Politics of a Guaranteed Income* is written from the point of view of a supporter of a guaranteed income, and Martin Anderson's *Welfare, The Political Economy of Welfare Reform in the United States*, Palo Alto: Stanford University. The Hoover Institution Press, 1978, critiques the concept. For other accounts, see James T. Patterson, *America's Struggle Against Poverty 1900–1985*, Cambridge, MA: Harvard University Press, 1986, chapter 12; Reichley, *Conservatives*, chapter 7; Kellerman, *The Political Presidency*, chapter 8; M. Kenneth Bowler, *The Nixon Guaranteed Income Proposal*, Cambridge, MA: Ballinger, 1974.
19 Burke and Burke, *Nixon's Good Deed*, p. 57.
20 See Moynihan, *Politics of a Guaranteed Income*.
21 Burke and Burke, *Nixon's Good Deed*, p. 65.
22 Ibid., p. 67.
23 George Shultz, Memo to the President, 7 May 1969; Daniel Moynihan, Memo to the President, 22 April 1969; Maurice Stans, Memo for the President, 7 May 1969; Paul McCracken, Memo to the President, 24 April 1969. All from the White House Central Files (WHCF), Confidential Files, Family Security Plans, box 69, Nixon Archive. David Kennedy, Memo to the President, 31 July 1969; Spiro Agnew, Memo to John Ehrlichman, 24 April 1969. White House Special Files (WHSF) – JDE, boxes 38 and 40, Nixon Archive.
24 John Ehrlichman made extensive verbatim notes of all the meetings he held with the president during his period in office. Some of these are unavailable, because Nixon's lawyers have successfully withheld them. The number withheld in this policy area is relatively small, however. White House Special Files – JDE, boxes 1, 2, and 3, Nixon Archive.
25 Dan Rather and Gary Paul Gates, *The Palace Guard*, New York; Harper and Row, 1974, pp. 64–7; Evans and Novak, *Nixon in the White House*, pp. 225–8; Reichley, *Conservatives*, pp. 138–43; John Osborne, *The First Two Years of the Nixon Watch*, New York: Liveright, pp. 148–54.
26 Memo from John Ehrlichman to Ed Morgan, 10 July 1969, WHSF – JDE, box 38.

27 Address to the Nation on Domestic Programs, 8 August 1969, *Public Papers of the President 1969*, Nixon, Washington, DC: US Government Printing Office, 1970, p. 640,

28 *Public Papers of the President 1969*, p. 324.

29 Ibid., p. 351.

30 Burke and Burke, *Nixon's Good Deed*, p. 220–2.

31 *Public Papers of the President, 1969*, p. 324.

32 Reported in *Congressional Quarterly, Weekly Report,* 15 August 1969, pp. 2–3.

33 Burke and Burke, *Nixon's Good Deed*, pp. 69–70.

34 Rather and Gates, *The Palace Guard*, pp. 63–7.

35 Burke and Burke, *Nixon's Good Deed*, p. 31.

36 Evans and Novak, *Nixon in the White House*, pp. 11–12; Stephen Hess, *Organizing the Presidency*, Washington, DC, The Brookings Institution, 1976, chapter 7; William Safire, *Before the Fall*, New York: Doubleday, 1975, p. 116.

37 Daniel Moynihan's own colourful account is very much written from the perspective of a major participant, *Politics of a Guaranteed Income.* For more dispassionate reviews, see Barbara Kellerman, *The Political Presidency: Practice of Leadership from Kennedy Through Reagan*, New York: Oxford University Press, 1984, chapter 8; Reichley, *Conservatives*, chapter 7; Rather and Gates, *The Palace Guard*, pp. 84–100; Evans and Novak, *Nixon in the White House*, chapter 8; Burke and Burke, *Nixon's Good Deed*, chapters 7 and 8; Bowler, *Nixon Guaranteed Income Proposal*, chapter 4.

38 Burke and Burke, *Nixon's Good Deed*, pp. 159–68.

39 Kellerman, *The Political Presidency*, pp. 139–40.

40 Moynihan's comments caused a considerable stir, both in the press and in the country, see the *New York Times*, 1 March 1970, pp. 1 and 69.

41 Kellerman, *The Political Presidency*, pp. 137–8.

42 John Ehrlichman, Notes on Meetings with the President, 27 August 1972, WHSF – JDE, box 4, Nixon Archive.

43 Notes on Meetings with the President, 2 September 1972, WHSF – JDE, box 4, Nixon Archive.

44 Notes on Meetings with the President, 2 April 1971, together with attached memos, WHSF – JDE, box 5, Nixon Archive.

45 California Welfare Reform Program Fact Sheet, WHSF – JDE, box 5, Nixon Archive.

46 Notes on Meetings with the President, 14 November 1972, WHSF – JDE, box 6, Nixon Archive.

47 12 September 1972, WHSF – JDE, box 6, Nixon Archive.

48 Memo for John Ehrlichman and Ken Cole from the President, 28 December 1972, President's Personal Files, box 4, Nixon Archive.

49 *Public Papers of the President, Richard M. Nixon,* 1969 through 1972. Of eighty-three references to welfare and the FAP, only five involved a major speech on the subject.

50 *The Nixon Presidential Press Conferences,* New York: Earl M. Coleman Enterprises, 1978.

51 Figures are from James T. Patterson, *America's Struggle Against Poverty, 1900–1985,* Cambridge, MA: Harvard University Press, 1986, pp. 197–8.

52 US Congress, Social Security Amendments of 1971, House Ways and Means Committee, Report on HR 1, 92nd Congress, 1st Session, pp. 208–9.

53 Quoted in Tom Joe and Cheryl Rogers, *By the Few for the Few: The Reagan Welfare Legacy,* Lexington, MA: D. C. Heath, 1985, p. 28.

54 *Public Papers of the President 1969,* pp. 642–5.

55 Henry Clay first proposed it as part of his 'American System', see Reichley, *Conservatives in an Age of Change,* p. 154.

56 See Melvin Laird's contribution to the *Republican Papers.* Walter Heller set out his position in 'A sympathetic Re-appraisal of Revenue Sharing', in Harvey S. Perloff and Richard P. Nathan (eds.), *Revenue Sharing and the City,* Baltimore: Resources for the Future Inc. and The Johns Hopkins Press, 1968, pp. 3–38.

57 As reported by William Safire in *Before the Fall,* New York: Quality Paperbacks, 1988, part 4, chapter 1.

58 Quoted in Reichley, *Conservatives,* p. 156.

59 Ibid., p. 156.

60 See Paul Dommel, *The Politics of Revenue Sharing,* Bloomington, IN: Indiana University Press, 1974, part 4.

61 Memo from Richard Nixon to John Ehrlichman, 14 January 1971, President's personal files, box 3, Nixon Archive.

62 John Ehrlichman, *Witness to Power: The Nixon Years,* New York: Simon and Schuster, 1982, pp. 207–9.

63 These papers were later published in *Publius, The Journal of Federalism,* 2:1 (1972), 98–137.

64 Publius, 'New Federalist Papers No. 1', *Publius* 2:1 (1972), 98–115.

65 Cato, 'Federalism Old and New', *Publius* (1972), 116–31.

66 Ibid., pp. 122–8.

67 Dommell, *Politics of Revenue Sharing,* part 2.

68 Samuel Beer, 'The Adoption of General Revenue Sharing: A Case Study in Public Sector Politics', *Public Policy,* 24:2 (1976), 157–71. Samuel Beer claims that the 'intergovernmental lobby played a crucial role in the adoption of general revenue sharing', but this occurred *after* the bill was introduced into Congress. Samuel Beer,' Federalism, Nationalism and Democracy in America', *American Political Science Review,* 72 (1978), 9–21.

69 Telegram from Nelson Rockefeller to the President, 12 January 1971, WHCF, FA 7 revenue sharing, box 32, Nixon Archive.
70 Memo from Richard Nixon to John Ehrlichman, 14 January 1971, President's personal files, box 3, Nixon Archive.
71 Notes on Meetings with the President, 14 February 1972, WHSF – JDE, box 6, Nixon Archive.
72 *Public Papers of the President 1969–1974*. Revenue sharing is mentioned more than seventy times by the President, but rarely in major speeches.
73 Bussing was an issue prominent in the leading participant's biographies, see Nixon, *Memoirs*, pp. 439–45; John Ehrlichman, *Witness to Power*, pp. 220–2, 234–5; Safire, *Before the Fall*, part 4, chapter 2.
74 Taken from David McKay, 'A Reappraisal of Public Choice Theory of Intergovernmental Relations', *Environment and Planning C: Government and Policy*, 3:1 (1985), 173.
75 For a discussion of this point, see Herbert Stein, *Presidential Economics: The Making of Economic Policy From Roosevelt to Reagan and Beyond*, New York: Simon and Schuster, 1984, pp. 94–5.
76 See, for example, the Senate Hearings on the subject reported in *Congressional Quarterly, Weekly Report*, 31 July 1970, pp. 1948–9.
77 Russell Long predicted that the 'doubling of the welfare rolls' and the 'guaranteed wage for not working . . . would destroy this country', quoted in Bowler, *Nixon Guaranteed Income Proposal*, p. 127.
78 Publius (William Safire), 'New Federalist Paper No. 1', *Publius*, 2:1 (1972), 103.
79 Patterson, *America's Struggle Against Poverty*, p. 168.
80 James Buchanan, 'Financing a Viable Federalism', in Harry L. Johnston (ed.), *State and Local Tax Problems*, Knoxville: University of Tennessee Press, 1969, chapter 1; Walter Heller, *New Dimensions of Political Economy*, Cambridge, MA: Harvard University Press, 1966; see also his contribution to Harvey Perloff and Richard Nathan (eds.), *Revenue Sharing and the City*, pp. 3–38.
81 See the discussion in Michael Reagan and John Sanzone, *The New Federalism*, New York: Oxford University Press, 1981, chapter 4.
82 See Robert D. Reixhauer, 'General Revenue Sharing – The Program's Incentives', in Robert P. Immon *et al.*, *Financing the New Federalism: Revenue Sharing, Conditional Grants, and Taxation*, Baltimore: Resources for the Future Inc. and the Johns Hopkins Press, 1975, pp. 40–87.
83 For a full discussion of this argument, see David McKay, 'A Reappraisal of Public Choice Theory of Intergovernmental Relations', *Environment and Planning C: Government and Policy*, 3:1 (1985), 163–74.

84 Lester Thurow, in Advisory Commission on Intergovernmental Relations (ACIR), *The Federal Role in the Federal System: The Dynamics of Growth; An Agenda for American Federalism Restoring Confidence and Competence*, Washington, DC: ACIR, 1981, p. 54.
85 Michael Reagan and John Sanzone, *The New Federalism*, chapter 4.
86 Nixon, *Memoirs*, p. 426.
87 There are repeated references to these themes in John Ehrlichman's Notes on Meetings with the President, boxes 1 to 4, Nixon Archive.
88 See in particular, Ehrlichman's comments on the deep-seated nature of Nixon's racism, Ehrlichman, *Witness to Power*, pp. 223–4.
89 *Public Papers of the President, 1969*, p. 696.
90 Publius and Althusius, in 'The New Federalist Papers', *Publius*, 1973.
91 Cato in 'The New Federalist Papers', *Publius*, 1973, 124.
92 Ehrlichman, *Witness to Power*, pp. 209–10.
93 For example, Bill Cavala and Aaron Wildavsky argue that interstate differences and the work-incentive problem render welfare reform unworkable, 'The Political Feasibility of Income by Right', *Public Policy*, 18 (1970), 321–54.
94 Richard P. Nathan, *The Plot that Failed: Nixon and the Administrative Presidency*, New York: Wiley, 1975, chapter 4.
95 State of the Union Message, 1971, *Public Papers of the President*.
96 The list is taken from Nathan, *The Plot that Failed*, pp. 70–6.
97 Nathan, *The Plot that Failed*, chapter 1; Nathan develops this theme and applies it to later Presidents in *The Administrative Presidency*, New York: Wiley, 1983. See also James P. Pfiffner, *The Strategic Presidency: Hitting the Ground Running*, Chicago: The Dorsey Press, 1988, pp. 91–3.
98 Nathan, *The Plot that Failed*, chapters 4 and 5; Joel D. Auerbach and Bert A. Rockman, 'Clashing Beliefs Within the Executive Branch', *American Political Science Review*, 70 (1976), 456–68.
99 Richard L. Cole and David A. Caputo, 'Presidential Control of the Senior Civil Service: Assessing the Strategies of the Nixon Years', *American Political Science Review*, 73 (1979), 399–413.
100 Ronald Randall, 'Presidential Power versus Bureaucratic Intransigence: The Influence of the Nixon Administration on Welfare Policy', *American Political Science Review*, 73 (1979), 785–810.
101 *Final Report on Violations and Abuses of Merit Principles*, House of Representatives, parts 1–4, pp. 1–244.
102 Quoted in Haynes Johnson, *In the Absence of Power; Governing America*, New York: Viking Press, 1980, p. 63.
103 *Final Report on Violations and Abuses of Merit Principles*, House of Representatives, part 3, pp. 139–70.
104 Ibid., pp. 166–70.

105 Nathan, *The Administrative Presidency*, p. 66.
106 Notes on Meetings with the President, 16 November 1972, WHSF – JDE, box 13, Nixon Archive.
107 Notes on Meetings with the President, 17 November 1972, WHSF – JDE, box 13, Nixon Archive (meeting between Nixon, Weinberger and Ehrlichman).
108 Notes on Meetings with the President, 14 November 1972, Nixon Archive (meeting between Nixon, Ash, Malek, Haldeman and Ehrlichman).
109 Notes on Meetings with the President, 17 November 1972.
110 Notes on Meetings with the President, 2 and 8 February 1973 (meeting between Nixon, Weinberger, Earl Butz, James Lynn and Ehrlichman) WHSF – JDE, box 14.
111 Memo from Tod Hullin to John Ehrlichman, 16 March 1973, WHCF – confidential files, box 27, Nixon Archive.
112 Memo from Jerry Jones to Bob Haldeman, WHCF – confidential files, box 27, Nixon Archive.
113 Stephen Hess, *Organizing the Presidency*, Washington, DC: The Brookings Institution, 1976, p. 136.
114 John H. Kessel, *The Domestic Presidency: Decision Making in the White House*, North Scituate, MA: Duxbury, 1975, chapters 2 and 4.
115 Most of these names are taken from Hess, *Organizing the Presidency*, p. 138.
116 Hugh Heclo, *Government of Strangers: Executive Politics in Washington*, Washington, DC: The Brookings Institution, 1977, p. 79.
117 Ibid., p. 80. On the transformed role of OMB also see Richard Rose, *Managing Presidential Objectives, Management and Budget and the Presidency*, Princeton, NJ: Princeton University Press, pp. 105–27.
118 Quoted in Otis L. Graham Jr; *Toward a Planned Society: From Roosevelt to Nixon*, New York: Oxford University Press, 1976, p. 255.
119 See Safire, *Before the Fall*, part 4, chapter 1; Evans and Novak, *Nixon in the White House*, chapters 1 and 2.

5 Carter and the politics of confusion

Origins

As is well known, Jimmy Carter's domestic-policy agenda was much less well structured than either Johnson's or Nixon's.[1] Johnson could exploit the Great Society slogan which served as a sort of rhetorical portmanteau for a wide range of policies. Nixon's agenda was shorter and in large part could be accommodated under the general heading of the 'New Federalism'. In his campaign speeches and statements, Carter promised a great deal, but there was little either ideologically or rhetorically to bind his commitments together. Given his general style (anti-Washington; populist; low key) and the changed nature of the times (low public expectations of the presidency; a growing federal deficit problem), it would have been difficult for Carter to have announced anything equivalent to the Great Society, but, as the first newly elected Democratic President since 1964, he was expected to be more innovative and reformist than Nixon or Ford.

His campaign pledges are easily summarized, because once elected he ordered adviser Stuart Eizenstat to compile every promise he made during the campaign. The list was not only long, it was also to become the basis of an ambitious domestic programme.[2] The main promises were:

(a) To re-organize the federal bureaucracy, cut down on government regulations and generally simplify the way in which the government deals with the citizenry.

(b) To introduce zero-based budgeting or a requirement that every agency justify any increase in spending before approval is granted.

(c) Comprehensive tax reform to simplify the existing system.

(d) A major overhaul of energy policy to improve conservation and efficiency.

(e) Comprehensive welfare reform.

(f) A confirmation and strengthening of the economic stimulus package passed by Congress in 1976 to help the economy generally and distressed cities and communities in particular.

Points (a) to (c) hardly look like part of a 'traditional' Democratic programme. Instead, they have all the features of a technocratic and fiscal conservative one. As such, they could as easily have been proposed by a Republican President.[3] Welfare reform and economic recovery were more familiar Democratic policies, although they did not dominate the Carter domestic agenda. So, in contrast to the Johnson and Nixon presidencies, the central concerns of this book – federalism, welfare and urban policy – did not become the hallmarks of the Carter domestic presidency.

The inclusion of energy was predictable in the light of recent events. Eventually, the Carter administration was to be associated more closely with the forging of a national energy policy than with any other area of domestic politics. There are a number of reasons for this. First, very early in his administration (15 April) he declared in a television address that 'our decision about energy will test the character of the American people and the ability of the President and Congress to govern this nation. This difficult effort will be the "moral equivalent of war".'[4] This rhetorical flourish attracted much attention and elevated the issue in the minds of public and Congress alike. Second, energy was by its very nature a highly complex and politically charged policy area. De-control of natural gas prices together with conservation measures for oil challenged the most powerful organized interests in America. At the same time the particular package of policies in the Carter energy programme promised few specific rewards for any section of society. The President had, therefore, to appeal to the public interest rather than to specific interests. Politically it was close to being a no-win situation.[5] Carter nonetheless set great store by the programme. He was later to recall that: 'Throughout my entire term, Congress and I struggled with energy legislation. Despite my frustration, there was never a moment when I did not consider the creation of a national energy policy equal in importance to any other goal we had.'[6]

The emphasis in this last line is important, for it reveals Carter's reluctance to set clear priorities or to acknowledge that one policy area, such as energy, was in fact deserving of much more attention than others. As many observers have documented, Carter literally flooded Congress with proposals and policy packages during 1977 and 1978.[7] Some were to fare poorly and others well, but at no time was the Carter agenda carefully ordered or structured. In this chapter we will examine two substantive policy initiatives of the Carter years which relate closely to the federalism and welfare policy arenas: welfare reform and urban policy. In addition we will study the main adaptive strategies of the Carter presidency and in particular Carter's attempts to reform the federal bureaucracy.

In terms of management structure and organization, Carter was determined to make an immediate impact on the office. As James Pfiffner has noted, 'Carter was the first presidential candidate to prepare in any detailed way for taking over the government.'[8] This took a number of specific forms. First, Carter embarked, with the assistance of Jack Watson, who had worked on his campaign, on an extensive talent search for gifted – mainly young – people to staff his administration. Second, he was pledged to a decentralized White House structure and to Cabinet government. Hence he favoured the 'spokes of a wheel' staffing system, without a Chief of Staff, and he accorded Cabinet members considerable discretion both over appointments to their departments and with respect to policy-making power. Nine key assistants were appointed, each responsible for major policy areas (domestic, national security) or for Cabinet liaison, personnel, Congressional liaison and so on.[9] A final feature of the Carter appointment process, which contrasted strongly with previous Presidents, was its exposure to public scrutiny and debate. Columnists, organized interests and other public figures were given the opportunity to comment on the new appointees. (This was, of course, part of Carter's open style of government.)

Two problems emerged very quickly as a result of this strategy. First, Carter's organizational structure effectively institutionalized a conflict inherent in any administration – that between the White House staff and Cabinet secretaries. This manifest itself in the form of in-fighting between Hamilton Jordan who, as Assistant to the President on Personnel Matters and his long-time associate, was best placed to perform the *de facto* job of Chief of Staff, and Jack Watson who, as Cabinet Secretary, was responsible for convening weekly Cabinet meetings.[10] Second, the whole process was slow and cumbersome. Carter in his public pronouncements implied some sort of political equality between a variety of policy areas, as well as to the ten Cabinet departments and what eventually became White House task forces on a number of key policy areas. Welfare reform and Carter's attempt to forge a national urban policy bring out some of these problems well.

Welfare reform

Why did Carter attempt to produce comprehensive welfare reform? Unlike energy policy, there was no immediate pressure to do so. The issue had been politically dormant following the demise of Nixon's Family Assistance Plan, President Ford having specifically rejected yet another reform scheme in late 1974. Moreover, although he had promised a new welfare plan (along with numerous others) during his run for the presidency, Carter had deliberately fought a low-key campaign where the specifics of intended reforms were hidden beneath the rhetoric of an anti-imperial, anti-Washington, populist candidate.[11] In other words, even though as a Democrat Carter was expected to be active in social policy generally, there was no urgency about taking on the difficult and politically dangerous task of re-vamping the welfare system. In the broader society, the failures of the Great Society, Watergate and economic dislocation had greatly altered the liberal agenda dominant until the early 1970s. Opinion polls reflected the shifting concern from social issues and Vietnam to questions of economic recovery and governability.[12] Whilst the Democratic Party platform had called for 'an income floor both for the working poor and [for] the poor not in the labor market',[13] party platforms have never exercised a great influence, let alone been binding on Presidents. Organized interests and state and local governments certainly continued to be interested in the subject, but not in ways which demanded a comprehensive review. The Governors sought fiscal relief; if this meant relieving them of the 'burden' of welfare, fair enough. Labour unions and the AFL–CIO wanted to link welfare reform to a full-employment job-creation programme, while the National Welfare Rights Organization favoured the creation of a national minimum income irrespective of family status or geographical locale. Within the academic community and among HEW officials support for some sort of negative income tax remained high.[14] Support in Congress for a national re-vamping of the system was by no means assured, for although FAP enthusiast Daniel Moynihan was by then a Senator and Chairman of the Senate Finance Sub-Committee on Public Assistance, Russell Long remained Chairman of the Finance Committee and remained firmly opposed to comprehensive reform.[15]

In other words, Carter was under no great political pressure to take on a project which was fraught with potential political dangers. Indeed the dangers had increased considerably by 1976 as a result of the Nixon administration initiatives and the generally higher benefit levels which Congress had authorized since the late 1960s. Income maintenance had become an extraordinarily complex package of programmes involving AFDC, food stamps, EITC, SSI, Medicare, Medicaid, and a host of smaller educational, housing and health programmes. Any major reform would have to coordinate at least the more important of these, and to do so nationally would require reform of the diversity of state benefits as well. Given his Democratic constituency, Carter could execute such a reform only by insuring that benefit levels were maintained in the more generous states and raised considerably in the less generous states. Welfare reform would, therefore, not only be potentially politically costly, it would also cost a lot of money.

These problems acknowledged, there seems little doubt that Carter was concerned about the poor. As Governor and a citizen of rural Georgia, he had seen at first hand the social consequences of low welfare benefits, and he spoke and wrote frequently of the disparities and anomalies characteristic of the present system.[16] His was, however, a populist's and technocrat's concern. His views on welfare were not integrated into a broader ideology of what needed to be done to achieve the good society.

Unlike Nixon, Carter delegated the job of drawing up comprehensive reform to a Cabinet Secretary, HEW chief, Joseph Califano, who had worked in both the Kennedy and Johnson administrations. Califano was given until 1 May to produce a reform plan. Califano naturally turned to his own department for help and appointed a welfare study group headed by Henry Aaron, the new Assistant Secretary for Planning and Evaluation. Aaron in turn sought the help of the Income Security Policy (ISP) staff in HEW who had worked on welfare reform in the Ford administration. There then followed a period characterized by bureaucratic infighting and turf protection – and what could only be called policy confusion – which culminated in the announcement on 6 August 1977 of Carter's Better Jobs and Incomes Plan (BJIP).

Two basic difficulties were encountered. (a) By assigning the job of reform to Califano and by requiring that reform be comprehensive Carter was sowing the seeds of interdepartmental conflict. As Califano retells it, first HUD Secretary Patricia Harris objected (with great anger) to the suggestion that rent supplements and other housing subsidies be phased

out and replaced with income benefits. Then Agriculture
Secretary Bob Bergland objected to any attempt to incorporate
food stamps into the reform package. Labor Secretary Ray
Marshall cooperated with Califano because providing a jobs
programme to supplement welfare payments was part of the
original brief given by Carter.[17] The President did, in fact,
favour the phasing out of housing subsidies, but was eventually dissuaded by a reluctant Califano and by Domestic
Advisor Stuart Eizenstat and Budget Director Bert Lance that,
as Califano put it, 'the misery is not worth the fight'.[18]
(b) Carter insisted that any reform would both have to eliminate
all the anomalies and inequities in the existing system *and*
impose no extra cost on the budget. Almost all those involved
in the welfare policy network agreed that these were totally
irreconcilable objectives, because, as with the early versions of
the Nixon FAP (or, for that matter, Milton Friedman's original
negative income tax scheme), a no-cost reform would have led
to sizeable reductions in benefits for large numbers of existing
welfare recipients.[19] For some weeks, Carter was obdurate on
this point and seemed to find it intellectually difficult to grasp
the fact that a major reform *had* to cost more money.[20]

In some respects Carter had worked himself into a policy
impasse. He was pledged, as will be discussed later, to
increased federal aid for the cities and Congress had already, in
September 1977, voted large increases in urban aid.[21] There is
no question that these commitments were threatening other
administration proposals including welfare and plans for
national health insurance.[22] When he eventually announced,
on 2 May, that he was going ahead with a comprehensive
reform of the system, he listed twelve basic objectives. These
are worth listing in full because of the clear incompatibility
between objective 1 and most of the others. In addition,
promises of a guaranteed income could be reconcilable with
the insistence on work incentives only if all federal (and state)
benefits were somehow incorporated into the scheme (of
which more later).

(1) No higher initial cost than the present system's.

(2) Under this system every family with children and a member able to work should have access to a job.
(3) Incentives should always encourage full-time and part-time private sector employment.
(4) Public training and employment programmes should be provided when private employment is unavailable.
(5) A family should have more income if it works than if it does not.
(6) Incentives should be designed to keep families together.
(7) Earned Income Tax Credits should be continued to help the working poor.
(8) A decent income should be provided also for those who cannot work or earn adequate income, with federal benefits consolidated into a simple cash payment, varying in amount only to accommodate differences in costs of living from one area to another.
(9) The programmes should be simpler and easier to administer.
(10) There should be incentives to be honest and to eliminate fraud.
(11) The unpredictable and growing financial burden on local governments should be reduced as rapidly as federal resources permit.
(12) Local administration of public job programmes should be emphasized.[23]

Carter's insistence on presenting this agenda to the nation (where it was generally well received) some time before any details had been worked out, presented Aaron and the ISP team with the impossibly difficult job of filling in the details in ways compatible with the basic objectives outlined by Carter. Moreover the strong emphasis on 'workfare' and job creation elevated the Department of Labor and Ray Marshall to the centre of the policy process. Indeed, from May onwards, it was not obvious whether Califano's HEW or Marshall's Department of Labor was in charge.[24]

From May to 6 August, when the BJIP plan was announced, HEW and Labor officials worked hard to formulate the details of what remained a major domestic initiative of the Carter administration. However, as Lynn and Whitman document in their *President as Policy Maker*, both departments were hampered not only by conflicting objectives, but also by not knowing what, among these objectives, the priorities of the President were.[25] In the end, Carter conceded that the reform package would have to involve some extra cost, but he provided little guidance beyond that.

What eventually transpired was a reform proposal which bore all the hallmarks of compromise between departments. The major features of BJIP were:

A new program of public service employment would provide up to 1.4 million jobs for poor adults in families with children. HEW and DoL estimate that a program of this size should provide for one job per family for all low-income families in which an adult is expected to work to contribute to family support. This jobs program would replace the work incentive (WIN) program, which has not been successful in moving welfare recipients into jobs, and the CETA Title VI jobs program, which only recently began to target jobs primarily on low-income, and long-term unemployed workers.

A simplified, fairer cash assistance program would provide aid to all Americans with inadequate family income, either as a basic support payment or as a supplement to low earnings. This new program would replace AFDC, SSI, and food stamps, which now provide assistance in an uncoordinated and fragmented way, with an integrated cash assistance plan that would reduce the great benefit disparities across the country and among different groups of the poor. Its simplified structure also should greatly reduce possibilities for error, fraud, and abuse, and maintain strong work incentives.

An expanded earned income tax credit (EITC) would provide additional supplementation to low-income workers in private sector employment. This would be an integrated component of the new system, along with the jobs and the cash assistance program.[26]

The most ambitious provision in the plan was the proposal to consolidate AFDC, SSI and food stamps into one income-maintenance payment. Crucially, however, this payment would be made up of a federally funded minimum to be supplemented by state payments. The minimum would be set low enough to require all states to make supplements, so some variations between states would continue. Three other features of the plan are worthy of note. First, the division of the poor into working and non-working categories. The latter – the disabled, old, blind and single parents with pre-school children – would be guaranteed a minimum income. All other adults including those in otherwise 'non-working' families would be required to work and would receive income supplements if their earnings were below a minimum level. This constituted the negative income tax aspect of the plan. Third, where private-sector employment was unavailable, new public-sector jobs, no less than 1.4 million of them, would be made available via a new federal jobs programme.

Although at first well received, the plan soon ran into serious trouble on the Hill. For although the extra cost was stated at a relatively modest $2.8 billion a year in payments, plus $3.4 billion from an expanded EITC,[27] it did involve increasing the number of welfare recipients massively. Some sixteen million individuals, mainly beneficiaries of food stamps, would be 'added' to the welfare rolls. Clearly this was a political liability, given the public's ideological aversion to the welfare concept. The BJIP also failed to link the new benefits to those housing and medical payments which were triggered by income thresholds. Enormous pressure would be created to extend such benefits to all recipients of BJIP – potentially an addition of several million people. As an Urban Institute report claimed in early 1978, this would increase the federal financial commitment greatly.[28] If medical benefits were excluded, it would undermine the incentive of the poor to work, or to bring their earnings up to and beyond that point where they would be ineligible for Medicaid.

Reaction from Congress and in particular from Finance Chairman Russell Long was predictable. He attacked the concept of a national minimum benefit and also argued for the 'workfare' measures to be extended to mothers with pre-school children.[29] Most estimates of the cost of the programme were, moreover, substantially higher than the original $2.8 billion (or $6.2 billion, including the lost tax credits). One Congressional Budget Office study put them as high as an additional $19 billion by 1982.[30] No one will ever know what the true cost could have been, of course, but the plan had certain built-in assumptions (such as an unemployment rate of just 5.6%) which were likely to increase the cost over time. House Ways and Means Committee Chairman Al Ullman was generally rather better disposed to the plan, but he, too, baulked at the high cost involved.[31]

According to Califano it was these revised costings which finally killed BJIP, but not so much in Congress as in the mind of Jimmy Carter. As Califano put it: 'There was a more serious obstacle [than Russell Long and the Senate Finance Committee]. The President no longer cared, and it was showing . . . In the wake of Proposition 13, Carter was determined to regain his frugal budget-balancing image.'[32] In a sense, the President's failure to continue his support for welfare reform is not surprising. Although he initiated the move, neither he nor any member of the White House staff was closely involved in formulating the plan. Carter personally disliked the whole policy area; it was complex but not easily understood. For a man with an intensely problem-solving intellect, this was distasteful.[33] Had one of his closest aides been involved and able to brief the President on the issue, the outcome might have been different. As it was, Stuart Eizenstat and Hamilton Jordan's essentially competitive relationship with Cabinet Secretaries such as Califano and Marshall undermined the prospects of strong presidential support even further.

BJIP was not reported out of the House Ways and Means Committee, although one relatively minor provision in the plan was enacted in truncated form by the 95th Congress. EITC was expanded to allow working welfare recipients to receive up to an additional $100's worth of credits a year. During 1979 a much modified welfare plan was re-introduced by the administration – but this time the proposals were of a step-by-step nature and emanated largely from within the White

House. However, this new package, which would have required all states to allow two-parent families welfare benefits if the main wage earner was unemployed, also fell foul of Russell Long in the Senate – even though it did pass the House by 222 to 184.[34]

Urban policy

Unlike welfare, Carter was under pressure to produce new and expanded policies in the general area of aid for states and, more especially, for cities. Between 1970 and 1977 fiscal crises had become commonplace among the nation's larger and older cities. In response to this, the Democratic Congress has passed a number of short-term relief measures – often over President Ford's veto. Three of these – the Comprehensive Employment and Training Act (CETA), Countercyclical Revenue Sharing and Public Works Grants, had grown rapidly with appropriations of over $15 billion between them in fiscal 1977. In October 1977, Congress increased funding for the Community Development Block Grant programme, with strong support from the administration.[35] Much earlier, Carter had made a specific attempt to project himself as a champion of the cities, promising at the US Conference of Mayors in June 1976 that if elected they would have 'a friend, an ally and a partner in the White House . . . I believe that working together, we can turn the tide, stop the decay and set in motion a process of growth that by the end of this century can give us cities worthy of the greatest nation on earth.'[36] Carter had proceeded to appoint as Secretary of HUD a woman who quickly proved to be a champion of the cities, Patricia Harris. Harris worked assiduously to promote urban programmes, and was instrumental in elevating the Urban Development Action Grant legislation (UDAG) near to the top of the administration's agenda early in 1977.[37] UDAG, which provided cities with grants for downtown commercial and civic development, was in the tradition of the Great Society.

As with other areas of public policy, Carter was attracted by the idea of producing a *comprehensive* policy for the cities. No President had attempted this before. Johnson had subsumed his specific objectives under the general banner of the 'Great Society'. An urban policy (or an energy or welfare policy for that matter) implied coordination, structure and planning — processes which struck a sympathetic intellectual chord with Carter. At first Carter used a similar policy formulation method to that used for welfare — he delegated HUD Secretary Patricia Harris to convene an Urban and Regional Policy Group (URPG). In memos to Harris and other Cabinet Secretaries Carter designated HUD as the 'lead agency', which would be required to coordinate with Labor, Commerce, HEW, Transport and the Treasury to produce an urban policy.

According to the leading participants in this process in HUD, in setting up this strategy Carter was not only confirming his preference for Cabinet government, he was also eschewing the secretive and closed style of policy-making typical of the Johnson and Nixon administrations.[38] Carter's approach represented an inductive approach to policy-making which contrasted with the pre-conceived notions of what was best for urban America implicit in such initiatives as the War on Poverty, Model Cities and the Nixon FAP. Put another way, the Carter urban policy was to be an intelligence-gathering exercise rather than an intellectual one. Unfortunately it was also, at least in the first months, almost leaderless. The problem was obvious. Carter had given the job of leadership to HUD Secretary Harris, who, although a forceful personality acting on the specific instructions of the President, held no sway over senior Cabinet Secretaries representing Commerce, Treasury, Labor and HEW. Some division of labour was tentatively agreed: Commerce was responsible for economic development, HUD for neighbourhood development and the Treasury for public finance. OMB was also involved and given a co-ordinating brief to assess the fiscal implications of any proposals.

Between March and July 1977 very little happened. Departmental Secretaries had delegated the job to deputies who found it difficult to agree among themselves. During July Vernon Jordan, Executive Director of the Urban League, upbraided the President for doing so little for the cities. His sentiments were echoed by members of the Congressional black caucus a few days later.[39] All the participants in the process agree that this galvanized the President into taking firmer action. Patricia Harris replaced Assistant Secretary Donna Shalala, who had been given the job of convening URPG with Robert Embry. Embry was at the time Assistant Secretary for Community Planning and Development. He had close links with the White House and had even been considered by Carter for the secretaryship of HUD. As important, Stuart Eizenstat began to take a keen interest in the issue and sat in as co-chair of URPG during their weekly meetings in the old Executive Office Building. This culminated in a first draft of a national urban policy in September and the publication of a second draft with rough cost estimates in November. Following intervention by Eizenstat and his deputy Bert Carp a final draft appeared in late November, without cost estimates. This change of strategy was prompted by OMB's estimate that the long list of projects in the document would cost an estimated $10 to 20 billion in federal commitments. As its title, 'Cities and People in Distress', suggests, this final draft focussed on the problems of declining cities, and in particular on unemployment, fiscal stress, physical environment, institutional capacity and equal opportunity.[40]

'Cities and People in Distress' was circulated widely – in fact 'to almost all the interested parties in the country', as one of its major authors, HUD consultant Marshall Kaplan, put it.[41] Again this was deliberate strategy on URPG's part. They wanted to produce an urban policy that reflected the genuine needs of America's urban areas, rather than the pre-conceived ideas of a small group of academics based in the White House. Predictably, the ensuing reaction was often hostile. Those areas and interest excluded from the policy fought hard for inclusion.[42] Between December and the final announcement of the Urban Policy in March, almost every public-interest organization representing cities, counties and states pleaded their particular cause. The Mayors of older northern cities objected to the apparently low level of aid being offered. Governors were concerned that the approach was too local-government oriented, leaving the states relatively worse off than before.[43] Smaller towns and cities in the south and west pleaded that targeting aid on larger northern urban areas would effectively shut out some of the poor.[44] Put another way, the pluralistic, inductive style of the Carter administration served as an invitation to seek lowest-common-denominator solutions in public policy. Thus urban policy was not only required to cost little, but also to please everybody.

During and following these protests, the URPG adapted its strategy once more. In early December, a further draft was produced with an extended list of objectives – most of them carefully costed. Carter reacted angrily to this, reminding them that they were required to construct an *integrated* urban policy, not just a shopping list of existing and a few new programmes. Interestingly, several of the participants claim that this was the first time that Carter actually read one of the urban-policy drafts. Until then, Eizenstat and Carp (who claim that 30 to 40% of their time was devoted to this issue during these months) had acted on behalf of the President. On Carter's instructions Eizenstat then proceeded to produce a long memo, with the help of Patricia Harris and her staff, outlining the basic principles in the Carter urban policy. This became known as the 'Pat/Stu' memo, the authors having signed their names thus on the document.[45] Carter read the memo and effectively endorsed it in late January 1978, instructing URPG to 'analyze existing programs and to recommend new program initiatives'.[46]

This became the foundation of what came to be known as *Base Evaluation* or an attempt
(a) to measure the impact of all federal programmes on urban areas, and
(b) to recommend how they could be re-organized to help cities.

Crucially, the Pat/Stu memo had recommended that all cities be included and all levels of government. Naturally this appealed to Carter's ambition that any policy be comprehensive. Some targeting would remain, but in theory, at least, all communities with a problem might benefit. Another aspect of the Pat/Stu memo was its emphasis on defining broad policy principles and objectives leaving the detail to be worked out by those departments and agencies whose programmes had urban impacts.

Embry and the URPG duly produced a lengthy base evaluation which listed the urban impacts of everything from Community Development Block Grants, to air pollution to small business loans. From this and the Pat/Stu memo, a draft urban policy was forged. However, Carter, much preoccupied with foreign policy at the time, did not see the draft until 23 March 1978 and he was scheduled to announce his urban policy just four days later. In the event, Eizenstat and Harris condensed their recommendations into a briefing book with boxes indicating presidential options for approval, preceded by the pros and cons for each choice. Some examples affecting key economic development policies with Carter's annotations are given below:

1. Creation of an Urban Development Bank
   Decision
           Option 1.
   _____ Approve Bank located in commerce.
           Option 2.
   _____ Approve Bank located in HUD.
           Option 3.
   _√c_ Approve Interagency Bank (on an interim basis).
           Option 4.
   _____ Announce Bank, defer legislation.
           Option 5.
   _____ Do not approve Bank.

2. Introduction of Differential Tax Incentives
   Decision
   _____ Support HUD's proposed differential ITC.*
   __√ᶜ__ Support limited differential ITC.
   _____ No differential tax incentives.
   *Investment Tax Credit

3. Increase in Economic Development Grants
   Decision
   _____ Support increase in funding for UDAG in amount of
   $500 million.
   _____ Support increase in funding for Title IX in amount
   of $400 million.
   __√ᶜ__ Support increase in funding for both Title IX and
   UDAG in amounts of _____
   2,750m eachᶜ
   _____ No additional funding for economic development
   grants.

4. Proposal for interest subsidies for Section 108
   Decision
   _____ Provide interest subsidy and change eligible activities of Section 108.⁺
   __√ᶜ__ Do nothing.[47]
   ⁺Section 108 allowed HUD to guarantee bonds
   issued by local governments.

ᶜ = Carter annotations

The argument for and against each of these options clearly reflected the preferences of URPG staff members. When Eizenstat and Harris received the President's responses, they were obliged at the last minute to return to him with objections to some of his decisions. With respect to urban development grants, for example, Carter's decision in favour of a $275 million increase in each of the programmes was eventually rejected and replaced with increases of $400 million and $500 million as 'recommended' in the memo.

It would be unfair to Carter to imply that he was simply rubber-stamping bureaucratic decisions. As indicated, he had earlier insisted that the urban policy help all cities in need, and he also favoured greater involvement by state governments, which was included in the final report. Even so, the policy system created by Carter – open access, decentralized decision-making, rigid timetables – left the President with forty-eight hours to make a number of difficult decisions, while at the same time trying to attend to visits by Prime Ministers Menachem Begin of Israel and James Callaghan of Britain.

Carter's urban policy came to be known as 'A New Partnership to Conserve America's Communities'. It attracted wide publicity – much more than welfare reform – and was given a high profile by the administration. Few of the specific proposals involved new programmes; most recommended the adaptation of existing programmes towards the needs of cities. Loans for housing rehabilitation were to be increased, public works enhanced under CETA, employment-tax credits were to be targeted on companies hiring the long-term unemployed and counter-cyclical revenue sharing and the UDAG program-mes extended. The one major new programme was to be the creation of a national development bank which would guaran-tee loans of up to $11 billion over three years to companies investing in distressed areas (both urban and rural). Finally, the states were to receive monies from a $200 million fund for helping distressed communities within their borders.[48]

Carter's urban policy made little progress. Within two months it became clear to administration officials that further targeting on the most needy cities was necessary if the costs of programmes were to be kept down. This applied *tout force* to the national development bank and the investment tax credit programmes,[49] neither of which were enacted by Congress. Housing rehabilitation, CETA and the UDAG programme were extended, but counter-cyclical aid was not renewed in 1978.

Carter's urban policy was in part a victim of the times. Proposition 13 was passed in June 1978 and heralded a new era of tax-cutting and fiscal conservatism. But the initiative's

failure must also be related to the political process by which it
was created and to the leadership role played by the President
himself. We will return to these points later.

Coherence

Economic theory

Carter's welfare plan had the advantage of federalizing a large
part of the AFDC programme, and incorporating the already
largely federalized SSI and food stamps into the scheme clearly
made sound economic sense. More problematic was the
reform's failure to involve Medicaid, housing and a whole host
of other in-kind and state welfare benefits. While these
remained outside the scheme, numerous anomalies were likely
to persist. By 1978, Medicaid had grown into a $12 billion
dollar programme, having cost less than $2 billion as recently
as 1968.[50] By comparison, AFDC's *federal* costs were just $5.7
billion in 1977, with state and local contributions bringing the
total up to $10.3 billion.[51] Indeed, by the late 1970s AFDC had
been relegated from the role of dominant welfare programme to
just one of many. Only 15.5% of total federal welfare spending
was accounted for by AFDC in 1977.[52] Clearly any rational
comprehensive reform had to take account of all welfare
benefits. The Carter scheme was likely therefore, to result in a
number of anomalies. Martin Anderson – not to mention many
members of Congress – was probably right in claiming that,
had it been adopted, Carter's BJIP would eventually have led
to an overhaul of Medicaid, housing and other benefits.[53] This
in turn would have genuinely transformed the status of federal
income-maintenance provision in the United States. Had such
an overhaul *not* occurred, BJIP could have persuaded many
individuals to keep their earnings below the Medicaid eligibility thresholds and thus have constituted a disincentive to
work.

Even without such an overhaul, Anderson argued that BJIP

was 'revolutionary' because it nationalized the idea of welfare benefits for any individual without income, not just the disabled, blind, old and single parents with young children. He argued this partly on economic grounds – it would have led to increased federal expenditure – and partly on philosophical grounds (which we will return to later).[54] Whether BJIP was fiscally irresponsible seems highly doubtful. It would at most have led to $6 to $10 billion additional welfare spending which, given the magnitude of the reform, was not a large sum. But considerable political pressures existed which eventually would have led to further commitments by the federal government. The size of these can only be guessed at.

Because state supplements were to be retained, BJIP would not have achieved the most economically rational solution – total federalization (for a discussion see chapter 4, p.87). HEW officials were aware of this and fought hard against the retention of state supplements. But their objections were based more on considerations of equity than on economic grounds.[55]

A priori, the division of the poor into working and non-working categories was a sensible economic distinction. Work incentives would be applied to the former group, but not to the latter. In reality, however, individuals and families move out of the one category and into the other with great frequency. Administering (and policing) such a system would have been very difficult. Nixon's FAP, with a guaranteed income and potentially a negative income tax for all recipients, was a much simpler and more workable scheme. The creation of up to 1.4 million public-sector jobs to ensure that the working poor would work was, of course, a non-market-type economic device, but one which could have helped ameliorate the growth of a large, spatially concentrated, dependent population. Even so, implementing such a scheme would be fraught with difficulties. Job creation schemes until then – most notably CETA – had been characterized by a host of administrative and political problems. It was unlikely the Carter plan would have fared any better.

Carter's urban policy was designed to revive economic

activity in distressed cities, or parts of cities. Its focus was clearly on investment and job creation led by federal (and to a lesser extent, state) incentives, subsidies and grants. Unfortunately, this is an area of economics fraught with uncertainties and doubts. In 1977–8 it would be accurate to say that economists had generally made the transition from interventionist Keynesianism to free-market liberalism. This affected urban affairs as much as any other area of economic policy. Judged by the canons of free-market liberalism, Carter's measures were doomed to failure. They were not, in the main, designed to control externalities or negative spillovers such as pollution or crime, which liberal economists may have conceded as legitimate areas of intervention for a national government. Urban development banks, tax breaks and community-development programmes would simply distort market forces and lead the economy further away from *Pareto optimality*. This view was rapidly gaining currency in the late 1970s, even among those not usually associated with such a 'hands-off' approach. For example, in their contribution on 'the cities' in the annual *Setting National Priorities* series produced by Brookings, Richard Nathan and Paul Dommel pointed out:

Just because urban hardship exists does not necessarily mean that new federal programs should be initiated, or old ones expanded, to aid hardship cities. This point is often made in the following terms. Most people do not choose to live in old and densely populated cities with high-rise life styles. The growth of new areas and new settlement patterns (both in suburbs and increasingly in small cities) reflects individual choices, which are perfectly appropriate, and in fact desirable, in a democratic society. The role of the old inner cities, it is argued, has to change and in fact is changing; public policy should not swim against the tide.[56]

Judged by Keynesian, interventionist standards, the Carter urban policy was also lacking. The move towards provision of aid for all cities, large and small, clearly compromised the avowed intention to target subsidies and grants on the most needy. This shift in emphasis was, of course, politically motivated as was the decision – reached after much heartache on Carter's part – to locate the new Development Bank in no less than three agencies – HUD, Commerce and Treasury. Such an expedient would surely have undermined the Bank's effectiveness and led to yet more bureaucratic in-fighting and turf protection.[57] This accepted, the notion of 'targeting' did spread to a number of federal departments and agencies during the Carter years, and spending on urban-associated program-mes did increase. Indeed the Community Development Block Grant programme increased by 60% and following legislative amendments in 1977 and 1978 much of the aid available under this increase was directed towards low- and moderate-income citizens.[58]

At a more general level, it is doubtful that even if fully implemented, Carter's urban policy would have arrested, still less reversed, the fortunes of distressed cities. Most urbanists now agree that the forces accounting for the rise and decline of cities – technological change, demographic trends, the general health of regional and national economies – are simply not amenable to successful manipulation by governments in democratic countries.[59] The most that can be hoped for is some amelioration of the worst consequences of decline through specific programmes. With its complex intergovernmental structure and highly politicized policy process, the United States is probably a less suitable case for such programmes than some other countries. Certainly the experience of the Great Society warned of the perils and pitfalls of highly com-promised policy implementation.

Perhaps in recognition of this, the Carter urban policy talked of the need for 'partnership' with local and, especially, state governments and with the private sector – and in so doing anticipated the shift towards state and private sector solutions favoured by the Reagan administrations.

Political theory

BJIP would have made some progress towards removing some of the worst inequities associated with AFDC. But by retaining state supplements and failing to integrate the plan with Medicaid and other in-kind benefits, considerable inequities would have been retained. While accepting this, BJIP did represent a major deviation from the New Deal regime. Americans were to be provided with a guaranteed minimum income by right irrespective of family status or geographic locale. Unemployed males and childless couples would have been eligible for welfare. Like Nixon's FAP, BJIP would thus have instituted a limited form of equality of condition which, education apart, had no precedent in American social policy. In this sense, the plan was entirely consistent with Carter's pledge to help poorer Americans and to purge the American welfare system of its worst anomalies. Martin Anderson rightly labelled this a fundamental change:

What is being proposed is not a 'reform' of the current welfare system. What is being proposed is a radical, fundamental change in our entire approach to welfare. The American people have believed that those who cannot support themselves – particularly the blind, the disabled, the aged and mothers with small children – should receive welfare. Our welfare programs have been designed to provide help for such people. But Americans, in general, have never felt that healthy single individuals, childless couples and families with both parents present deserve much welfare. There seems to be little barrier to employment for those with no childrearing responsibilities.[60] (emphasis in original)

It was not just prophets of the right such as Martin Anderson who oppposed comprehensive reform. Some of the very officials whom Anderson in his book condemns as manipulative, liberal HEW bureaucrats themselves had serious doubts about the philosophical foundations of a minimum income by right.[61] Most notably, economist Henry Aaron, Chief of the ISP staff, disliked the notion because of its lack of public support. He favoured incremental benefits – in-kind programmes such as food stamps.[62] Califano chose Aaron because of his reputation as a good economist who had studied the welfare problem. He was not a champion of reform but an expert on it. It seems very doubtful that Carter or any official in the White House was aware of this.

Few would dispute that welfare is a difficult area to reform – indeed some political scientists have even argued that it is impossible to reform.[63] Carter's BJIP was flawed but represented a real break from the old regime. There is little doubt that by delegating the details of the plan first to a Cabinet Secretary and then to HEW officials he did nothing to advance its political prospects. Carter and the White House were only obliquely involved in the policy process – a fact which was to influence not just the eventual outcome of BJIP but also its content.

As far as federalism was concerned, Carter subscribed to no general theory of how best to divide responsibilities between the various levels of government. BJIP would in fact have been a centralizing influence, as would some elements in the urban policy (targeting to specific cities, the creation of a national Development Bank). However, Carter also championed the enhancement of the state role in urban policy and favoured – and was successful in winning support for – an extension of block grants with their implied elevation of the states in the federal system. Carter repeatedly pledged to bring 'the government back to the people', but talk of partnership with states and communities aside, this was hardly apparent in the policies he actually supported and pursued. If anything, his urge for participation showed itself in the process of policy formulation rather than in the substance of policy and its implementation. Hence his insistence not only that the Departments play a leading role in making policy, but also, as with the urban policy, that they should consult with all the parties and interests affected. This helped to politicize the policy process and gave organized interests especially the intergovernmental lobby – a greater role than they would otherwise have had. Contemporary claims of the rise of a 'topocracy' government by state, local and county officials and their organizations were fuelled by the Carter policy-making style.[64]

What of administrative efficiency? In a range of substantive policy areas and in legislation submitted to Congress for

executive branch re-organization and civil service reform,
Carter was strongly committed to rooting out what he saw as
waste, duplication and inefficiency in the federal government.
The President's position on this subject reveals both an anti-
Washington, populist urge to bring government closer to the
people and a technocratic desire to simplify government. Re-
organization and civil service reform will be dealt with later,
but in neither welfare nor urban policy were the programme
designs compatible with the Carter efficiency imperative. BJIP
was, of course, intended to simplify what was a hopelessly
complex system. Had it been implemented, however, the
whole question of incorporating state and federal in-kind and
supplementary benefits into the plan would have had to be
approached. The outcome would have increased administrative
complexity. Carter's urban policy, too, may have added to the
bureaucratic and political complexity characteristic of the
federal government. It promised expanded but targeted
categorical programmes and the creation of a quasi-
governmental institution, the urban development bank. The
URPG did make a specific attempt to avoid the mistakes of the
Great Society by stressing economic development rather than
launching new programmes based on a rhetoric of absolute
solutions and vague notions of participatory democracy. Even
so, the concept of targeting itself requires information,
coordination and, above all, discrimination between jurisdictions and recipients. Few would dispute that this is a recipe for
politicization and hence for increased complexity.

Adaptation

In some respects it is difficult to talk of the Carter
administration's adopting a strategy in reaction to legislative
and policy implementation failures, for the President was
committed to a major rationalization of the executive branch
from the very beginning. He wanted, above all, to simplify and
reduce the size and complexity of the federal bureaucracy.
During his campaign he had insisted that 'our government in

Washington now is a horrible bureaucratic mess . . . We must give top priority to a drastic and thorough reorganization of the Federal bureaucracy.'[65] Accordingly Carter launched a number of re-organization initiatives, the most important of which resulted in the passage of the Civil Service Reform Act in 1978. This law, which enjoyed strong Congressional support, potentially gave Presidents much greater control over the bureaucracy. It replaced the Civil Service Commission with two new agencies, the Office of Personnel Management (OPM) and the Merit Systems Protection Board (MSPB) and instituted a new senior corps of federal employees – the Senior Executive Service (SES). Effectively, SES managers would constitute the key level of policy-making administrators. They were very specifically not designated civil servants; the idea was to give the President more control over the civil service and thus render it more efficient.[66] Up to 10% of SES employees could be President-nominated political appointees, who could be placed almost anywhere in the federal bureaucracy. Agency heads could create or re-assign existing administrators to the new SES grade and thus potentially transform the top management of federal departments. At a stroke, therefore, Congress gave to Presidents greatly enhanced powers to change – and possibly transform – the operating values and objectives of the federal bureaucracy. In addition, merit pay increases for civil services grades GS-13 to GS-15 were introduced and federal managers were given more freedom to fire incompetent workers. Although unions and other groups lobbied hard against the bill it eventually passed the Senate on a voice vote, and the House by 365 votes to 8.[67]

In 1980, Congress passed another potentially important bill, as part of Carter's drive for greater efficiency. The wonderfully named 1980 Paperwork Reduction Act, established an Office of Information and Regulatory Affairs (OIRA) within OMB which had wide powers to limit the information generated by departments and agencies and ensure that it was needed, collected efficiently and not duplicative. In effect, this gave OIRA and the Budget Director wide powers to limit departmental and agency rule making. An amendment by Senator Edward Kennedy recognized this and required that the Budget Director comment on proposed rules within sixty days of their publication, after which he forfeited his power to veto or amend them.[68] But even given this caveat, the act gave very considerably stronger gatekeeping powers to OMB – a fact which the Reagan administration was to be quick to recognize just one month later, in January 1981.

These centralizing measures were motivated by the high premium placed by Carter on organizational efficiency. As such, they had no ideological content. Although the bills had origins early in the Carter administration, they were not passed until late 1978 and late 1980. Carter had little or no opportunity to put them into practice, therefore. Perhaps the most curious feature of this drive for centralization and efficiency is its manifest incompatibility with the early management strategy set by Carter from the White House. Carter had favoured a 'spokes-in-the-wheel' managerial style and the delegation of broad policy-making and appointment powers to Cabinet Secretaries. Studies of White House decision-making during the Carter years confirm that this was a highly inefficient way of doing business – possibly because it was inherently inefficient or because of Carter's personality and style. He failed to get to know his Cabinet members well and departmental/White House liaison was poor.[69] In the face of repeated policy failures, Carter conceded the need for a Chief of Staff, Hamilton Jordan, in 1979. At the same time, in a remarkable gesture of frustration (or contrition?), he demanded the resignations of his entire Cabinet in July 1979. He accepted five, including that of HEW secretary, Joe Califano.

Whether the 'July massacre' actually helped Carter is doubtful. Press reaction was generally critical – Carter's gesture reinforced rather than removed his image as an unstable and indecisive leader.[70] As far as the substantive issues of welfare reform and urban policy were concerned, these charges meant little. Patricia Harris was transferred to HEW and Moon Landrieu became HUD Secretary. Neither had much time to make an impact on their departments before the elections just over a year later. In effect, then Carter had little opportunity to pursue an administrative strategy even if he had wanted to. He had left most sub-Cabinet appointments to his departmental secretaries and by 1979 he was seriously diverted by foreign-policy concerns. At a more general level, the domestic policy agenda did change during these last two years. The budget deficit was increasing, not declining towards zero as Carter planned, and this put pressure on such departments as HEW and HUD to keep spending down. Indeed during both 1979 and 1980 budget projections for social programmes included substantial cuts on original estimates. This expenditure-trimming imperative tended to raise the role and status of OMB within the White House. By 1980, indeed, Carter himself acknowledged that these concerns were the dominant domestic issue.[71]

Conclusions

The federalism and welfare-policy agendas did change during the Carter years. State-oriented solutions gained some influence, as did the use of block grants. Comprehensive welfare reform received a serious setback following the failure of the Carter initiative. There is little doubt that this failure is related to the policy-making process favoured by Carter during his first two years in office. Plans and proposals were drawn up slowly, mainly by departmental officials who in turn were encouraged to consult widely with outside interests. The White House in general, and Carter in particular, played virtually no leadership, priority-setting role. This process also probably contributed to some of the anomalies and omissions characteristic of the plans. If this was partly true of welfare policy it was even more applicable to urban policy. It was almost certainly a mistake to promise a comprehensive urban policy. The area is simply too complex and the problems too intractable to be amenable to the simple unitary solutions implicit in the label 'National Urban Policy'. This aside, the open, decentralized lowest-common-denominator approach favoured by Carter was bound to result in an incoherent set of policies with limited political prospects.

It is easy to claim with the benefit of hindsight that both policies were doomed to failure, irrespective of the White House incumbent or managerial/leadership style assumed. But at the time of both plans' birth, opinion was by no means unanimous on this point. Indeed Senator Alan Beall Jr of Maryland claimed in the spring of 1977 that 'the political climate for achieving comprehensive welfare reform would seem to be almost perfect',[72] and initial reactions to the urban policy proposals were generally enthusiastic. Passive presidential leadership helps to explain why welfare reform failed and why those measures most central to the urban policy died in Congress.

Carter's problem was not only one of style and management. His views on domestic policy also lacked ideological and intellectual coherence. He wrestled constantly with the fact that it was not possible to formulate major social-policy reforms without spending more money. By the end of his embattled presidency it was the fiscal imperatives which held sway over his ambition to achieve reforms. Even more than Nixon, his agenda lacked ideological unity. He had no clear vision in domestic policy. Nixon did subscribe to an anti-bureaucracy philosophy which he was able to marry to his distaste for liberals and putative subversives. As pointed out in the last chapter, this was to have some, if limited, programmatic consequences when the second Nixon administration pursued an administrative strategy. Carter lacked even this degree of ideological consistency. He disliked the organizational untidiness of the federal behemoth, but his objections were rooted in an engineer's preference for order and unity. He was, in other words, largely unable to see the necessity of pursuing clear policy objectives early in his administration with great vigour and persistence. Paradoxically, his urge to re-organize led to the passage of two laws, civil service reform and paperwork reduction, which were to be used in a highly ideological and political manner by his successor, Ronald Reagan.

NOTES

1 For general reviews of Carter's domestic policies, see Dilys M. Hill, 'Domestic Policy', in M. Glenn Abernathy, Dilys M. Hill and Phil Williams (eds.), *The Carter Years: The President and Policy Making*, London: Frances Pinter, 1984, pp. 13–34; Haynes Johnson, *In the Absence of Power: Governing America*, New York: The Viking Press, 1980, book 2; Austin Ranney, 'The Carter Administration', in Austin Ranney (ed.), *The American Elections of 1980*, Washington, DC: American Enterprise Institute, 1980, pp. 1–36.

2 Reported in Robert Shogan, *Promises to Keep: Carter's First Hundred Days*, New York: Thomas Crowell, 1977, pp. 117–18.

3 See James W. Caesar, 'The Theory of Governance of the Reagan Administration', in Lester M. Salamon and Michael S. Lund (eds.), *The Reagan Presidency and the Governing of America*, Washington, DC: The Urban Institute Press, 1984, pp. 57–87.

4 *Public Papers of the President, 1977*, 'Address to the Nation', 18 April 1977, Washington, DC: US Government Printing Office, p. 656.

5 For reviews of Carter's energy policy, see Michael J. Malbin, 'Rhetoric and Leadership: A Look Backward at the Carter National Energy Plan', in Anthony King (ed.), *Both Ends of the Avenue: The Presidency, the Executive Branch and Congress in the 1980s*, Washington, DC: American Enterprise Institute, 1983, pp. 212–45; Eric M. Uslaner, 'Shale Barrel Politics: Energy Policy and the Institutional Decentralization of Congress', unpublished paper, University of Maryland, 1982; Shogan, *Promises to Keep*, chapter 9; Barbara Kellerman, *The Political Presidency: Practice of Leadership From Kennedy Through Reagan*, New York: Oxford University Press, 1984, chapter 10; Charles O. Jones, 'Keeping Faith and Losing Congress: The Carter Experience in Washington', *Presidential Studies Quarterly*, 14 (1984), 437–45.

6 Jimmy Carter, *Keeping Faith: Memoirs of a President*, New York: Bantam Books, 1982, p. 91.

7 See Ranney, 'The Carter Administration', pp. 17–20; Caesar, 'Reagan Administration', pp. 61–8.

8 James P. Pfiffner, *The Strategic Presidency: Hitting the Ground Running*, Chicago: The Dorsey Press, 1988, p. 117.

9 For accounts, see Colin Campbell SJ, *Managing the Presidency: Carter, Reagan and the Search for Executive Harmony*, Pittsburgh: University of Pittsburgh Press, 1986, chapter 3 and 4; R. Gordon Hoxie, 'Staffing the Ford and Carter presidencies', in Bradley D. Nash, *Organizing and Staffing the Presidency*, New York Center for the Study of the Presidency, Proceedings, vol. 3, no. 1, 1980, chapter 3; Bruce Adams and Kathryn Kavanagh-Baron, *Promise and Performance: Carter Builds a New Administration*, Lexington, MA: D. C. Heath, 1979, chapters 2 and 3.

10 Hoxie, 'Staffing the Ford and Carter Presidencies', pp. 72–7.

11 See Ranney, 'The Carter Administration', pp. 5–7, also Johnson, *In the Absence of Power*, chapter 1.

12 See the poll data present in *Public Opinion*, 1:2 (May/June 1978).

13 Democratic National Platform, 1976, Reported in *Congressional Quarterly, National Party Conventions, 1831–1976*, Washington DC: Congressional Quarterly Press, 1979, pp. 101–2.

14 For sources and a full discussion, see Laurence E. Lynn Jr and David de F. Whitman, *The President as Policy-Maker: Jimmy Carter and Welfare Reform*, Philadelphia: Temple University Press, 1981, pp. 35–42.

15 Lynn and Whitman, *The President as Policy Maker*, p. 37.

16 Ibid., p. 35. See also Jimmy Carter, 'Its the Poor Who Suffer', in the compilation of his speeches, *A Government is as Good as its People*, New York: Simon and Schuster, 1977, pp. 65–8.

17 Joseph A. Califano Jr, *Governing America: An Insider's Report From the White House and the Cabinet*, New York: Simon and Schuster, 1981, pp. 330–4.

18 Califano, *Governing America*, p. 331.

19 Califano, *Governing America*; Martin Anderson, *Welfare: The Political Economy of Welfare Reform in the United States*, Palo Alto: Stanford University, The Hoover Institution Press, 1978, pp. 170–5.

20 Califano, *Governing America*, pp. 334–5.

21 Increases were voted for Community Development funds and a $400 million Urban Development Action Grant Program was created, *Congressional Quarterly, Weekly Report*, 1 October 1977, pp. 2079–83.

22 'Cities' Needs May Scuttle Carter's Budget Plans', *New York Times*, 6 November 1977, pp. 1 and 66.

23 *Public Papers of President Jimmy Carter, 1977*, Remarks at a news briefing, pp. 771–2.

24 Lynn and Whitman, *The President as Policy-Maker*, chapter 8.

25 Ibid., chapters 8 and 11.

26 This summary is adapted from James R. Storey, *The Better Jobs and Incomes Plan: A Guide to President Carter's Welfare Reform Proposal and Major Issues*, Washington, DC: The Center Institute, Welfare Reform Policy Analysis Series, 1 November 1978, p. 25.

27 *Congressional Quarterly, Weekly Report,* 13 August 1977, p. 1702.
28 The Urban Institute, *The Welfare Reform Proposal: Implementation Issues,* Washington, DC: Urban Institute Working Paper 5102–01, 1977, pp. 17–18.
29 *Congressional Quarterly, Weekly Report,* 'Senate Finance Committee Doing its Own Thing on Welfare Reform', 3 September 1977, pp. 1865–72.
30 Quoted in Anderson, *Welfare,* p. 185.
31 Ullman produced his own reform package which would have cost less than the Carter plan: *Congressional Quarterly, Weekly Report,* 4 February 1978, pp. 11–15.
32 Califano, *Governing America,* p. 363.
33 Anderson reports how frustrating Carter found the whole issue. '"It's all very difficult", he [Carter] complained, "I came over to my office this morning at 5.30 and I spent three hours on the welfare question before my first appointment. And this afternoon I have two more hours of study and work with Cabinet members on the welfare question . . ."' Anderson, *Welfare,* pp. 174–5.
34 *Congressional Quarterly, Almanac,* 1979, Washington, DC, 1980, pp. 509–10.
35 *Congressional Quarterly, Almanac,* '$12.5 billion Urban Aid Authorization Voted', vol. 33, 1977, Washington DC, 1978, pp. 127–37.
36 Quoted in Harold L. Wolman and Astrid E. Mergret, 'The Presidency and Policy Formulation: President Carter and the Urban Policy', *Presidential Studies Quarterly,* 10 (Summer 1980), 403.
37 'HUD Chief Gaining Power and Urban Leaders' Respect', *New York Times,* 15 May 1978, p. D9.
38 This next section is based partly on interviews with the following officials in Washington between November 1977 and April 1978:
    Robert Duckworth, Director of the Office of Urban Policy, HUD
    Judith May, Assistant to Robert Duckworth, HUD
    Robert C. Embry Jr, Assistant Secretary for Community Planning Development, HUD
    Carla Cohen, Special Assistant to Robert Embry, HUD
    Donna E. Shalala, Assistant Secretary for Policy Development and Research, HUD
    Lynn Curtis, Executive Director, Urban and Regional Policy Group, HUD
    Marshall Kaplan, Consultant, HUD
    Larry Houston, Special Assistant to Juanita Kreps, Commerce
    David Walker, Assistant Director, Advisory Commission on Intergovernmental Relations.
    Bert Carp, Deputy to the Assistant for Domestic Policy Affairs, The White House

Bo Cutter, Office of Management and Budget
Holly Staebler, Staff Director, House Sub-Committee on the City
39 *New York Times*, 25 July 1977, p. 43; and 30 July, p. 8. Carter announced his intention to produce an urban policy on 1 August. See the *New York Times*, 1 August 1977, p. 1.
40 'Cities and People in Distress', Department of Housing and Urban Development, mimeo, November 1977.
41 Interview with Marshall Kaplan, 12 April 1978.
42 'Cities Uneasy About Carter Plans', *New York Times*, 6 December 1977, pp. 1 and 17.
43 'Carter's Urban Policy is Delayed, with Mayors and Governors Split', *New York Times*, 1 March 1978, p. 36.
44 'Cities Say Plan to "Target" U.S. Aid Might Shut Out Some of the Poor', *New York Times*, 3 February 1978, p. A12.
45 Memo from Patricia Harris and Stu Eizenstat to the President, 9 January 1978, mimeo.
46 Quoted in memo from Robert C. Embry Jr to Stuart Eizenstat, HUD, mimeo, February 1978, p. 1.
47 Reproduced from a White House document, undated.
48 *A New Partnership to Conserve America's Communities: a National Urban Policy*, Department of Housing and Urban Development, March 1978.
49 'White House Offers Urban Plan Covering Only Neediest Areas', *New York Times*, 24 May 1978, P. A1 and 19.
50 For a discussion, see Louis B. Russell, 'Medical Care Costs', in Joseph A. Pechman (ed.), *Setting National Priorities: The 1978 Budget*, Washington, DC: The Brookings Institution, 1977, pp. 177–206.
51 For a discussion, see George J. Carcagno and Walter S. Corson, 'Welfare Reform', in Joseph A. Pechman (ed.), *Setting National Priorities*, pp. 249–81.
52 Carcagno and Corson, 'Welfare Reform', table 8.1, p. 253.
53 Anderson, *Welfare*, pp. 205–6. See also, House of Representatives, Welfare Reform sub-Committee, 12 October 1977.
54 Anderson, *Welfare*, pp. 190–4.
55 Lynn and Whitman, *The President as Policy Maker*, pp. 184–6.
56 Richard P. Nathan and Paul R. Dommel, 'The Cities', in Pechman (ed.), *Setting National Priorities*, pp. 310–11.
57 As claimed President Ford's ex-Secretary for Housing and Urban Development, Carla Hills in 'On Urban Policy', *New York Times*, 15 May 1978, p. A23.
58 For a discussion, see Paul E. Peterson, Barry G. Rabe and Kenneth K. Wong, *When Federalism Works*, Washington, DC: The Brookings Institution, 1986, pp. 42–4.
59 Anderson, *Welfare*, pp. 192–3. For a general sense of how perceptions

have changed, see the collection of essays edited by George E. Peterson and Carol W. Lewis, *Reagan and the Cities*, Washington, DC: Urban Institute, essay by George E. Peterson, pp. 11–35.

60 For a more recent discussion of this distinction and the dilemmas it raises, see Hugh Heclo, 'General Welfare and Two American Political Traditions', *Political Science Quarterly*, 101 (1986), 179–96.

61 Anderson, *Welfare*, pp. 177–8; 183–8.

62 Aaron had actually written a study entitled *Why Welfare is so Hard to Reform*, Washington, DC: The Brookings Institution, 1973, in which he argues that the interstate variations and other complexities characteristic of the system make it virtually impossible to reform the area and at the same time establish work incentives and keep the cost reasonable (chapters 4 and 6).

63 Bill Cavala and Aaron Wildavsky, 'The Political Feasibility of Income by Right', *Public Policy*, 18 (1970), 321–54.

64 See Samuel H. Beer, 'Federalism, Nationalism and Democracy in America', *American Political Science Review*, 72 (1978), 9–21; David McKay, 'The Rise of the Topocratic State: U.S. Intergovernmental Relations in the 1970s', in Douglas E. Ashford (ed.), *Financing Urban Government in the Welfare State*, London: Croom Helm, 1980, pp. 50–70.

65 *Congressional Quarterly, Weekly Report*, 16 October 1976, p. 3009.

66 For a discussion and further details, see *Congressional Quarterly, Almanac, 1978*: 'Congress Approves Service Reforms', Washington, DC, pp. 818–34.

67 *Congressional Quarterly, Almanac, 1978*, p. 18.

68 *Congressional Quarterly, Almanac, 1980*, 'Paperwork Reduction', p. 529.

69 Accounts of the Carter management style include Bruce Adams and Kathryn Kavanagh-Bonar, *Promise and Performance: Carter Builds A New Administration*, Lexington, MA: Lexington Books, 1979, chapters 3, 4 and 5; Campbell, *Managing the Presidency*, chapter 3; R. Gordon Hoxie, 'Staffing the Ford and Carter Presidencies', pp. 55–85; Pfiffner, *The Strategic Presidency*, pp. 55–8; 93–4; 117–18; chapters 7 and 8; Charles O. Jones, 'Keeping Faith and Losing Congress: The Carter Experience in Washington', *Presidential Studies Quarterly*, 14 (1984), 437–45; Robert A. Strong, 'Recapturing Leadership: The Carter Administration and the Crisis of Confidence', *Presidential Studies Quarterly*, 16 (1986), 636–50.

70 See Strong 'Recapturing Leadership', 646–8.

71 Carter, *Keeping Faith*, pp. 526–9.

72 Quoted in Lynn and Whitman, *The President as Policy Maker*, p. 33.

6 Disengagement under Reagan: I. The New Federalism

Uniquely among Presidents under discussion in this volume, Ronald Reagan came into power armed not only with an apparently coherent legislative programme promising radical change, but also with a determination to transform the ways in which the federal government administers existing programmes. In this sense, it is misleading to talk of how the administration adapted following legislative success or failure, for an administrative strategy was fully in force from the very beginning. Both strategies were informed by the same ideological imperatives – disengagement of the federal government from the American economy and society. This chapter will deal with the major legislative programme designed to achieve this end – the New Federalism. Chapter 7 will analyse the Reagan administrative strategy and its consequences, not only for federalism but also for the broader society and polity.

The New Federalism: content and origin

By the time he came into office, Ronald Reagan's conception of American federalism and/or the proper role for the federal government in social policy was very well developed. Unlike Nixon and Carter, Reagan was intensely interested in the question. Repeatedly during his career and increasingly during the 1970s, he had talked of the need to return power to the states. As early as 1969 he had pleaded that 'after a third of a century of power flowing from the people and the states to Washington, it is time for a New Federalism in which power, funds and responsibility will flow from Washington to the states and to the people'.[1] As was noted in chapter 4, as Governor of California he had become convinced that the states could play the major role in running domestic programmes such as welfare. Indeed, he had instituted a major reform of California's welfare system which resulted in a reduction in the welfare rolls by over 350,000 individuals.[2] In his 1976 campaign for the presidency, Reagan, acting on the advice of welfare expert Martin Anderson, had proposed returning all welfare programmes to the states – the idea and cost of which attracted derision from all but a few on the Republican right.

By 1980, however, right-wing ideas had received fresh impetus following the incoherence and failures of both liberal and putatively conservative administrations. Moreover, both the quality and quantity of right-wing theorizing were high. Numerous books and papers had been produced on virtually every aspect of domestic policy; all in their different ways pointed to the same conclusion: national government in the United States had become too large. The way forward for a just and efficient economy and society was through a return to the market. Moreover, virtually every aspect of domestic policy could be reformed in accordance with market ideology. Welfare, social security, federal aid to states and localities, regulation, macro-economic strategy were all subject to market forces – thus, domestic policy reforms could all follow similar directions.[3]

In one sense, radical reformers of the left as well as the right should have welcomed this change, for it heralded a departure from the sterile incrementalism and political expediency which, it is often claimed, were typical of policy-making in most recent administrations. For those interested in theoretically informed policy, both incrementalism and political expediency should be anathema. Incrementalism prevents responsible policy-making and assumes that only small policy changes are optimal. Political expediency (or an unsavoury obsession among politicians with political survival) can have all sorts of deleterious consequences including inflation, budget deficits, short-sighted economic management and the undermining of public confidence in political institutions.[4] Reformers of the left and right accept these criticisms as, indeed, do all politicians whose policies are informed more by ideas and vision than by pragmatism and opportunism.

Devolving powers and responsibilities from the federal to state governments was a constant theme in the 1981–5 Reagan administration. No other recent President has shown as much interest in federalism or has acted so resolutely to reform the intergovernmental system. Nevertheless, as earlier chapters indicated, most recent Presidents have expressed disquiet at the way in which intergovernmental relations (IGR) have evolved. The most vocal criticisms have been directed at the greatly enhanced federal role (in 1980 federal aid amounted to approximately 25 % of all state and local expenditure);[5] at the confusion and apparent waste which characterizes the system (most federal programmes have evolved on an *ad hoc* basis with no clear rationale); and at the alleged unresponsiveness of the system to the needs of citizens (surveys repeatedly showed a higher degree of public antipathy to federal than to state and local programmes).[6] As a result, successive Presidents have proposed a number of rationalizations and reforms – although, as we saw with both the Nixon and Carter administrations, the few which have been implemented have tended to add to the complexity of the IGR system rather than simplify it.[7]

The Reagan proposals were of a quite different order. They were, first of all, a crucial part of an interrelated programme of domestic-policy reforms. Reducing the size and scope of the federal government involved lowering federal taxation and domestic spending, deregulation and returning power to the states. Devolving responsibilities to state governments was motivated by both economic and political argument. Over the years, the administration argued, the federal government has assumed partial or complete responsibility for a number of policy areas which were not 'legitimately' a federal concern. Both an economic and a political/democratic rationale for a major 'sorting out' of responsibilities existed. Economic theory points clearly to the need for central (or federal) governments to run some types of services, while lower-level governments run others. One branch of public-choice theory goes further and suggests that the more devolved and fragmented the jurisdictional delivery system is, the more efficient the provision of public goods will be. If, as the administration claimed, the system is overcentralized, then it must be economically inefficient. With devolved responsibilities, the same level of service could be provided more cheaply. So, quite independently of the claim among market economists that governments at every level do too much, the size of government could be reduced simply by decentralizing taxation and expenditure functions for a specified range of services. We shall return to these points later.

Political theory does, of course, provide weighty justification for decentralized government. In a country as large and diverse as the United States, highly centralized government is almost certainly incompatible with democratic responsiveness and accountability. The extent of decentralization in the United States has long been the subject of controversy, although it is considerable by the standards of many countries. Every administration since 1968 has attempted to give state and local governments more discretion over the running of federal programmes, in the belief that these governments know what is in the best interests of their citizens.[8] At the same time, liberals and conservatives have continued to join battle on this question, which raises the most fundamental issues in political theory. The trade-offs between equality and efficiency, justice and accountability, are all too apparent in the American intergovernmental system. In the past, liberal ideology and local fiscal crisis have combined to provide powerful justifications for redistributive federal programmes. But what might be called 'decentralist' ideology is even more influential in the United States. And in the context of the *national* fiscal crisis which has affected all federal governments since the late 1960s, it is not surprising that this tradition has been on the ascendant.

The strictly political (as opposed to economic) basis of decentralist ideology is simple and familiar. State and local governments are more closely in touch with citizens' needs and demands. The waste and confusion deriving from a remote and overbearing central authority is likely to be avoided. Bureaucracies are likely to be smaller, more efficient and more accountable.[9] A further and related political justification for decentralization exists. Put simply: if more distributional questions are settled at the sub-federal level, the load on an already overburdened federal government will be lighter. State and local governments can get on with the essentially micro-political job of managing myriad interest-group pressures, leaving the federal government free to formulate macro-policy in economic and foreign affairs.[10] This can be seen as more than mere political expediency. If central or federal governments are overloaded, they cannot function effectively. Devolving decision-making to sub-national units is therefore not only politically convenient but also leads to more efficient decision-making.

There is no doubt that the Reagan administration came into office convinced by these economic and political arguments for decentralization. As one commentator has put it:

No administration during its first year in office can be expected to have all its arguments and governing theories finely honed, but Reagan Administration officials have developed a tentative but firmly articulated set of administrative, constitutional and political defenses for the President's goals regarding federalism and the division of responsibilities among federal, state and local governments.[11]

1981 reforms

During 1981, the administration assigned highest priority to economic reforms – tax and expenditure reduction – leaving the major federalism initiative to 1982. However, some important reforms were proposed in 1981, namely:
(1) The consolidation of all or part of eighty-three categorical

programmes into six human services block grants – health services, preventive health services, social services, energy and emergency assistance, local education services and state services. If implemented, 30% of all federal aid would be in the form of block grants, compared with 16.6% in the Carter budget.[12]

(2) A reduction in the total grant commitment to state and local governments by approximately 25% – including a 13.5% reduction in fiscal year 1982 alone (from $99.8 billion in the Carter budget to $86.4 billion).[13]

Devolving some of the 500 or so categorical grants to state and local governments was a natural objective, given that categorical programmes tend to establish and nurture direct and potentially uncontrollable linkages between federal departments or agencies and myriad state and local governments. Washington-based policy networks consequently emerge, with constellations of interest groups jockeying for position and power.[14] By directing lump-sum grants to the states, the administration hoped to break these linkages and policy networks and thus achieve both decentralization and a much simpler policy environment in Washington.[15] Reducing the total amount of aid was almost certainly inspired as much by the need to achieve cuts in government expenditure as by a desire to strengthen federalism. As is well documented, 'grants to state and local governments' are part of the 'other expenditures' category in national accounting. Unlike entitlement programmes (income-related transfer payments direct to individuals), debt interest and, at least in the context of the early 1980s, defence, some reductions in this area were politically feasible. As it turned out, substantial cuts were achieved, but mainly in those programme areas with least political support and influence – welfare, food stamps and housing assistance.[16] This was not simply a matter of the administration taking the easiest course. It was stated policy to cut welfare and food stamps. The President's block grant proposals did not fare so well. What eventually transpired by the end of 1981 was a compromise package of block grants and 'quasi' block grants. Congress, playing its traditional role as defender of particular interests, retained a number of politically influential categorical programmes while conceding the consolidation of other programmes, especially in the health area, into block grants.

1982 reforms

As the centrepiece of the 1982 State of the Union message, the President's 'New Federalism' proposed a number of sweeping changes, the most important of which were:

(1) A 'swap' of the three main welfare programmes funded by the states and federal governments on a matching basis. The states would assume full responsibility for AFDC (the main welfare programme) and food stamps, while the federal government took over Medicaid (medical care for the poor). So the existing federal cost of AFDC and food stamps (some $16.5 billion) would be absorbed by the states, while the federal government would take on the full cost of Medicaid ($19.1 billion).

(2) A 'turnback' to the states of some forty social, community-development and transport programmes, together with, initially, the revenues to pay for them. Beginning in fiscal year 1984 a new federal trust fund would be created, to be financed by taxes on windfall oil profits, tobacco, gasoline, alcohol and telephones. Totalling $28 billion in 1984, this trust-fund money could be drawn on by the states until 1987, when state taxes would gradually replace federal revenues, so that by fiscal year 1991 the states would be virtually 'self sufficient' in these programme areas. One estimate put the total amount of federal aid contributing to state and local aid at 3 to 4% for that year, compared with 25% in 1980.[17] Figure 1 shows how the turnback would operate, together with the estimated Medicaid savings the states would make from the Medicaid/welfare swap. Also, part of the trust fund would be used to compensate those states who were net losers as a result

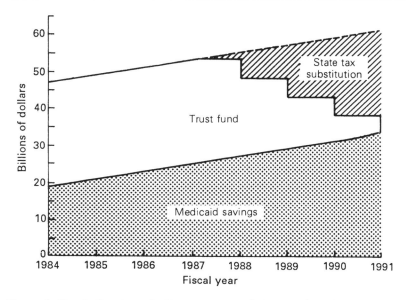

Figure 1. Funds for states in Reagan proposal. Source: based on figure 1, *Congressional Quarterly*, 30 January 1982, p. 152.

of the swap. A relatively small number of programmes were specifically excluded from the package, including the funding of interstate highways, higher education and education for pre-schoolers, the disadvantaged and handicapped.

(3)   States were to be given a choice as to how they adapted to self-sufficiency. They could either continue to participate in existing categorical programmes – in which case the relevant federal agencies would be reimbursed from the trust fund – or they could receive their trust money as a single federal grant. The administration favoured the latter and, in theory at least, so would most states, for this new super revenue-sharing programme would give considerable discretion to state administrations. Indeed, the only proviso was that any existing monies going direct to local governments (such as mass transit) would have to continue to do so.

Taken together, the 1981 and 1982 proposals amount to a radical restructuring of intergovernmental relations in the United States. Summarizing the extent and implications of the proposals, we can conclude as follows:

(1) A reduction in the federal role was the most obvious administration objective. Between 1981 and 1984 overall federal aid was to be reduced by 25% and between 1987 and 1991 federal grants were to be virtually dispensed with. The block-grant reforms were designed only as transitional stop-gap measures. By implication, at least, the administration least liked categorical aid, followed by block grants, followed by no aid whatsoever.

(2) The states, rather than localities, were to be the key units in the intergovernmental system. For notwithstanding requirements that states continue to fund some existing federal/local programmes, many of the distributional decisions previously taken by the federal government were to be devolved to the states. Urban policy, in particular, would become a state rather than federal responsibility.[18] This change marks out the Reagan initiative as unique among recent reforms of federalism. As indicated in chapters 4 and 5, all previous reforms either strengthened or maintained federal/local links, especially in urban policy.[19]

(3) The proposals contained virtually no specific guidance on the distributional effects of radical devolution, although the general assumption was that these would be neutral. On regional differences David Stockman, the OMB director, claimed that the programme was 'completely neutral'.[20]

(4) The reforms did not suggest how a highly devolved intergovernmental system would increase accountability and responsiveness at the state and local levels. The assumption was the devolved administration would *ipso facto* produce more accountable and sensitive government.

The policy process

Like Carter and Nixon before him, Ronald Reagan came into office determined to make full use of his Cabinet Secretaries and on 26 February 1981 seven Cabinet Councils were approved, the most important of which was the Cabinet Council for Economic Affairs (CCEA). The councils were, above all, designed to act as policy-formulation bodies. The general direction of policy was to be set by the White House, including budgets and personnel matters, while the detail of policy was to be left to the councils. Although they met no less than 112 times during 1981,[21] the councils never monopolized even the detail of policy. This is well demonstrated by the way in which Reagan's New Federalism proposals were drawn up. Four key sets of actors were involved: the Office of Policy Development (OPD), OMB, the Legislative Strategy Group headed by Chief of Staff James Baker and the CCEA.

At first, the OPD under the leadership of Martin Anderson was centrally placed. Anderson was, of course, the author of the 1978 polemic, *Welfare*, which had made stinging criticisms of Nixon and Carter's welfare reform plans.[22] As a strong supporter of returning AFDC and other welfare programmes to the states, Anderson was well qualified to lead the New Federalism drive both in 1981 and 1982. But Anderson proved to be an ineffective political operator within the White House and left the administration shortly after the announcement of the New Federalism plans in February 1982.[23] Anderson favoured not so much a swap of responsibilities, but a total devolution to the states together with some proportion of federal income-tax revenues.[24] As David Stockman recounts it, Anderson was 'the only White House staffer who understood any of it (the welfare and social security system); and like me, he was an ideological libertarian who wanted to contract the system as extensively as was politically feasible and then some'.[25]

Most of the 1981 reforms were subsumed under the budget cuts of that year; as such, OMB became the lead agency presenting its programme of budget reductions to CCEA at weekly meetings. According to David Stockman, the cuts in aid to states and localities that were eventually proposed were to some extent compromised by the opposition of such Cabinet Secretaries as Drew Lewis at Transportation and Sam Pierce at HUD.[26] The much more comprehensive 1982 reforms were also in large part a product of OMB. For although the legislation was formally drafted by a White House working group, that group was headed by Donald W. Moran, a close associate of Stockman within OMB.[27] Treasury was also involved and the final details were approved by the Legislative Strategy Group chaired by James Baker.[28] So, like most other areas of domestic policy, the focus of power had shifted from OPD to OMB and to a lesser extent, the Legislative Strategy Group.[29] Indeed, one of the most outspoken advocates of the New Federalism, Edwin L. Harper, was moved from his senior post at OMB to become Reagan's assistant for policy development in late 1982, so cementing the OMB/White House link.[30] In the event, OMB was able to accept the idea of the swap, because the arrangement gave OMB control over one of the most rapidly growing federal programmes – Medicaid. It was assumed that Medicaid expenditure could be 'capped' by OMB, which was, indeed, one of Stockman's main objectives during the 1981 budget-reduction discussions.[31]

In sum, Reagan's New Federalism plan was the product of specific ideological preferences (decentralization, a reduced federal role) together with the perceived budget imperatives of 1981 and 1982. It was drawn up by right-wing OMB economists acting under general guidelines provided first by Anderson and then by Stockman. James Baker's role seems to have been one of moderating the more extreme elements in the plan in order to enhance its legislative success. Indeed, at this time, at least, the Reagan White House was strong on strategy; it had not only adopted clear priorities, it was also working hard on placing this agenda before the people and Congress. The President himself played a crucial role in this process. Following his 1982 State of the Union Message, he embarked on a national campaign of publicity to sell his New Federalism package.[32] Within the White House, the President's assistant for Intergovernmental Affairs, Richard S. Williamson, was assigned the job of liaison with the governors to ensure that the reforms succeeded.[33] As it turned out, very little of Reagan's New Federalism package was to survive 1982. As will be discussed later, opposition from just about every affected party was vocal, the congressional response was lukewarm or hostile and public opinion was unmoved. Part of the reason for this failure relates to the fact that even judged by the values which the administration held dear, the reforms lacked intellectual coherence in terms of prevailing economic and political theories.

Coherence

Economic theory

The theoretical justification for the administration's 1981 proposal greatly to extend the block-grant method of allocating funds to the states has been discussed in an earlier chapter (see chapter 4, pp.88–90). But the block-grant consolidations were merely a prelude to the much more radical 1982 proposals. This section will, therefore, concentrate on these proposals.

Fortunately, those economists interested in the division of functions among different levels of government are almost invariably mainstream neo-classical or equilibrium scholars. In other words, their analysis is informed by the same economic paradigm as that claimed by the Reagan Administration. Any inconsistencies in the Reagan programme can, therefore, be measured against the standards of an economic theory which is broadly accepted as legitimate by politicians and academics alike.

One of the administration's boldest proposals – the swap of welfare programmes for medical aid – makes little or no economic sense. Liberal economics does accept a role for government in the area of income redistribution. As Herbert Stein, a conservative and former Chairman of CEA under Richard Nixon, notes:

In general classical economists have supported progressive income taxation as a means of reducing inequality and have supported measures to reduce poverty. By 1960, progressive income taxation on the one hand and income support measures for the poor on the other hand were accepted by all but the most unreconstructed conservatives.[34]

Judging by official policy statements, the Reagan administration was in accord with this general position, the President himself having vowed always to provide for the 'truly needy'.[35] However, the specific means of doing this was to allocate virtually all of the welfare function to state governments. More than enough evidence exists to suggest that, considerations of justice and fairness apart, this is the least economically efficient way of allocating welfare funds. (For a full discussion, see chapter 4, pp.86–7).

By on the one hand accepting the need for welfare, but on the other proposing a devolution of all major welfare programmes (AFDC and food stamps) to the states, the Reagan administration was acting irrationally. In fact, the most efficient welfare system would by-pass state and local governments altogether, for as long as they were involved (as in the existing system on a matching basis) some variations would persist and therefore the costs of some externalities would be borne. Notwithstanding the problem of the optimal *level* of welfare aid, the ideal system would be a national system of benefits distributed direct to individuals.

If medical aid for the old and the poor is considered an aspect of income redistributive welfare, the other part of the Reagan swap – the administration assuming responsibility for Medicaid – apparently makes good economic sense. However, it is clear that if one crucial welfare benefit is administered by one level of government, then all aspects should be. Few dispute that income maintenance and health care are the most important and the most interlinked. As Richard Nathan, a liberal Republican, noted with respect to Carter's welfare plan:

You cannot enact a welfare bill until you have a health bill because you have a difficult problem of people going into their job programme and losing Medicaid benefits. Until the Administration tells you what they are going to do with Medicaid, you cannot seriously consider their welfare bill.[36]

For the administration to propose a further administrative separation of the two areas, therefore, was to invite serious confusion, as highly disparate state income-maintenance benefits would have to be linked with federal medical aid. Again, this problem can be expressed in strictly economic terms. Under the Reagan plan, generous income benefits in some states would not (and administratively almost certainly could not) reduce eligibility for federal medical aid. Yet the Pareto-optimal welfare package would provide (say) medical aid only for those who could not afford private health insurance. If the criteria for this level were to vary from state to state and benefits were not linked to disparate income-maintenance programmes, then no rational medical programme could be formulated.

The swap arrangement, although important, was part of a much grander 'turnback' plan to devolve most major federal programmes to the states. What was the economic rationale, if any, behind this reform? We should note that the means of achieving this end – the creation of a temporary federal trust fund to help the states in the transition to self-sufficiency – was not in itself very important in spite of the publicity it attracted at the time. Much more significant was the radical proposal, in effect to dismantle the intergovernmental grant system. From an economic perspective two possible motivations can be identified. First, and obviously, the proposal would reduce federal expenditures. Second, and less obviously, the reform would reduce the total of *all* government spending because once taken up by the states and localities, the programmes would be funded at a lower level than by the federal

government. In the administration's view, sub-national governments would not provide inferior services but simply more
efficient ones. As the President put it in his State of the Union
Message:

In a single stroke, we will be accomplishing a realignment that will
end cumbersome administration and spiralling costs at the federal
level while we ensure these programmes will be more responsive to
both the people they are meant to help and the people who pay for
them.[37]

While we accept that 'responsive' may mean more accountability or equality rather than more efficiency — a point we
shall return to later — there is no doubt that economic
considerations were prominent in the President's thinking.[38]

Economic theory does provide some guidance in this area,
but not, unfortunately, very clear guidance. Resuming the
public-good argument discussed in chapter 4, we might infer
that transferring virtually all grant programmes to the states
and localities was an ill-thought-out plan, for different services
produce different externalities or different spillovers (benefits
or costs) to neighbouring jurisdictions. Table 3 represents an
attempt to categorize services by the geographic scope of
benefits (a similar chart could be produced for the spillover
costs which would, if anything, extend the scope of national
policies).

Obviously this is a controversial taxonomy, and it hardly
dovetails neatly into the existing, jurisdictional structure.
There are, for example, relatively few regional authorities in
the United States, and the size of local and state jurisdictions
varies so greatly that the scope of benefits would vary in a way
which would place some services in the local category in one
place but in the regional category in another. More seriously,
some economists have challenged the very concept of externality as a basis for dividing government functions, claiming
instead that the intergovernmental grant system is essentially a
political rather than an economic phenomenon. Lester Thurow
has put this point well:

Table 3. *Estimated geographic scope of benefits for selected government services*

Service	Scope of benefits		
	Local	Regional	National
Fire protection	×		
Police protection	×		
Water distribution	×		
City streets	×		
Public libraries	×	×	
Air and water pollution		×	
Water supply		×	
Sewage and refuse disposal		×	
Mass transit		×	
Arterial streets and intercity highways		×	
Airports		×	
Urban planning and renewal		×	
Education			×
Aid to low-income groups			×
Communicable disease control			×
Research			×
Manpower retraining and labour market policies			×
Parks and recreation	×	×	×

Source: Adapted from George F. Break, Intergovernmental Fiscal Relations in the United States, Washington, DC: The Brookings Institution, 1967, p. 69.

[The concept of externalities] is simply not a convincing explanation of the provision of most domestic public goods. Once a society gets beyond basic public health measures and communicable diseases, medical care does not generate externalities. Death is the most private of all activities, and an individual's health has no non-market economic effects on the general population. Neighbourhood externalities certainly exist in housing, but internalizing these externalities does not lead to the types of housing programmes that have been legislated. The externalities have nothing to do with minimum housing standards for each family. Similarly, I find the arguments that education generates externalities unconvincing once one gets beyond elementary education (literacy etc.). Fire protection is like medical care. Some amount of fire protection and code enforcement is necessary to prevent conflagrations, but beyond this a donor has no more interest in his neighbour's fire protection than in his neighbour's fire insurance.[39]

Intergovernmental aid programmes emerge, therefore, as a result of a familiar mix of responses to interest-group pressure, demands for equality or fairness or, possibly, potential revolt.[40] Strictly economic rationales for intergovernmental aid, including state/local assistance, fall apart completely once the externality argument is rejected.

In the context of this discussion, the Reagan proposals make little sense. If the externality argument is accepted, the reforms are irrational – education, manpower retraining as well as welfare should be taken *away* from state and local governments, not given to them (table 3). Of course this assumes a rationality in existing jurisdictional boundaries which is patently absent. If the externality argument is rejected, no proper economic rationales for the reforms exist,[41] so it was quite misleading for the administration to invoke them. Of course, there is another economic justification for the President's proposals, but it is grounded more in political expediency than in economic theory. Put simply, the reforms would have significantly reduced the federal budget and increased state and local fiscal commitments by an amount much less than the federal decrease. The public-finance literature on intergovernmental grants is quite unequivocal on this question: block grants have a lower stimulative effect on state/local spending than do categorical grants, because the greater fungibility of block grants encourages flexibility and the transfer of federal money into programmes previously funded by states and localities.[42] Moreover, the (temporary) switch to block grants apart, the general effect of the transfer of programmes to lower-level authorities would reduce total government spending, as few politicians like raising taxes, which (after the transitional period financed out of the trust fund) they inevitably would have to do.[43]

Such an outcome would be quite compatible with the administration's belief that voters at the state and local level should decide the level of state and local services without federal help. However, no argument can be made to support the claim that these changes would produce a more *efficient* delivery of services. Fewer or less adequately funded services yes, but not more efficient ones. Generally speaking, the public-finance literature is not concerned with economic efficiency as measured by moves towards or away from Pareto optimality (which, like it or not, is the only theoretically ambitious measure of economic efficiency we have). Instead, public finance scholars busy themselves with the essentially descriptive issues of tax collection and expenditure patterns among different levels of government.

We can conclude, therefore, that the Reagan reforms were not supported by economic theory. We have no reason whatsoever to infer that the proposals would have led to a more economically efficient system of service delivery in a range of vital programmes and services. We can, however, conclude that they would have reduced the absolute size of government, even if state and local spending would have increased. Would this, in the words of the President himself, have led to a more 'responsive' and 'accountable' government?

Political theory

In a 1981 report, the Advisory Commission on Intergovern- mental Relations (ACIR) identified two distinct theoretical traditions in American federalism: the Jeffersonian and the Madisonian,[44] to which we will add a third, redistributive centralism.

The Jeffersonian perspective is simple and familiar: the more local is the level of government, the more able are citizens to participate in decision-making and thus to hold political authorities accountable for their actions. To eighteenth- and nineteenth-century political thinkers the choice was a simple one between centralization and decentralization; there was little sense of complex intergovernmental linkages and fiscal relations affecting a vast range of government services. In this simple world, the Jeffersonian perspective was almost certainly valid. Elementary education, road maintenance, public order and a few other services were better performed by small, usually isolated, communities. Inefficient or corrupt local governments were quickly identified and soon replaced. State governments actually did very little in this period except lay down the framework of law within which localities operated. Federal authorities were left with the essentially 'macro' functions of providing national security and currency control.

Few observers deny that what has been called the 'intergovernmentalization' of public policy has seriously undermined the accountability of local government. Localities have themselves become much larger and more remote. More importantly, very few services are now exclusively local in character. All the key programmes receive state and federal aid with strings of varying length and strength attached. Voters cannot therefore hope to hold local politicians and officials accountable for programmes over which they have but limited control.[45] Any major 'turnback' of programmes to the states and localities should in theory increase accountability. In this case, Reagan's New Federalism was absolutely coherent. With complete control over major services, lines of responsibility along lower-level governments would be clearer. States and localities, moreover, have more highly developed structures for citizen participation than federal government. By almost every measure – the existence of the instruments of direct democracy (recalls, initiatives, referendums), the frequency of elections, the number and level of posts subject to election, access by citizens to meetings, records and hearings – state and local governments are more 'democratic' than the federal government.[46]

But it is not quite as simple as this in practice. In the first place, it is important to distinguish between state and local governments. Jeffersonian notions of accountability applied to local rather than state governments. Indeed, so vast are many of today's state governments that they would be unrecognizable to an early Jeffersonian Democrat. And the New Federalism proposed a major devolution of power to state not local government. Block grants were to be administered from the Governors' mansions, not by the Mayors. Eventually, virtually all federal aid would be phased out leaving the states in glorious isolation. While we cannot estimate what effects this could have on *local* autonomy and responsiveness in any precise way, some inferences from past attempts at devolution can be drawn. In particular, the move towards block grants initiated by the Nixon, Ford and Carter administrations has been the subject of considerable research.[47]

Unfortunately, however, most of this research is informed by values distinct from those central to discussion in this section. The major concern of most researchers is the effect of block grants on specific *interests* or on the distribution of income and resources within areas. In other words the analysis relates to questions of equity (the subject of the next section) rather than accountability and participation.

Most of the relevant work applies, in any case, to federal/local rather than state/local relations. Generally, shifts to federal block or formula grants and away from categorical or project grants favour smaller and more fiscally secure communities.[48] However, should the states take over these programmes the consequences can only be guessed at. There may indeed be more participation in the sense that more communities would benefit from state aid. For as we shall discuss later, the states are less prone to redistribute resources from rich to poor. A more even distribution of grants available to all communities irrespective of need, is therefore likely.[49] Another probable consequence of devolution is a further politicization of state government as those distributional questions now settled in Washington are resolved at the state level.

Finally, the elevation of the states to a key role in the intergovernmental system is likely to increase centralization within states. This would be especially true if local incomes were reduced – as inevitably they would be with cessation of federal aid. Much of the experience from the tax-cutting measures of the 1978–82 period points in this direction – with reductions in local income, states were often obliged to take on a more prominent, often *dirigiste*, role.[50]

We can conclude, therefore, that although Reagan's New Federalism would in theory move the intergovernmental system some way in the direction of Jeffersonian democracy, in practice the present size and complexity of governments of all types in the United States makes any such outcome uncertain, to say the least. The virtual termination of federal grants and the crucial role allocated to the states is as likely to make local governments – the key units in the Jeffersonian system – more remote from the people, rather than less.

It is, of course, both over-simple and idealistic to equate local accountability and opportunities for participation with the remoteness or immediacy of taxing and spending authorities. There is a second and conflicting tradition in American federalism which, although not explicitly centralist, does equate a free and fair system with interdependence between central, state and local authorities. Hence in Madison's notion of the 'Compound Republic', the larger the jurisdiction the less likely the oppression of minorities:

Extend the sphere, and you take in a greater variety of parties and interests; you make it less probable that a majority of the whole will have a common motive to invade the rights of other citizens or if such a motive exists, it will be more difficult for all who feel it to discover their own strength and to act in unison with each other. In the extent and proper structure of the Union, therefore, we behold a republican remedy for the diseases most incident to republican government.[51]

In the context of federalism, this Madisonian notion implies that national authorities should check the activities of state governments, so it might be inferred that the New Federalism, by returning autonomy to the states would allow them to resume their frequently criticized role as oppressors of minorities. Such an inference would be quite inappropriate, however, for Madison was concerned with liberty and justice rather than with modern conceptions of equality. He was, of course, correct in thinking that left to their own devices, many states and localities would become intolerant of minorities and contemptuous of the rule of law. American history is littered with examples of such intolerance and contempt. But the New Federalism did not address itself to constitutionally defined freedoms; its main objective was a massive fiscal decentralization. We have no reason to suppose that the rights of individual citizens would be more or less protected under the new system. Presumably, hard-fought-for constitutional guarantees of liberty, endorsed by numerous Supreme Court decisions, would continue.

Madison's idea of the 'Compound Republic' has however been adapted – even transformed – in a way which defines liberty in terms of citizens' access to material goods. This third tradition of American federalism, which we will call redistributive centralism, was dominant between the 1930s and 1970s. The reasoning was simple: only federal governments with truly national constituencies can be motivated to pass laws designed to redistribute resources from rich areas or groups or individuals to the less advantaged. Through a combination of corruption, mal-apportionment and the 'capture' of lower-level governments by local elites, many states will favour regressive and unresponsive policies. Ethnic minorities, the poor and women will be ignored or exploited. Furthermore, basic educational and social provision for the population will, generally, be hopelessly under-funded and inefficiently administered. Writers as varied as William Riker, Grant McConnell, Mancur Olson and James Sundquist concurred in this conclusion.[52] Until the 1960s, evidence from the south alone appeared to vindicate the charges. Federal aid and intervention was, therefore, absolutely essential to establish minimum standards, root out corruption, and above all provide citizens with sufficient economic opportunity to participate fully in American democracy. Grant McConnell summed up the spirit of the times well:

The effect of a small constituency is to enhance the power of local elites, whatever their character or sources of power . . . [T]he claims that small units ensure democracy are erroneous . . . Decentralization to local units does not make for democracy; indeed in the sense that democratic values centre about liberty and equality, the tendency inherent in small units to stratification of power relationships and to protection of established informal patterns of domination and subordination is almost alien to equality.[53]

Federal aid was, therefore, *ipso facto* a good thing. States and localities would be jolted out of their corruption and indifference. Aid would, above all, reduce social, political and economical inequalities.

Without resolving one of the oldest and liveliest debates in political theory – the relationship between size, democracy and equality[54] – it is possible to make some interesting comments on how Reagan's New Federalism might be situated in the debate. As suggested earlier, pleas for decentralization in the late 1970s and early 1980s were largely inspired by disillusionment with the massively increased federal aid of the previous thirty years. Critics claimed that rather than inequalities being reduced and problems solved, the intergovernmental system had sunk into a morass of administrative chaos and interest-group opportunism. The obvious solution, therefore, was to abandon federal intervention in favour of a massive devolution of power to the states. The choice was put to the public in very simple terms: administrative chaos and waste or efficiency and simplicity. Equality as such was rarely mentioned. Instead the assumption was that the 'old' (existing) system had failed and had to be replaced. For those interested in theoretically informed policy-making this sequence of events raises two key questions:

(1) Would the decentralization of the New Federalism increase inequality?

(2) Assuming that equality as such was not assigned a high value by the administration, would equality be worth exchanging for some other value, such as increased economic efficiency, political accountability or administrative simplicity? We must assume that if (1) can be shown

to be empirically valid and if there was no trade-off between equality and other values, then the end result of the reforms would simply be less equality. Naturally, such an outcome would render the reforms both unnecessary and undesirable.

Both these questions can be answered quite easily. The New Federalism would certainly have increased inequality in the provision of a wide range of public services. Virtually all the evidence from existing and past programmes confirms that the more discretion is left to the states, the greater will be the variation in levels and quality of services. AFDC, Medicaid, and a number of other programmes presently provided on a matching basis with the states, display gross inequalities. For example, in 1979, Hawaii provided benefits for a family of four of up to 96% of the adjusted official poverty level, compared with only 49% in Mississippi. [55] Generally, the southern and Rocky Mountain states provide the lowest benefits (below 60% of the locally defined poverty level) while the north-eastern, Pacific and upper mid-west states provide the highest (over 80% of the poverty level). These disparities do, of course, apply to *matching* programmes. It could well be that total devolution to the states would increase inequalities further as well as reduce the general level of benefits. We will return to this point in chapter 7.

The first major study of the likely effects of the Reagan decentralization on different social groups confirms that the losers in the poorer states would be the disadvantaged, and the winners the business groups:

Based on existing structures of decision making in the states, a thorough decentralization of federal decision making would result in a pattern of policy output which would vary significantly across the states. In particular, the interests of the poor, labor, pupils and teachers would be poorly served in states with low *per capita* income, states with a high percentage of their population in poverty, and states in which minorities constitute a high percentage of the population. Not only would the interests of these groups be poorly served in these states compared to the wealthier, low minority states, but, with the exception of teachers, their interests would also be weak *relative to other groups within these states*. The interests of business would be *best* served (and be stronger relative to other groups) in these same states.[56]

The major reason for this likely pattern is that poverty and social policy interests find it extremely hard to organize in the often hostile arenas of state politics. Instead, over the years, they have struggled to establish national lobbying networks based in Washington.[57] Through established contacts with members of Congress and bureaucrats, these lobbyists have helped nurture and protect myriad programmes. With the proposed demise of these programmes – initially through the adoption of block grants and eventually by a complete decentralization to state revenues – the poverty and urban lobby would be forced to re-organize at the state level. Few academics or political commentators doubt that this would amount to a drastic reduction in the scope and influence of social-policy programmes.[58]

Of course these changes do not apply to Medicaid, which would have become a federal responsibility, but they apply to almost all other programmes and policies, most of which have a strong redistributive element – an unsurprising fact given the problems of establishing redistributive policies at the sub-national level.

Finally, what of the planned temporary shift to block grants? Block-grant funding is less amenable to central control and resources tend to be spaced more evenly between geographical areas than under categorical grants.[59] Distribution under block grants is based less on criteria of need, therefore, and more on the particular patterns of political influence dominant in the fifty states. Again, we will return to this point in chapter 7.

To return to the second question raised earlier: given that decentralization would increase inequality, what is the trade-off between this cost and other values? We have already dealt with the question of economic efficiency and have concluded that the Reagan reforms had no convincing rationale founded in economic theory. We further concluded that decentralization would have no easily demonstrable benefits in terms of political accountability. This leaves administrative simplicity, or the claim that decentralization would, by helping to clear up the extraordinary complexity of the American intergovernmental grant system, bring great benefits in terms of administrative efficiency. Unfortunately it is not easy to locate 'administrative efficiency' in either economic or political theory. Economists ignore the concept unless it is linked to the functioning of markets. They have no interest in government bureaucracy beyond the assumed advantages of allocating certain functions which the market cannot perform to particular levels of government – a point we have already dealt with.

Political theory also contributes little, and debate on the subject within public administration is inconclusive.[60] One thing, however, is clear: if we accept the confusion characteristic of the present American system, it is not obvious that decentralization is the best rationalization strategy. A complete transfer of programmes would create fifty separate systems, and within states jurisdictional fragmentation would guarantee a continuing administrative complexity. *A priori*, and ignoring the political obstacles, it would be more sensible to propose *centralization*, with federal government, regional and area field offices operating programmes directly. Such a system exists for most social security benefits; few accuse these programmes of inefficiency. In other words the administrative efficiency critique of the *status quo*, while valid, does not carry with it just one simple solution – decentralization. Centralization is almost certainly as convincing a remedy. Of course should decentralization bring other benefits – increased accountability, reduced inequality, improved economic efficiency – then it may be preferable. But none of these *desiderata* can be shown to follow logically from the Reagan plan.

Social theory, public policy and political feasibility: some conclusions

The broad conclusions of this analysis are simple and obvious: the decentralization proposals of the Reagan administration could not be accommodated within existing economic and political theories – including many theories to which the administration itself adhered. One vital question remains: to what extent did the theoretical incoherence of the proposals contribute to their political failure? The usual characterization of the American political system is one in which fragmentation and pluralism render major reforms or policy shifts untenable. Only incremental change is possible. This model is not historically specific, although its most recent version certainly is. In sum, pluralism and multiple access points encourage the steady expansion of government spending and of the scope of government services. The only way to break this trend is through radical reform, which the system does not readily permit. It was this paradox which persuaded some on the right to abandon any 'rational' welfare reform. Martin Anderson, in particular, argued in his book on the subject (1978) that the 'rational' welfare reform – for the federal government to take over the area and institute a negative income tax for income maintenance – was unworkable because, during both formulation and implementation, the reform would be compromised in ways which would greatly increase government expenditure.[61] The sensible course to take, therefore, was to cut back slowly on welfare spending, while leaving the basic structure untouched. This was not the optimal theoretical solution, but the only choice which political expediency allowed.

The Reagan administration clearly did not heed this advice in the area of intergovernmental relations. By embarking on an ill-thought-out but radical reform it was inviting the worst of both worlds. As with almost all radical policy change in the United States, it was likely to be compromised and weakened in Congress and opposed by at least some states and localities. But its obvious incoherence greatly increased the chances of failure. The welfare/Medicaid swap met with considerable opposition from the Mayors and Governors. Within a few months, the President conceded that the federal government would retain the food stamps programme, and that some Medicaid costs would continue to be borne jointly by state and federal governments. By 1983 even this modified plan had been effectively dropped, and so had the more grandiose design of the federal trust fund. Instead, what transpired was a familiar mix of consolidation of programmes into block grants accompanied by continuing cuts in federal support for a range of programmes. Why were the most radical of the reforms so hurriedly abandoned? At least five reasons can be identified:

(1) The illogicality of the welfare/medical aid swap was quickly recognized and condemned by governors. Predictably many Governors welcomed the Medicaid takeover, but they found it hard to reconcile this with their required assumption of welfare costs. Governors in those states with generous Medicaid benefits opposed the plan because the administration proposed benefit levels below the highest.

(2) The swap, together with the plan to transfer virtually all programmes to the states eventually, was condemned on equity grounds. Big-city Mayors and the Governors of larger industrial states predicted considerable cuts in services and benefits for the poor and disadvantaged.[62]

(3) The proposals came at a time of particular fiscal stress for many states and localities. As they involved real reductions in income, they were likely to meet with considerable opposition.

(4) References in the reforms to accountability and responsiveness were quickly dismissed by the affected interests. For while a consensus on the need for simpler administration and more dencentralized control almost certainly did exist in the states and localities, dramatic reductions in federal funding were far too high a price to pay for these new 'freedoms'. Being held accountable for dramatically reduced services is not the sort of account-

ability any politician wants. And, as was demonstrated earlier, the trade-offs between efficiency and accountability on the one hand, and equality on the other, are complex and difficult. More inequality is evidence of a non-responsive policy in some jurisdictions, while being labelled exactly the opposite in others. Certainly, there was little in the way of public pressure for more accountability. The public may distrust federal programmes more than state and local services, but they are also very reluctant to accept cuts in long-established federal grants and benefits.[63]

(5) Finally, during the quite extensive consultations with the Governors which followed the announcement of the plans, the administration gradually retreated from its original position and for the first time conflicts within the White House played a part in undermining the prospects for success. As indicated, in June the federal government conceded that some formula for sharing Medicaid costs was acceptable. Predictably, this was anathema to David Stockman, who engaged in a number of 'Table thumping' sessions with intergovernmental affairs advisor Richard Williamson on the issue.[64] Williamson won because he recognized that without such concessions the whole reform package was dead. If this was the 'Triumph of Politics' (to borrow the title of Stockman's book), it also marked the beginning of the end of the New Federalism. For under the new arrangement, state costs would still have increased.[65] Opposition from the Governors remained, therefore, but was bolstered by doubts within the White House and in particular, OMB, about the cost implications of the compromised package.

Reagan's New Federalism proposals constituted a fundamental challenge to the New Deal regime. They were indeed an attempt to turn the clock back to the 1920s and before by effectively abandoning the federal role in intergovernmental aid. As such, they were likely to arouse opposition in the states, counties, localities and in Congress. It is difficult to attribute the eventual failure of the reforms to the process by which they were forged. They originated from within the White House and OMB, Cabinet Secretaries played a residual, reactive role, and consultations with interested parties were avoided until after the package was announced. Had such consultations occurred, the reforms would almost certainly have suffered the same fate as Jimmy Carter's National Urban Policy. A feeble, lowest-common-denominator package would have emerged which pleased nobody. This patently was not the administrations's objective. Because they were radical, the reforms had to be drawn up in secret by a small group of like-minded officials. Ultimately, the problem was not procedural but intellectual and political. It simply was not feasible to reconcile greatly reduced expenditure with wholesale de-centralization. It is, however, testimony to the ideological determination of Reagan and his team that the Governors would probably have accepted the plan had there been guarantees of no cost reduction or had there been firmer promises of new revenue sources.[66] In other words, Reagan could have successfully challenged the New Deal regime had the New Federalism been both more coherent and had the reforms not been so intimately related to the administration's overriding obsession with budget cutting. Moreover, he would have done so in the context of a virtual political vacuum. There was, as indicated, disquiet with the inef-ficiency of the existing system, but no social movement or pressure existed for a radical overhaul. The public were largely indifferent. In a March 1982 *New York Times*/CBS poll taken immediately after the publicity drive for the New Federalism, only two respondents out of a national sample of 1,545 named federal-state relations as the country's most important problem.[67]

In fact, the New Federalism was by no means a total failure. Grant-in-aid expenditure did decline in 1982. As a percentage of state local expenditures, federal aid fell from 26.3% in fiscal year 1980 to 21.0% in fiscal year 1985.[68] Moreover, eventually some nine block grants were created, involving the consolidation of seventy-seven categorical grant programmes. In addition, the Reagan administration embarked on a very-well-defined administrative strategy which was largely designed to decentralize – or remove completely – a range of federal programmes.

NOTES

This chapter is based partly on the author's 'Confusion and Reality in Public Policy: The Case of Reagan's New Federalism', *Political Studies*, 33 (1985), 181–202.

1 Quoted by William Safire, 'The Newest Federalism', *New York Times*, 28 January 1982, p. A23.

2 See Ronald A. Zimbraun, Raymond M. Momboisse and John H. Findley, 'Welfare Reform: California Meets the Challenge', *The Pacific Law Journal*, 4 (1973), 740–1; Martin Anderson, *Welfare*, Palo Alto: Stanford University, The Hoover Institution Press, 1978, pp. 154–5.

3 For examples of such thinking applied to domestic policy, see Anderson, *Welfare;* George Gilder, *Wealth and Poverty*, New York: Basic Books, 1981; P. Duignan and A. Rabushka (eds.), *The United States in the 1980s*, London: Croom Helm, and Palo Alto: Stanford University, The Hoover Institution Press, 1980, Part 1.

4 These are the claims of the political/business cycle theorists and to some extent the 'overload' advocates. For a discussion, see James E. Alt and K. Alec Chrystal, *Political Economics*, London: Harvester; Berkeley and Los Angeles; University of California Press, 1983, chapter 5.

5 US Department of Commerce, *Survey of Current Business, April 1982*, Washington, DC: US Government Printing Office, table 3.3.

6 See Advisory Commission on Intergovernmental Relations (ACIR), *Changing Attitudes Towards Governments and Taxes*, Washington, DC: ACIR, 1980, for a comprehensive review of public attitudes.

7 For a good review of the reform attempts, see David E. Walker, *Toward a Functioning Federalism*, Cambridge, MA: Winthrop, 1981, chapter 4.

8 Ibid. and Advisory Commission on Intergovernmental Relations, *Citizen Participation in the Federal System*, Washington, DC: ACIR, 1979, chapter 6.

9 The best statement of this position is by Claude E. Barfield, *Rethinking Federalism: Block Grants and Federal, State, and Local Responsibilities*, Washington, DC: American Enterprise Institute, 1981.

10 Harold Wolman and Fred Teitelbaum, 'Interest Groups and Interests in the Reagan Era', in Urban Institute, *Project on Changing Domestic Priorities*, Discussion Paper, September 1983, section B.
11 Barfield, *Rethinking Federalism*, p. 23.
12 Ibid., p. 25.
13 Ibid., p. 27.
14 For a good discussion of this phenomenon, see Hugh Helco, 'Issue Networks and the Executive Establishment', in Anthony King (ed.), *The New American Political System*, Washington, DC: American Enterprise Institute, 1978.
15 Wolman and Teitelbaum, 'Interest Groups'.
16 For details, see Fred I. Greenstein, *The Reagan Presidency: An Early Assessment*, Baltimore: The Johns Hopkins Press, 1983, chapter by Nathan. Also, F. Fox Piven and R. A. Cloward, *The New Class War: Reagan's Attack on the Welfare State and its Consequences*, New York: Pantheon, 1982, chapter 1.
17 Quoted in George E. Peterson, 'The State and Local Sector', in James L. Palmer and Isabel V. Sawhill (eds.), *The Reagan Experiment*, Washington DC: Urban Institute Press, 1982.
18 With the notable exception of the proposal to create Enterprise Zones modelled on the British experience. However, Congress rejected Enterprise Zone bills in 1981, 1982 and 1983.
19 This in part reflects the strong electoral links between the cities and the Democrats in general and Democratic Presidents in particular. So while Jimmy Carter attempted to cut federal spending and consolidate categorical programmes into block grants, he was unwilling to sever federal/local ties.
20 Quoted in *Congressional Quarterly*, 30 January 1982, p. 152.
21 For full accounts, see Colin Campbell, *Managing the Presidency: Carter, Reagan and the Search for Executive Harmony*, Pittsburgh: University of Pittsburgh Press, 1986, chapter 3; James P. Pfiffner, *The Strategic Presidency: Hitting the Ground Running*, Chicago: The Dorsey Press, 1988, pp. 58–64; see also the account in Anderson's *Revolution*, San Diego: Harcourt Brace Jovanovich, 1988, chapter 19.
22 Anderson, *Welfare*.
23 'Policy Office is Short on Clout and Long on Critics', *New York Times*, 11 January 1982, section 2, p. 7; 'Conscience of Administration to Resign', *Los Angeles Times*, 4 February 1982, p. 14.
24 Quoted in 'Early Action to Decontrol Price of Domestic Crude Oil Predicted', *New York Times*, 15 January 1981, pp. 1 and 11.
25 David A. Stockman, *The Triumph of Politics: Why the Reagan Revolution Failed*, New York: Harper and Row, 1986, p. 186.
26 Ibid., chapter 5.

27 Dick Kirschten, 'Reagan Hits the Road to Sell his Proposal', *National Journal*, 14 (February 27, 1982), 379–81.
28 Ibid., pp. 380–1.
29 See 'Policy Office is Short on Clout', *New York Times*.
30 Kirschten, 'Reagan Hits the Road', pp. 380–1.
31 Stockman, *The Triumph of Politics*, pp. 208–9.
32 Kirschten, 'Reagan Hits the Road', pp. 380–1; 'Reagan Administration Opens Campaign to Sell its "New Federalism" Initiative', *New York Times*, 28 January 1982, p. 1.
33 'A Voice for Moderation Amid Budget Cutters', *New York Times*, 23 December 1981, part 2, p.4.
34 Herbert Stein, *Presidential Economics: The Making of Economic Policy From Roosevelt to Reagan and Beyond*, New York, Simon and Schuster, 1984, chapters 8 and 9.
35 This follows the advice of Martin Anderson on welfare reforms; see Martin Anderson, 'Welfare Reform', in Duignan and Rabushka (eds.), *The United States in the 1980s*. Reagan had earlier always talked about the need to help only the truly needy and this was the basis of his reforms in California; see Zimbraun, Momboisse and Findley, 'Welfare Reform'.
36 R. P. Nathan, statement before the House Welfare Reform Subcommittee (12 October 1977), pp. 1291–2, quoted in Anderson, *Welfare*, p. 206.
37 Quoted in *Congressional Quarterly*, 30 January 1982, p. 148.
38 This has been inferred by a number of commentators; see for example W. C. Stubblebine, 'The Economics of the New Federalism', in W. C. Stubblebine and T. D. Willett, *Reaganomics: A Mid-Term Report*, San Francisco: Institute for Contemporary Studies, pp. 143–51.
39 Quoted in ACIR, *The Federal Role in the Federal System: the Dynamics of Growth; An Agenda for American Federalism: Restoring Confidence and Competence*, Washington, DC: ACIR, 1981, p. 54.
40 For a discussion of this and related points, see David H. McKay, 'The Rise of the Topocratic State', in Douglas Ashford (ed.), *Financing Urban Government in the Welfare State*, London: Croom, Helm, and New York: St. Martins, 1980, pp. 50–70.
41 There is in fact a further argument for decentralization deriving from public-choice theory, but it is fraught with inconsistencies and underpinned by unrealistic assumptions. This is C. Tiebout's 'Pure Theory of Local Expenditures'. Tiebout argues that a fragmented local government structure approaches the ideal condition for the distribution of public goods. Via local taxes, the voter/consumer at the local level is more directly linked to the politician/producer responsible for the public good and the voter can move should he/she not be satisfied with the level or quality of service provided. *Variety* among local

governments is analogous to the variety of producers in the economic market place, therefore. As such, contrasting local governments sort out preferences. Tiebout and his followers fail to take account of the fact that different public goods have different externalities and should therefore be provided by different-sized jurisdictions. Nor do they accommodate the fact of grossly imperfect residential mobility and they ignore labour mobility. For an extensive discussion, see David H. McKay, 'A Reappraisal of Public Choice Theory of Intergovernmental Relations', *Environment and Planning C: Government and Policy*, 3:1 (1985), 163–74.

42 See Wallace E. Oates, 'The New Federalism: Economists' View', *CATO Journal*, 2 (1982), 180–3.

43 Ibid., 487–8.

44 ACIR, *The Federal Role in the Federal System: The Dynamics of Growth, An Agenda for American Federalism, Restoring Confidence and Competence*, pp. 78–9.

45 The ACIR in its literature and public statements repeatedly makes these points; see the 11-volume, *The Federal Role in the Federal System: The Dynamics of Growth*. It should be stressed, however, that the ACIR has a political commitment to decentralization. Research showing how complex are the trade-offs between equity and accountability in centralized and decentralized government programmes in the US has simply not been conducted.

46 This is true only of the *formal* structures of power. The still-flourishing pluralist/power-elite debate shows that in terms of equity, fairness and access to decision-makers by all social groups, state and local governments are not unequivocally established as more democratic than the federal government.

47 For a complete literature review, see Harold Wolman, 'The Effect of Block Grants', *Urban Institute Paper Number 3083–1*, Washington, DC (September 1981). See also 'The Community Development Block Grant', Special issue of *Publius*, 13 (summer 1983).

48 See James W. Fossett, *Federal Aid to Big Cities: The Politics of Dependence*, Washington, DC: The Brookings Institution, 1983; Richard P. Nathan, 'State and Local Governments under Federal Grants: Towards a Predictive Theory', *Political Science Quarterly*, 98 (1983), 47–57.

49 This tendency also exists at the federal level, of course, but is less pronounced. See D. M. Hedge, 'The Effects of Alternative Grant Mechanisms on the Distribution of Federal Aid to the Cities', *American Review of Public Administration*, 18 (summer 1981), 38–49.

50 J. J. Kirlin's *The Political Economy of Fiscal Limits*, Lexington, MA: D. C. Heath, 1982, comes to this conclusion for California. For a general review of tax-cutting measures, see J. P. Blair and D. Nachmias (eds.),

Fiscal Retrenchment and Urban Policy, Beverly Hills: *Sage Urban Affairs Annual Review*, vol. 17, 1979, part 2.

51 *The Federalist*, number 10, New York: New American Library, 1961, p. 83.

52 William Riker, 'Federalism', in *Handbook of Political Science, Vol. 5*, Reading, MA: Addison-Wesley, 1975; Grant McConnell, *Private Power and American Democracy*, New York: Alfred Knopf, 1966; M. Olson, 'The Principle of Fiscal Equivalence: the Division of Responsibility among Different Levels of Government', *American Economic Review*, 59 (1969), 479–87; James Sundquist, *Making Federalism Work*, Washington DC: The Brookings Institution, 1969.

53 Quoted in ACIR, *An Agenda for American Federalism: Restoring Confidence and Competence*, p. 80.

54 For a general discussion, see Kenneth Newton, 'Is Small Really So Beautiful? Is Big Really So Ugly? Size, Effectiveness and Democracy in Local Government', *Political Studies*, 30 (1982), 190–206. Also, Robert Dahl and Edward Tufte, *Size and Democracy*, Palo Alto: Stanford University Press, 1973.

55 Made up of AFDC and food stamps payments. Total benefits in Hawaii came to $7,884, compared with $3,540 in Mississippi. The official poverty level so adjusted according to differing costs of living in different states. See ACIR, *The Federal Role in the Federal System: The Dynamics of Growth, Public Assistance: The Growth of a Federal Function*, Washington, DC: ACIR, 1980, table 14, p. 112.

56 Wolman and Teitelbaum, 'Interest Groups', p. 77.

57 Ibid., sections A and B.

58 The Reagan reforms would also (and indeed did) hit the activities of public-interest liberal advocacy groups whose activities have been critical in increasing take-up rates, expanding eligibility criteria and encouraging applications for federal programmes. Federal aid for such groups has been seriously curtailed. See Richard P. Nathan, P. M. Dearborn, C. A. Goldman and Associates, 'Initial Effects of the Fiscal Year 1982 Reductions in Federal Domestic Spending on State and Local Governments', in J. W. Ellwood (ed.), *Reductions in U.S. Domestic Spending*, New Brunswick: Transaction Books, 1984, pp. 315–50.

59 Wolman, 'The Effect of Block Grants: a Review of the Literature'. See also S. J. Szanszlo, *Block Grant Implementation: Mid '83 Review Executive Summary*, Tulane Law School, Center for Legal Studies on Intergovernmental Relations, Conference Series, 1983.

60 See Newton, 'Is Small Really So Beautiful?', section 1 and sources cited.

61 Anderson, *Welfare*, chapter 6.

62 Richard P. Nathan, 'The Reagan Presidency in Domestic Affairs', in Fred I. Greenstein (ed.), *The Reagan Presidency: An Early Assessment*, Baltimore: The Johns Hopkins Press, 1983, pp. 66–70; See also Neil R.

Peirce, 'Federalism Reborn: Huge Funding Shift is a Giant Stride and a Pandora's Box', *Los Angeles Times*, part 2, 27 January 1982, p. 5; and a series of articles in the *New York Times*, 10 January 1982, p. 1; 12 January, part 4, p. 17; 17 January, p.1.

63 In a 1982 article, Hugh Heclo argued for a more politically educated public which will accept reduced levels of domestic spending – or accept higher taxes or inflation. This seems a curious way of approaching the problem, however. Quite apart from the fact that the US has easily the lowest level of domestic spending of any major OECD country (including, now, Japan) surely what is needed is education on how competing goals and values can be achieved given particular revenue sources. This may or may not involve reduced domestic expenditure. See Hugh Heclo, 'Fiscal and Political Strategy', in Fred I. Greenstein (ed.), *The Reagan Presidency, An Early Assessment*, Baltimore: The Johns Hopkins Press, 1983, pp. 42–4.

64 'New Federalism Proposals Could be Fiscal Time Bomb', *New York Times*, 26 July 1982, p. 11. See also 'A Voice for Moderation Amid Budget Cutters', *New York Times*, 22 December 1981.

65 'White House Revises New Federalism Proposals', *New York Times*, 24 June 1982, part 4, p.22.

66 Richard Snelling of Vermont as leader of the Governor's Group supported decentralization, as did a number of other Governors. Cost considerations remained paramount, however. See Neal R. Peirce, 'The States Can Do It But is there the Will?, *National Journal*, 14:9 (27 February 1982), 374–8; 'Negotiators Say Accord is Near on Federalism', *New York Times*, 5 May 1982, pp. 1 and 22.

67 Reported in the *New York Times*, 19 March 1982, p. 20.

68 *Special Analyses, Budget of the United States*, fiscal year 1987.

7 Disengagement under Reagan: II. A centralist strategy for devolution

The Reagan administrative strategy

In a 1985 paper, Terry Moe noted that

more than any other modern president, Ronald Reagan has moved with dedication and comprehensiveness to take hold of the administrative machinery of government. At the heart of his approach are the politicization of administrative arrangements and the centralization of policy related concerns in the White House: developments in the institutional presidency with origins in past administrations, but now significantly accelerated and expanded.'[1]

This is the unanimous conclusion of a public administration community whose collective mind has been much concentrated by the Reagan experience.[2]

In most instances, the main objectives of Reagan's politicization effort were (1) to devolve or decentralize power from the federal government to state and local governments, or (2) at a more general level, to the market. The White House was, therefore, engaged in an attempt to change bureaucratic (and judicial) values and standards of practice and decision-making in line with well-specified ideological preferences. In this context, this chapter has three main objectives. First, to chronicle the means whereby this disengagement exercise was attempted. Second, to discuss the effectiveness of disengagement, and third, to speculate on the longer-term consequences of the strategy.

As suggested in chapter 6, Reagan's administrative strategy was not created as a reaction to legislative failure. It was put into effect from the very beginning and was designed to complement legislative changes. On the federalism front, for example, reforms were specifically constructed in ways which reduced the federal role (the New Federalism) or provided state governments with greater discretion over how federal funds were to be spent (the move to block grants). As earlier indicated, this legislative agenda was intimately related to the administration's economic objectives. And the administrative strategy was similarly related to the perceived needs of the economy. De-regulation, for example, could in part be achieved by giving state governments more control over enforcement in such areas as environmental protection and occupational health and safety. Even the moral agenda could be advanced in this way, through the appointment of federal judges favouring greater state discretion in a range of social issue areas. In sum, Reagan's administrative strategy for decentralization was inextricably entwined with his economic and political objectives. Six devices were employed to advance these aims:

(a) The creation of a transition bureaucracy unprecedented in size and scope.
(b) The creation of administrative devices – the OPD, the Office of Planning and Evaluation (OPE) and the use of Cabinet Councils to aid strategic policy planning.
(c) Expanding the OMB's non-budgeting role – especially as a bureaucratic gatekeeper in the field of regulation.
(d) Greatly increasing the number of political appointees both within the EOP and in the federal bureaucracy generally.
(e) Consistently ensuring that appointees adhered to the administration's ideological position.
(f) Applying similar criteria to judicial appointments.

Some of these have been the subject of extensive research. What follows is a brief summary of some of the more salient of these findings, together with some new evidence on points (c) to (f).

(a) The Carter/Reagan transition team

James Pfiffner reports that the Reagan administration took the opportunities offered by the transition period much more seriously than other administrations. Reagan spent more (over $3 million, including $1 million in private funds) on the effort and gave it his highest priority.[3] The major changes included a freeze on those Carter appointees who had been offered jobs but had not formally been employed (up to 20,000 individuals), the appointment of Ed Meese III as Chief of Staff of all transitional arrangements, the screening of all Cabinet members for political and ideological loyalty, the removal from Cabinet members of the right to appoint sub-Cabinet personnel, and the appointment of Donald Devine as Director of the newly created (in 1979) OPM. As OPM Director, Devine had considerable control over lower-level management appointments in the civil service.[4] Chester Newland further notes the importance of nearly a hundred transition task forces whose job, with the aid of the OPM, was to interview senior administrators in every major department and agency, and generally to investigate the prevailing ideological temper of the bureaucracy.[5]

While not always successful – ideological loyalty was frequently compromised for other values, such as competence and experience – this exercise was a uniquely thorough exploitation of the transition period.

(b) Strategic planning

The experience of the transition period convinced Meese that the EOP should have at its disposal an institutional structure of strategic policy planning. Three devices were utilised: the old Domestic Policy Staff was transformed into an Office of Policy Development, whose job was to execute short-term policy. In addition, an OPE was created to deal with longer-term strategy and within the OPD five Cabinet Councils (later seven) were charged with the responsibility of preparing policy reports and implementing the presidential agenda.[6] On the face of it, this new structure looks like a technocratic response to complex policy issues. But it was hardly just this. Far from the new institutions being sources of policy intelligence, they were reactive, implementation systems. Over-riding the whole structure was Ed Meese, responsible for long-term policy and James Baker and Michael Deever, responsible for day-to-day implementation. Career professionals (even down to lowest grades) were effectively purged from the existing EOP, and replaced with Reagan loyalists.[7] Under the Baker – Deever – Meese troika, adherence to the presidential ideology was strictly required. As Newland puts it: 'The policy network, in short, does not set the general direction; it follows it, working out policy details strictly secondary to the president's fixed views of government.'[8]

Observers agree that the secondary role assigned to these institutions undermined their independent status considerably. OPD had three directors in three years; the frequency and importance of Cabinet Council meetings were more a reflection of presidential preference than anything else; the OPE could never really compete with Chief of Staff Baker's stated long-term priorities.[9] In sum, the Reagan innovations were not designed to create a permanent management structure in the White House which could be passed on to future Presidents. Instead, institutional reforms were crafted to further the President's preferences and policies.

(c) The Office of Management and Budget
A much more dramatic example of centralization involved the elevation of OMB to a critical role not only in budgeting, but also as a legislative and regulatory gatekeeper. OMB's budget-making function primarily involves relations with Congress and as such will not be dealt with here. Its regulatory/legislative function, although much noted in the literature, has not yet been placed in a specific policy content.[10] OMB has always had some control over legislation through its review of agency legislative proposals, but this power has been taken much further by the Reagan Administration. Budget Director David Stockman was attributed with the capacity to exercise an effective veto over some legislative

items by simply not allowing draft legislation to go before Congress. Individual agencies, and particularly the post-Burford Environmental Protection Agency, have had their powers to frame legislation considerably reduced. OMB's role in clearing prepared testimony given by agency employees to Congressional committees has also been changed in ways which strengthen the gatekeeper function.[11] In these ways both formal and informal links between bureaucrats and Congressional committees were weakened. This accepted, Congress can counterattack by questioning agency witnesses on their prepared testimony, and it can mould new legislation to overcome OMB's scrutiny of agency legislative proposals. Clearly such Congressional tactics imply confrontation with the executive, but there are other ways in which OMB can control the agenda by effectively by-passing Congress alto-gether. During the Reagan years, two devices have been used, executive orders and the re-interpretation of existing laws relating to OMB's management function.

As noted in chapter 5, the 1980 Paperwork Reduction Act was part of the Carter administration's attempt to reduce the excessive information available to the public and the burden-some over-regulation of society which Carter thought increas-ingly characterized the federal government. To this end, the act established an Office of Information and Regulatory Affairs (OIRA) within OMB to monitor what was originally proposed as a 15 % reduction in paperwork. In addition, OMB issued two circulars, A3 and A-130. A3 originated from 1972, but was expanded in May 1985 to require all departments and agencies to clear the publication of periodicals and non-recurring publications with OMB. A-130 (The Management of Federal Information Resources) was issued in December 1985 and had a much wider brief: to limit the dissemination of information to those areas 'specifically required by law' and 'necessary for the proper performance of agency functions provided that the latter do not duplicate similar products that are . . . provided by other government or private sector organisations'.[12] To-gether these measures have reduced the amount of paper circulating in Washington. One OIRA estimate is that under the Paperwork Act the 'burden' was reduced by 37.3% between 1980 and 1984.[13] Most significant is evidence that OIRA's activities have reduced the *dissemination* of inform-ation – especially on defence, social policy, consumer and environmental protection issues – rather than reducing the burden of extra paperwork on the public which was the act's original objective.[14] OIRA therefore acts as an information gatekeeper with an effective veto over publications it con-siders unnecessary or troublesome.

OMB control over agency rule-making has aroused more controversy than the paperwork question. Through the use of two executive orders, some critics charge that the adminis-tation has greatly reduced agency rule-making powers. Ex-ecutive Order 12,291 was issued in February 1981 in order to centralize the agency review process. OIRA was given the specific task of assessing the economic costs and benefits of new rules and regulations formulated under existing legisla-tive mandate. The review process was complex and secret – no rules were to be published before OMB review. Once submit-ted, OMB can delay deliberation on rules, and then either accept them, accept them with minor changes or return them for reconstruction. Agencies may also withdraw proposed regulations. OMB's own statistics suggest that the review process has become stricter and more selective over time (Table 4). Evidence also exists to suggest that some agency officials became increasingly reluctant to submit rules for review over this period. The statistical pattern here reveals something about the substantive impact of OIRA's review process. Agencies vested with major responsibilities for regulating industry showed the greatest decline in rules submitted between 1981 and 1984 (EPA − 58.9%; Labour − 57.8%; Energy − 52.8%). On the other hand, agencies primarily concerned with administering welfare and social policy pro-grammes for individuals and lower-level governments showed significant increases in the rules submitted (HHS + 69.2%; HUD + 45.9%; Education + 35.1%).[15] Narrowing eligibility requirements and generally increasing selectivity in the

Table 4. *Treatment of agency rules under EO 12,291 by OIRA 1981–5*

	1981	1984	1985
Consistent with EO 12,291	91.7	78.0	71.0
Consistent with minor changes	4.9	15.2	23.0
Returned for reconsideration	1.8	2.7	1.5
Withdrawn by agency	1.6	2.5	3.1
Not resolved	0.0	1.6	1.4
	100.0	100.0	100.0
% meeting OIRA resistance	8.3	20.4	27.6

Source: OMB Regulatory Programme of the United States, 1 April 1985 – 30 March 1986 at 581 (1981 and 1984 statistics); testimony of OMB Director, James C. Miller III before the Sub-Committee on Intergovernmental Affairs, Senate Committee on Governmental Affairs, 28 January 1986 (1985 statistics).

distribution of grants and benefits to individuals and lower-level government usually requires more rules; easing the 'burden' of regulation on industry requires fewer rules.

Some of the individual cases involved have attracted considerable publicity – especially over the easing of regulation in environmental protection and occupational safety and health. Detailed studies of these areas (mainly by Congressional committees) indicates that OMB has consulted the affected industries and, having found out which rules they do not like, attempted to abandon them. Investigations by the House Committee on Government Operations in 1983 into the Department of Labor's Occupational Safety and Health Administration's handling of toxic waste chemicals, and by the House Energy and Commerce Committee's Sub-Committee on Oversight and Investigations in 1985 into EPA's rules on the use of asbestos, strongly support this claim.[16]

OMB's review power was greatly strengthened following

the issue of a second executive order, 12,498, in January 1985. 12,498 requires agencies to submit plans and proposals, rather than already-formulated rules and regulations, to OMB. It also changes the criterion by which OIRA makes decisions from one of cost/benefit to 'consistency with the administration's regulatory priorities'. While it is too early to provide hard evidence on 12,498's impact, it will almost certainly weaken agency discretion further. This is the view of those Congressional committees charged with oversight and particularly those chaired by Senator Albert Gore (D. TN) and Representative John Dingell (D. MI). Partly as a result of their pressure, which included the threat of legislation to override OMB's new powers, OMB issued new public-disclosure rules in June 1986. While these go some way to combating the considerable secretary which shrouds the whole review process, they do not fundamentally alter the agenda-setting capabilities given to OMB by the two executive orders.[17]

Clearly OMB's powers are limited. Statutory directives cannot be ignored; Congressional committees are everwatchful; new legislation is always possible; judicial action can be threatened – and indeed has been used; the constitutionality of executive orders themselves is open to doubt. But in spite of all these, the effect of the Reagan administration's reforms in this area has been to weaken the independence of departments and agencies in relation to the most important institution of central power and control in the United States – the OMB. Congress has to delegate some rule-making power to the executive (and since the 1983 *Chadha* decision outlawing the legislative veto, its control over established agency rules has been weakened). President Reagan has made great efforts to ensure that what was a widely dispersed and fragmented executive discretion in many areas of domestic policy was centralized in the Executive Office of the President.

(d and f) The appointment power and the federal bureaucracy
In an important article published in 1979, Richard Cole and David Caputo concluded that President Nixon's attempts to change policy through appointing senior civil servants sym-

pathetic to the administration was 'doomed to insignificance from the outset. So few top officials are selected during any single presidency compared with the total number of senior executives that any numerical impact which those selected can have must be slight.'[18] By the end of Reagan's first term, however, the appointment power had been used in an unprecedented manner, in an attempt to change the operating values of a number of key domestic agencies. How did this come about? First, the Reagan administration had greater ideological purpose than previous administrations; screening appointees for political loyalty was easier, therefore. This involved not only appointing political allies as heads of agencies and departmental secretaries, but also ideologically sound officials at lower levels in the bureaucracy. Second, and related, is the fact that the 1978 Civil Service Act gave to the Chief Executive sweeping new powers to control the federal bureaucracy. More political appointees were sanctioned; political appointees could move career civil servants around more easily and incentive and merit payments could be granted to career officials. The OPM was charged with the task of implementing these changes and the Reagan administration was quick to appoint a determined and prosletysing cadre, Donald J. Devine, to the directorship of OPM. In terms of simple numbers, there is no doubt that the Reagan administration embarked on a major politicization exercise. This was not just a matter of utilizing the discretion made available under the 1978 Act. As the hearings into the re-nomination of Donald Devine show, the administration used every possible means of placing its own men and women in key positions through the bureaucracy and in changing the values and practices of career civil servants.[19] Four of the most careful studies of Reagan's personnel policies further support the politicization claim. Lynn's in-depth analysis of five prominently placed Reagan appointees is the only careful study of the *effects* of the administration changes. He concludes that, depending on the aptitudes of the appointee and the bureaucratic context, new personnel could and did sometimes change the 'core activity' of an agency,[20] and Goldenberg claims that 'on balance the Reagan Administration has succeeded in enhancing the role of the careerist as a passive extension of the presidency'.[21]

Further evidence of the uniquely political nature of the Reagan appointment strategy can be inferred from the National Academy of Public Administration (NAPA)'s survey of 536 presidential political appointees holding office in the Johnson to Reagan administrations. Questions in the survey addressed such issues as attitudes to career civil servants, Presidents and working environment. It transpires that most political appointees are favourably disposed to career officials, although fewer Reagan appointees considered civil servants 'competent' and 'responsive' than in any of the four previous administrations.[22] By Department, State, Treasury, Justice, Defence and EOP were characterized by a particularly high level of regard by politicals for career officials. Officials in Transportation, Interior, Labour, Energy and HUD were regarded significantly less highly.[23] Intra-departmental conflicts of values are generally lower in the first group and higher in the latter. It has, of course, been within the second group of agencies that some of the fiercest policy conflicts of the Reagan administration have been waged. Finally, a truly dramatic difference exists in the source of job satisfaction among Reagan political appointees, compared with all previous administrations. 63.6% of the Reagan officials put 'serving an admired President' among their three most important sources of job satisfaction. The average for all presidencies was 26.9%, the next highest figure being 25.5% for Gerald Ford.[24]

Finally, a comparative study by Joel Aberbach and Bert Rockman of the Nixon and Reagan civil-service appointees concludes that, in their interview sample of the top incumbent SES officials (those graded CA-1), more than two-thirds of those placed in the social services' agencies (HUD, HHS, Education) identified themselves as Republicans. This compares with 40% for all agencies. At the level below CA-1 only 11% classified themselves as Republicans in the social services' agencies.[25] The message is clear. Large numbers of

Republicans were appointed to these 'sensitive' agencies in order to exercise control over a liberal bureaucracy – a claim borne out by the ideological as opposed to party indicators in Aberbach and Rockman's data.[26]

Just how much more successful Reagan was in 'packing' the bureaucracy than Nixon is demonstrated by the fact that only 24% of a sample of the top social services' officials in the Nixon administration were Republicans.[27]

We can conclude, then, that the Reagan administrations used the management tools available very extensively. Previous Presidents, most notably Richard Nixon, have also utilized these tools (see chapter 4, pp. 94–100), but not with comparable determination reinforced by ideological cohesion. As Randall concluded, following an analysis of Richard Nixon's largely unsuccessful efforts to reshape welfare policy in the face of bureaucratic opposition: 'when presidents fail to influence policies, it is not usually for lack of administrative tools. Rather, the explanation may be a lack of time, lack of political or personal interest or lack of understanding of the bureaucracy and management tools at hand.'[28] On balance, Ronald Reagan had a good grasp of the available management tools: he certainly showed determination in applying them to the federal bureaucracy.

(f) Judicial appointments

In a 1986 paper, Frederic Waldstein pointed out that:

During his first term in office Ronald Reagan appointed to the federal bench one Supreme Court justice, 31 judges to the courts of appeal, and 129 district judges. In addition, there are currently an extraordinary number of vacancies due to attrition and the creation of 85 new judgeships in 1984 by Congress. Predictions that Reagan, by the end of his second term, will have appointed a majority of the federal judges sitting on the bench if current trends hold, has caused quite a stir among journalists, academics, and politicians.[29]

The stir has been caused not just by the *number* of appointees Reagan has made – any President would be in this position, given the high turnover of federal judges – but also by the character of the appointees. The first careful analysis of the Reagan first-term appointments points to two major developments: a dramatic change in the method of screening appointees, and the selection of judges politically and ideologically attuned to the President.[30]

As with the federal bureaucracy, this process involved a centralization of authority in the White House. Before Reagan, selection activity lay primarily with the Deputy Attorney General's Office. While still involved, the Deputy is now aided by a Committee on Federal Judicial Selection, which in the first term included Edwin Meese, the presidential counsellor, and Chief of Staff, James Baker. This committee, together with the President's personnel department has acted to screen nominees for ideological suitability. In addition, they have *independent* powers to recommend judges and to investigate nominees. As Goldman puts it: 'It is, perhaps, not an overstatement to observe that the formal mechanisms of the Committee have resulted in the most consistent ideological or policy-orientation screening of judicial candidates since the first term of Franklin Roosevelt.[31] Moving in quite the opposite direction from the Carter administration, Reagan declined to use the selection commission device designed to increase the representation of women and minorities on the federal bench, and also was the 'first Republican administration in 30 years not to utilise the recommendations of the American Bar Association's Standing Committee on the Federal Judiciary'.[32] In other words, when making judicial appointments, the administration has been actively working to exclude external advice and influence. Decision-making has been centralized by concentrating the appointment power in the White House.

The impact of these appointments is not yet clear, but some inferences can be drawn from the biographical data on the new judges. Goldman's analysis indicates that the District Court appointees show few dramatic departures from the past patterns (the Johnson to Carter presidencies) in terms of occupation, experience, party background (Republican presidents appoint overwhelmingly Republican judges, Democrats appoint Democrats to a slightly lesser extent), or American Bar Association (ABA) ratings. However, the Reagan appointees are unusual in that substantially more were educated in private, non-Ivy-League undergraduate and graduate colleges (around 40%, compared with an average of 36% for previous administrations). Fewer Jews were appointed (6.9%, compared with around 9% for previous Republican Presidents) and significantly more millionaires (22%, compared with only 4% for Carter).[33] Both Goldman and *Congressional Quarterly* have recorded a substantial drop in black appointees – even compared with the Nixon administration.[34] Overt racism is not the motive here. It is simply that very few black jurists are not liberals. Interestingly, the administration has appointed a number of women and hispanics (although not as many as Carter) – groups which tend to represent all shades of political opinion.

Goldman's analysis of appointments to the courts of appeal shows a similar pattern: few blacks, and more apparently wealthy nominess from non-establishment backgrounds. Goldman's sources do not provide data on ideology and apply only to the first term. A more recent source, *Almanac of the Federal Judiciary*, provides biographical data on sitting judges. These summaries categorize most judges as conservative, middle-of-the-road, or liberal. Where no label is mentioned, judges' ideology can be inferred from readings of the appeals court decisions and past records. The resulting pattern is shown in table 5. A startling 90.4% of the Reagan appointees were considered conservative – dramatically more than for the last Republican President, Richard Nixon. *None* were labelled liberal. Note also that many more Reagan appointees were educated at non-elite (non-Ivy League) private colleges. Many were conservative law professors. Douglas Ginsburg, the rejected 1987 Supreme Court nominee, was typical. Indeed, he had worked as chief administrator of OIRA before being elevated to the Court of Appeals in 1986.

The Reagan appointees are clearly on the right of the ideological spectrum, and were appointed for their adherence

Table 5. *Biographical data on judges sitting in US Circuit Courts of Appeal, August 1986, by presidential nomination*[a]

	Johnson N = 26	Nixon N = 31	Carter N = 55	Reagan N = 55
Education (graduate where applicable)				
Elite private	38.4	48.4	50.3	21.6
Non-elite private	15.1	16.1	10.3	47.6
States	46.5	35.5	38.4	30.9
Sex				
Male	100.0	100.0	80.0	89.0
Female	0.0	0.0	20.0	11.0
Race				
White	92.3	100.0	89.1	98.4
Black	7.7	0.0	9.1	1.3
Hispanic	0.0	0.0	1.8	1.3
Ideology				
Liberal	65.4	16.1	54.5	0.0[b]
Conservative	11.5	48.4	14.6	90.4
Middle-of-the-road	23.1	35.5	30.9	9.6

[a] FDR, Eisenhower, JFK and Ford nominees are excluded because of small numbers (FDR 1; Eisenhower 7; JFK 6; Ford 7)
[b] N = 52 for Reagan appointees, as ideology could not be inferred from the past record of three very recently appointed judges
Figures do not add up to 100 because of rounding
Source: Computed from *Almanac of the Federal Judiciary: Profiles of all Sitting Judges of the US Courts of Appeal,* Law Letters Inc., Chicago, Current Series

to judicial constraint – a style which Reagan and Meese called for during 1980 and 1981.[35] In most instances this is interpreted as giving to the state courts and legislatures rather than the federal courts the final say on a range of moral, social and economic issues. In this sense, the Reagan judicial strategy was also a decentralization strategy.

Consequences and coherence

Measuring the consequences of these changes is difficult, given the nature of the data and the short time-span involved. Moreover, the Reagan reforms involved all policy areas, a review of which is well beyond the scope of this study. Even if we confine the analysis to issues involving federalism, the scope remains large, because, as earlier indicated, most of the changes were designed to decentralize authority from federal to state governments. A further problem is identifying the specific motivations of the administration in pursuing an administrative strategy. At a general level, we can confidently conclude that they concerned the disengagement of federal power in a range of issue areas. But unlike legislative objectives, we cannot easily infer more specific aims. For example, OMB's screening of agency rules was probably motivated not only by a stated desire to simplify regulation, but also by a desire to devolve regulation to the states and to 'free' the market from burdensome federal rules. How each of these was weighted by OMB is difficult to establish, however.

In spite of these problems, we can draw some preliminary conclusions on the effects of these changes by drawing on the few studies so far conducted in the area. In 1983, the National Science Foundation sponsored a major study of the effects of rule changes in the intergovernmental grant system. This study is important because it distinguished between changes in the administration of grants resulting from (a) legislation, (b) administrative rules and (c) behavioural changes enforcing agency standards and procedures. Consequences were measured in terms of three variables – the quantity and complexity of rules, the flexibility of administration for recipient governments and the benefits to the client popu-lation.[36] These variables were measured by coding the re-sponses from state and local interviewees in very simple terms – whether the complexity of rules increased, decreased or stayed the same, with similar choices being presented on the flexibility and client-population issues. As might be expected, the findings confirmed the enormous complexity characteristic of the intergovernmental grant system.

Even so, some general patterns were discernible, which can be summarized as:

(a) the greatest changes resulted from legislation – most notably the block grants created by the 1981 Budget Reconciliation Act. In most policy areas covered by the block grants – including community development, education and health – state discretion over programmes was increased substantially. However, with few exceptions, benefits to client (very often low-income) populations were reduced or remained unchanged under state administration. Also, *local* government flexibility was often reduced under state rules.

(b) With categorical programmes, and especially those in the income-maintenance area (child nutrition, AFDC, food stamps), the 1981 Budget Act increased the quantity and complexity of rules, generally reduced the flexibility of recipient governments and reduced the benefits for client populations. This is, of course, in line with the tighter eligibility requirements and other changes imposed by the act.[37] Together, categorical programmes account for some 80% of intergovernmental aid and the income-maintenance programmes make up by far the largest portion of this total.

This conclusion is reinforced by the results of other research projects focussing specifically on welfare programmes. Changes in AFDC eligibility rules as a result of the 1981 act reduced benefits for a large number of recipients and in some cases removed individuals from the rolls (and therefore also often removed their eligibility for other benefits, including Medicaid).[38] The 1981 legislation additionally reduced the federal share of Medicaid costs and generally tightened the eligibility requirements of the programmes. As a result, interstate variations in the availability and quality of Medicaid provision increased considerably.[39]

A further study by Nathan, Doolittle and Associates

confirms most of these findings. Their nine-state analysis found that the most redistributive programmes – AFDC, food stamps, low-income jobs under CETA, housing subsidies – suffered most, although many states maintained Medicaid benefit levels because of the political influence of a large section of Medicaid recipients – the elderly.[40] Changes as a result of OMB's rule review process were very difficult to measure for the simple reason that many new rules were effectively vetoed by OIRA before they were proposed publicly. The reports' authors were impressed by the ideo-logical unity implicit in rule changes – clearly the adminis-tration was engaged in a major deregulation exercise, but measuring the impacts at the state and local levels was difficult. We do know from other studies, however, that rule changes have had some effect, especially in the areas of occupational safety and environmental protection.[41] Indeed, the issue has become sufficiently important to have inspired a number of Congressional hearings into the subject.[42]

(c) Behavioural changes in federal-agency enforcement values and standards were considerable, especially in civil rights and environmental protection. Hence EPA, Justice, HHS and CEQ relied not so much on rule changes to affect policy, but on interpretation of existing rules. This conclusion seems compatible with the publicity alleging or establishing lax rule enforcement by such agencies and especially EPA.[43] It also fits well with claims that personnel changes can and have had a major impact on policy.

At a more general level, the Reagan personnel changes may not have been as effective as he would have hoped because of the difficulties inherent in attempts to politicize the federal civil servance. 1984 hearings into the operation of the SES revealed, for example, that the administration's hostility to career bureaucrats had lowered morale and led to a very rapid turnover in personnel.[44] Of the SES officials who joined the service in 1979, 40% had left by 1981 and an estimated 65% would have left by 1985.[45] Merit and incentive bonuses were administered in a biased or capricious manner by OPM, with payments in some agencies (Defense, NASA, Justice, OMB) being far more common than in others (HHS, HUD, Commerce, Labor).[46] SES officials (only 10% of whom can, under the 1978 act, be political appointees) were disillusioned by the political favouritism characteristic of the administration, and career bureaucrats, in turn, had little regard for political appointees.[47] In sum, there are clear limits to politicization imposed by the managerial and organizational complexity of the federal bureaucracy. The 1978 act gave Presidents some additional political tools which could be used in a political manner – though this very specifically was not the act's intention. But if the result of such a strategy is lowered morale, rapid staff turnover and a blurring of the line between political and non-political officials, then the administration's primary objectives may not be well served.[48]

The judicial changes may be more long lasting, but even here, clear limits to what can be done exist. Many of the business-connected Reagan appointees will leave the bench over the next few years, leaving the next President room to appoint judges of a different (or similar) ideological profile. And, of course, Reagan was unable fundamentally to alter the ideological balance on the Supreme Court.

The effectiveness of these changes aside, do they add up to a coherent conception of federalism or a programme for devolution and decentralization? Not entirely. As was established, the clearest consequence of the 1981 and 1982 reforms by programme area was a *centralization* of administration in a range of income-maintenance programmes. Services provided under the new block grants were generally decentralized, but, in budgetary terms, these are much less significant than the welfare programmes. Moreover, as predicted in the last chapter, the block grants innovation led to a centralization of power within many states. It seems unlikely, then, that the net effect was to bring government in any sense 'closer to the people'. Further evidence of the administration's insensitivity towards any clear conception of federalism can be drawn from the 1986 decision to abolish GRS. GRS is the most decentralizing of the block-grants programmes, giving, as it does, great discretion to state governments on the use of federal funds.

Generally, the administrative and judicial appointment strategy favoured a decentralization of political and economic power. But even here, some centralization tendencies are apparent. With judicial appointments, for example, the administration favoured justices sympathetic to the creation or reinforcement of national standards in economic regulation. So a centralization of policy in such areas as banking and off-shore leasing was likely to result. Similarly, federal officials appointed to promote such policies by the administration are more likely to find themselves concentrating more rather than less power in Washington.

Conclusions

Reagan came into office with a very clear idea of what needed to be done to disengage federal power from the American economy and society. To achieve this, both legislative and an administrative/judicial strategy were necessary. For obvious reasons, the latter required a substantial centralization of power in the White House, even though the programmatic objectives were usually decentralist. But the urge to disengage was informed not so much by some coherent notion of American federalism as by a determination to reduce spending and the regulation of American society. If this meant devolving powers to state governments, so be it. If it meant centralizing administration, as with AFDC and food stamps, this too was a legitimate reform. By-passing Congress through administrative devices and the power of appointment did produce some important policy changes, but clear limits exist to the scope of such measures compared with innovative legislation. As far as intergovernmental affairs are concerned, it was an act of Congress, the 1981 Budget Reconciliation Act, which had the most impact on the American federal system. To be sure, all Presidents are now likely to utilize both legislative and administrative strategies, but non-legislative devices alone cannot transform the policy agenda. Reagan's attempt to challenge the very fundamentals of the New Deal regime failed in Congress. What was left was an opportunity to erode all those amendments and additions to the agenda resulting from the Great Society and its aftermath. This the administration successfully did, with those programmes designed to aid distressed cities and low-income citizens suffering most.[49]

While the administrative strategy's substantive programmatic impact was limited, it will almost certainly have longer-lasting consequences for American domestic policy in general and intergovernmental relations in particular. For one thing, Reagan's politicization of appointments and the centralization of power in the White House will in some form or other be passed on to the next President. A more liberal President could use the very same methods to shift the agenda back towards greater federal control and a stricter enforcement or reinterpretation of existing laws. Moreover, the continuing rapid turnover in both judicial and senior executive posts could give such a President considerable scope for such changes – especially given two terms in office. Furthermore, the Reagan administration produced this strategy quite independently of public or electoral opinion. Opinion polls have repeatedly shown a low level of support for most forms of social deregulation.[50] Indeed, a 1983 *Los Angeles Times* poll found that just 5% considered regulations 'too strict', but 42% thought they were 'not strong enough'.[51] A similar pattern exists with respect to most of the conscience issues – abortion, school prayer, equal rights, and affirmative action.[52] As was recorded in chapter 6, most Americans are singularly uninterested in federal/state relations. It is benefit levels that are important, not where the benefits come from. Only on bussing and most penal issues are the public in tune with the administration and neither of these achieved the status of major national issues between 1980 and 1986. If anything, the sometimes sensational publicity surrounding presidential appointments must have hurt rather than helped popularity and the President's re-election chances. But a few ill-advised senior appointments and nominations apart, the public are largely unmoved by administrative changes. The limits to such efforts are determined more by the internal dynamics of the policy system – the bureaucracy, state and local governments and organized interests – than by public opinion. 'Going Public', while a very necessary component of the President's legislative strategy, is less crucial when OMB's rule-making power is enhanced or the SES is used in a politically motivated way. Again, this should encourage future Presidents to use such devices – even given their limited scope for achieving the sort of radical change which national legislation can produce.

NOTES

1 Terry M. Moe, ' The Politicized Presidency', in John E. Chubb and Paul E. Peterson (eds.), *The New Direction in American Politics*, Washington, DC: The Brookings Institution, 1985, p. 235.
2 Richard P. Nathan, 'The Reagan Presidency in Domestic Affairs', in Fred I. Greenstein (ed.), *The Reagan Presidency: An Early Assessment*, Baltimore: The Johns Hopkins Press, 1983, pp. 48–81; Chester A. Newland, 'The Reagan Presidency: Limited Government and Political Administration', *Public Administration Review*, 43 (1983), 1–20; Chester A. Newland, 'Executive Office Policy Apparatus: Enforcing the Reagan Agenda', in Lester A. Salamon and Michael S. Lund (eds.), *The Reagan Presidency and the Governing of America*, Washington, DC: Urban Institute, 1984, pp. 125–68; Hugh Heclo, 'Comment: An Executive's Success Can Have Costs', in Salamon and Lund (eds.); *The Reagan Presidency and the Governing of America*, pp. 371–4; Bernard Rosen, 'Crisis in the U.S. Civil Service', *Public Administration Review*, 46 (1986), 207–14; Charles H. Levine, 'The Federal Government in the Year 2000: Administrative Legacies of the Reagan Years', *Public Administration Review*, 46 (1986), 195–204.
3 James P. Pfiffner, 'The Carter-Reagan Transition Team: Hitting the Ground Running', *Presidential Studies Quarterly*, 13 (1983), 625–6.
4 Ibid., 623–45; see also James P. Pfiffner, *The Strategic Presidency: Hitting the Ground Running*, Chicago: The Dorsey Press, 1988, pp. 16–18.
5 Newland, 'Executive Policy Apparatus', pp. 135–68.
6 Ibid., pp. 144–59.

7 Ibid., pp. 152–3.
8 Ibid., p. 160.
9 Newland, 'The Reagan Presidency', pp. 150–60.
10 Congressional Quarterly, *Weekly Report*, 'Budget Office Evolves into Key Policy Maker', 14 September 1985, pp. 1809–18; Newland, 'The Reagan Presidency'; Moe, 'The Politicized Presidency'; and sources cited. Larry Berman, *The Office of Management and Budget and the Presidency, 1921–1979*, Princeton, NJ: Princeton University Press, 1979, pp. 40–1.
11 *Congressional Quarterly*, 14 September 1985, Hearing Before the Sub-Committee on Intergovernmental Affairs, US Senate, *Oversight of the Office of Management and Budget Regulatory Review and Planning Process*, Washington, DC: US Government Printing Office, 28 January 1986.
12 Office of Management and Budget, Circular A-130, 12 December 1985 (Federal Register 52730, 12/24/85), Washington, DC, 1985.
13 Offices of Management and Budget, *Regulatory Program of the United States*, 1 April 1985, 31 March 1986, Washington, DC, 1986, pp. 2–3.
14 Committee on Governmental Affairs, US Senate, *Office of Management and Budget: Evolving Roles and Future Issues*, Washington, DC, US Government Printing Office, 1986, pp. 185–256.
15 Sub-Committee on Intergovernmental Affairs, US Senate, 1986, Testimony of James Miller.
16 Hearing Before the Sub-Committee on Oversight and Investigations, Energy and Commerce Committee, *OMB Review of EPA Regulations*, Washington, DC: US Government Printing Office, 1985.
17 OMB Watch, *Regulatory Review: OMB's New Public Disclosure Rules*, June 1986, pp. 1–9.
18 Richard L. Cole and David A. Caputo, 'Presidential Control of the Senior Civil Service: Assessing the Strategies of the Nixon Years', *American Political Science Review*, 73 (1979), 411.
19 Hearing into the Renomination of Donald J. Devine, US Senate, Committee on Government Affairs, April and June 1985, Washington, DC, US Government Printing Office, 1985.
20 Laurence E. Lynn, Jr., 'The Reagan Administration and the Penitent Bureaucracy', in Salamon and Lund (eds.), *The Reagan Presidency and the Governing of America*, p. 366.
21 Edie N. Goldenberg, 'The Permanent Government in an Era of Retrenchment and Redirection', in Salamon and Lund (eds.), *The Reagan Presidency and the Governing of America*, p. 402.
22 National Academy of Public Administration (NAPA), *Final Report of the Presidential Appointee Project*, Washington, DC: NAPA, 1985.
23 NAPA, *Final Report*.

24 Linda L. Fisher, 'Appointments and Presidential Control Importance of Role', paper delivered at the Annual Meeting of the Political Science Association, Washington, DC, 1985, table 4.

25 Joel D. Aberbach and Bert A. Rockman, 'From Nixon's Problem to Reagan's Achievement – The Federal Executive Reexamined', paper prepared for the Conference on the Reagan Legacy, 24–26 May 1988, Institute of Governmental Affairs, University of California, Davis, p. 10.

26 Aberbach and Rockman, 'From Nixon's Problem to Reagan's Achievement', p. 10.

27 Ibid., table 2A.

28 Ronald Randall, 'Presidential Power versus Bureaucratic Intransigence: The influence of the Nixon Administration on Welfare Policy', *American Political Science Review*, 73 (1979), 808.

29 Frederick A. Waldstein, 'The Impact of the Reagan Administration on the Federal Judiciary Working Notes', paper presented at the 1986 annual meeting of the American Politics Group, Oxford, January 1986, p. 1.

30 Sheldon Goldman, 'Reorganizing the Judiciary: The First Team Appointments', *Judicature*, 68 (1985), 313–29.

31 Ibid., 315.

32 Ibid., 315.

33 Ibid., table 1 and 2, pp. 318 and 322.

34 Ibid., table 1; *Congressional Quarterly*, *Weekly Report*, 'Reagan Seen Gaining Control of Entire Federal Judiciary', 8 December 1984, pp. 3075–6.

35 Waldstein, 'The Impact of the Reagan Administration', pp. 4–9.

36 C. H. Lovell, 'Intergovernmental Regulatory Changes Under the Reagan Administration', *Final Report*, National Science Foundation SES-84001, University of California, Riverside, June 1984, chapter 6. The following summary is based on this report.

37 See Tom Joe and Cheryl Rogers, *By the Few For the Few: The Reagan Welfare Legacy*, Lexington, MA: D. C. Heath, 1975; Peter Gottschalk, 'Retrenchment in Anti-Poverty Programs: Lessons for the Future', in B. B. Kymlicka and Jean V. Matthews (eds.), *The Reagan Revolution?*, Chicago: The Dorsey Press, 1988, pp. 131–61.

38 Judith Feder and Jack Hadley, 'Cutbacks, Recession and Hospitals' Care for the Urban Poor', in George E. Peterson and Carol W. Lewis, *Reagan and the Cities*, Washington DC, Urban Institute, 1986, pp. 37–61.

39 For a discussion, see Paul E. Peterson and Mark C. Rom, 'Federalism and Welfare Reform: The Determinants of Interstate Differences in Poverty Rates and Benefit Levels', Paper for delivery at the annual meeting of the American Political Science Association, Chicago, 1987, pp. 15–17.

40 Richard P. Nathan, Fred C. Doolittle and associates, *Reagan and the States*, Princeton, NJ: Princeton University Press, 1987, chapter 15.

41 See George C. Eads and Michael Fix (eds.), *The Reagan Regulatory Strategy*, Washington DC: Urban Institute, 1984, chapter by Robert A. Leone and Michael Fix.
42 See note 16.
43 For a summary, see Thomas Ferguson and Joel Rogers, *Right Turn: The Decline of the Democrats and the Future of American Politics*, chapter 4.
44 Hearings Before the Sub-Committee on the Civil Service, Post Office and Civil Service Committee, US House of Representatives, *The Senior Executive Service*, Washington DC, US Government Printing Office, 1984, Testimony of Charles A. Bowsher, Comptroller General of the United States, and Hugh Heclo, Howard University.
45 Hearings Before the Sub-Committee on the Civil Service, Testimony of Charles A. Bowsher, pp. 2–5.
46 Ibid., appendices 1–28.
47 Hearings Before the Sub-Committee on the Civil Service, Testimony of Hugh Heclo, pp. 336–41.
48 Hearings Before the Sub-Committee on the Civil Service, Testimony of Hugh Heclo and Hale Champion, pp. 333–5.
49 See Peterson and Lewis, *Reagan and the Cities*; Wolman and Teitelbaum, 'Interest Groups'.
50 CBS/*New York Times*, Polls 1983 and 1984, reported in Ferguson and Rogers, *Right Turn*, pp. 13–18.
51 Reported in Ferguson and Rogers, *Right Turn*, p. 15.
52 Ferguson and Rogers, *Right Turn*, pp. 16–18.

8   The presidency and regime fragmentation

Modern perspectives on American political development point to the ways in which Presidents can exploit critical periods in history marked by re-aligning elections, major shifts in elite perceptions of the prevailing order, and the eventual replacement of old regimes with new.[1] As indicated in chapter 1, the election of 1932 represented just such a change as, some have argued, did the election of 1980.[2] During such periods, Presidents have unusual freedom to repudiate the old order, to make major institutional innovations and to change the nature of the political agenda. As Stephen Skowronek, the leading exponent of this view, has convincingly argued, such Presidents may fail in the programmatic sense (Roosevelt's New Deal did not cure the Great Depression), but succeed in terms of providing administrations with great discretion over the terms and outcome of political debate. They can therefore, successfully engage in a 'Politics of Reconstruction'.[3]

Within established political regimes Presidents have much less potential for producing policy changes independent of societal and institutional constraints. Even so, for those incumbents fortunate enough to find themselves able to exploit what Skowronek calls the 'Politics of Articulation', when the prevailing regime remains strong and the President and his party are keen to develop it in some direction or other, the potential for policy leadership remains high. Hence according to this thesis, Lyndon Johnson could, in the guise of the Great Society, extend the New Deal regime according to his own priorities and preferences.[4] Other Presidents, such as Jimmy Carter and Richard Nixon, may find themselves somewhat at odds with the times either because (as with Nixon) they were elected during a regime with which they were ideologically out of tune, or (as with Carter) when the majority party's hold on the regime was deteriorating rapidly.[5] Although not explicitly invoked by Skowronek, the Reagan experience could well correspond to a new period of re-construction, with the President able to change the agenda, execute institutional reforms and repudiate the inadequacies of the old order.

While this general scheme has a certain intuitive appeal and empirical application, the evidence from earlier chapters suggests that as an explanation of the 1964–87 period it needs important modifications. As always with presidential scholar-ship, a major problem is separating out the personalities and capacities of individual incumbents from the structural con-straints imposed by the prevailing regime. Johnson un-doubtedly enjoyed a favourable environment in which to produce new policies compared with Nixon, but Johnson was better equipped than Nixon to exercise some independent influence on this environment. And if both Kennedy and Johnson experienced the same regime, why was Johnson able to make so much more of it (in domestic policy, at least) than Kennedy? The answer must relate to specific – and random – historical events such as the assassination, disarray among the Republicans in 1964, and the capacities and career experiences of the two Presidents.

Moreover, once the concept of a political regime is accepted, the tendency is to underestimate the independent policy role of Presidents like Nixon and Carter, who were either out of tune with the regime or unfortunate enough to be elected while the regime was in a state of (alleged) terminal decline. As we saw, Nixon, at least, advanced the policy agenda considerably and he did so in ways largely independent of his eventually fatal political problems. Again, Watergate was a specific political event relating to the particular way in which Nixon operated. It had little or nothing to do with the constraints imposed by a Democratic Congress, the power of liberal-interest groups, courts or public opinion. If such presidencies are effectively to be dismissed as failures or aberrations, the substantive content of policies and programmes they produced, including how these contributed to the agendas of subsequent administrations, will tend either to be underestimated or ignored altogether.

Finally, and most seriously, the whole concept of regime change may be inappropriate in an age of weak parties, fragmented interest representation and a media-infused politics. The eight-year experience of the Reagan administration is instructive here. Reagan failed to destroy the policies of the New Deal but he made important inroads into those of the Great Society. Public opinion, although shifting against welfare provision during the 1970s, actually shifted back towards support for welfare during the Reagan years.[6] This hardly looks like a successful repudiation of the old order. As indicated in chapters 6 and 7, Reagan's New Federalism and social deregulation policies were not popular with the public, nor were they substantiated by an important social movement based on party, region or social class. They were, above all, products of the administration itself. If politics continues to be characterized by fragmentation and weak parties, this experience may become typical rather than exceptional. In this sense, Nixon and Carter, rather than being primarily the victims of the regime environment, may have been as much the victims of their own shortcomings and personal failings.

None of this is to deny that all the Presidents under discussion in this volume have been constrained by the New Deal regime. As was stressed in chapter 1, although the social and political forces responsible for this regime have declined, the pattern of policies with which it is usually identified have not. There are three major reasons for this. First, as far as social policy was concerned, the New Deal created programmes which were broadly quite compatible with American political culture. Social security benefits would be based on regressive earnings-related payroll taxes. Welfare would be provided only for those unable to help themselves (mothers with dependent children) – and even then on an *ad hoc* basis. There was little in this scheme to challenge contemporary notions of self-reliance. When, later in history, new social policy programmes were introduced, they were more often than not organized on a similar basis. Hence Medicare became part of the social security system, while Medicaid became a welfare programme.[7] Second, the specific political and institutional factors which accounted for this pattern and for the particular way in which the states were incorporated into the system, prevails to this day. Mainly southern and western conservatives in Congress continue to oppose major welfare reforms and have been responsible for the maintenance – and even strengthening – of the federal/state matching-grants system typical of AFDC and Medicaid. To be sure, these and related programmes have grown enormously since the 1930s but the basic pattern remains largely intact. Third, those departures from the pattern which have occurred have usually been the result of presidential initiatives. In the case of Lyndon Johnson, the relevant programmes – the War on Poverty and Model Cities – were designed effectively to by-pass institutional constraints, but not to challenge prevailing notions of self-reliance. Both failed to achieve their objectives, but helped inspire the growth and creation of New-Deal-style programmes such as AFDC, Medicare and Medicaid.

It was Richard Nixon, however, whose policies were the most innovative and, ultimately, constituted the greatest move away from New Deal programme design. The EITC was a limited form of negative income tax available to all poorer working families. More important in terms of funding was SSI, which established a federal minimum level of income for the old. Both these measures could be regarded as the policy remnants of Nixon's failed FAP. Both still exist and, in the income maintenance area at least, are the closest the United States has to the guaranteed income, universalist policies typical of virtually all other developed capitalist states.

Revenue sharing was innovative in a different way. It did represent a break with the past by establishing the principle of a no-strings attached federal block grant for state and local governments. But unlike the New Deal measures, the primary recipients would be governments rather than individuals. In this sense it was the first attempt to institutionalize inter-governmental aid in the United States. Although revenue sharing has since been abolished, block grants as a percentage of all intergovernmental aid have increased steadily since 1971.[8]

Jimmy Carter's administration had the least independent effect on the federal role, not only because of a changing regime environment, but also because he lacked the necessary leadership and policy management skills. In terms of our discussion, his most important contribution was a devotion to fiscal rectitude which in combination with a changing societal and Congressional mood enabled him to begin a retrenchment in federal welfare and intergovernmental spending which Reagan was to continue.

Ronald Reagan's objective was a near-complete disengage-ment of the federal government from the social policy realm. He was personally committed to a dismantling of the New Deal and Great Society. He failed in both projects, although he was able substantially to reduce federal spending on welfare and intergovernmental aid. As was argued, this was not the result of the sort of re-alignment of voters and values which mark a regime change. Instead it reflected the personal ideology and priorities of the President and his immediate staff.

In sum, although the New Deal policy regime remains largely intact it has been modified and adapted as a result of a series of presidential initiatives. Congress, the courts and other political actors have also played a major role, although only rarely has Congress been able to set the agenda in ways which signal a redirection in a range of domestic policies. Instead, Congress has either been carried along by presidential leader-ship (as with Johnson and the early Reagan years), or it has fought a rearguard action against presidential initiatives (as with many of the Nixon and Carter policies). Either reaction can lead to the conclusion that Congress has acted in-dependently, but in most cases the agenda has been set by the President. This is not to deny that the national legislature can sometimes pass a bill which is apparently out of tune with the prevailing presidential agenda. In 1988, Congress extended coverage under Medicare to include catastrophic illness. This was a Congressional not a presidential initiative, and it was hardly reconcilable with the budget-cutting in social policy associated with the Reagan administration. Similarly, Congress blocked a number of Johnson initiatives during the 1960s, including the 1966 Civil Rights Bill. The Johnson years will be remembered not for this, however, but for the administration's legislative successes.

Only during the 1974–6 period did Congress successfully set the domestic policy agenda with the passage of a number of major anti-recession measures over President Ford's veto. But these were exceptional years characterized by a greatly emasculated presidency, and an unusually assertive Congress.

The presidency as autonomous policy maker

These examples of relatively autonomous presidential actions take on a special significance if, as has been implied, American politics is now characterized by what could be called *regime fragmentation*. Elements of the New Deal order remain both in policy terms and in political alignments. But others have long since passed into history. As a source of social and economic programmes reflecting the interests of a dominant section of voters – if not a coherent social movement – the Democratic Party has declined. But no new party grouping or movement has emerged to take its place. Instead, politics seems charac- terized by shifting and often ephemeral political coalitions based on constellations of special and single-interest-group power. According to the bargaining model of American politics outlined in chapter 1, these developments have weakened the presidency. So Presidents are increasingly constrained by a fragmented political environment and by the absence of the sort of connective tissue engendered by party cues. Although by some measures this seems indisputable, the new politics of fragmentation also offers Presidents opportu- nities for increased autonomy – especially in programme design. Evidence from earlier chapters supports this claim. Specifically, we can conclude the following:

(1)   With the exception of Jimmy Carter, Presidents exercised a high degree of control over initial programme design. Policy processes were for the most part highly internalized. And in Carter's case a more open style was a conscious choice rather than something imposed from outside. Political parties played virtually no part in this process – indeed Presidents seemed intent on specifically excluding party leaders from decision-making processes. Instead, Johnson, Nixon and Reagan depended in the main on personally appointed aides and experts who were given considerable freedom over the details of programme design.

Permanent officials also played a relatively minor role. Again, Carter stands out as the exception, mainly because he delegated so much to his Cabinet Secretaries, who in turn were obliged to turn to their officials for help. Permanent officials played no part in the early Great Society measures, were more involved in Nixon's Family Assistance Plan – but not as the initiators of basic concepts and values – and were almost by definition excluded from Reagan's New Federalism plans. Of course, new policy ideas are not the exclusive property of one group or interest. Increasingly they are common currency. But if, as many have claimed, the bureaucracy wields unjustified power in the United States, then it should have much greater agenda-setting capacity than is suggested by the evidence presented in earlier chapters. Indeed, the low morale and rapid turnover of officials characteristic of the Reagan administration seems more indicative of bureaucratic weakness than strength. More credence could be attached to the view that executive decision-making in the United States is dominated by experts and professors.[9] Certainly Johnson and Nixon depended on such people for much of their policy intelligence, and all the Presidents elevated professors to high positions in the White House. But these were presidential choices. They were not imposed on incumbents by outside groups and interests.

(2)   The question of expert advice relates to the coherence of public policies. In theory, at least, newly appointed Presidents with clear policy objectives should be able to exploit those experts whose theories and perspectives best fit these objectives. Such was the case with Johnson and his Keynesian advisors and Reagan with his New Right advisors. As was catalogued, however, the ideological marriage of programmatic President to the generators of ideas does not necessarily produce coherent policies. Reagan's New Federalism made little sense in terms either of prevailing economic or political theory. Johnson's War on Poverty and associated measures were ill thought out in terms of how they would relate to the economic and political realities of urban America. Carter's policies suffered from his preference for open decision-making. They were, as a result, often unworkable compromises. Most of the Nixon measures were, in contrast, coherent and carefully worked out. For although constrained by an inherited Great Society agenda, Nixon did appoint a group of high-quality advisors, who, in his first term at least, were given great freedom to advance the President's policy objectives. Congress eventually killed the centrepiece of the Nixon reforms – his Family Assistance Plan – but this failure stemmed in part from Nixon's own lack of commitment to the measure.

As was indicated, there are occasions when the coherence of particular measures or packages of measures relates to their eventual legislative or implementation success. So, quite apart from the intrinsic intellectual importance of well-thought-out policies, coherence can be critical in more mundane political terms. Again, newly elected Presidents have an opportunity unique in the contemporary American political experience to formulate coherent and consistent policies. They are less constrained by party and past political commitments in this general area than they were thirty or forty years ago. To be sure, Congress, courts, organized interests, state and local governments and public opinion will later almost certainly compromise plans. But the essentials of a new agenda will have been set by the President and his advisors.

Moreover, an accumulating body of knowledge on a wide range of policies now exists, which, while imperfect and often inconsistent, does provide some criteria by which to distinguish good from bad. Members of Congress can make these distinctions as well as Presidents. Take welfare. Expert opinion from all but those on the far right now agrees that welfare benefits should be federalized or nationalized.[10] Similarly, opinion on the sorting out of functions between different levels of government is much nearer to consensus today than it was ten or fifteen years ago.[11] Formulating and implementing major reforms in these areas will certainly not be easy, but the potential for bold and coherent executive-led policy-making remains high. Put another way, coherent policies are more likely to conform to some conception of the public interest than those characterized by confusion and internal inconsistencies. Few would argue that the existing system of welfare provision in the United States serves the public interest. So the need for such reforms is urgent.[12]

(3)   Presidents have much greater freedom over the use of what have been called adaptation strategies than previously. This also relates to regime fragmentation. Party cues on the appointment of officials and judges are now quite weak, leaving Presidents with more choice over whom they appoint and for what purpose. More importantly, institutional reforms which have been centralizing power in the White House at least since the creation of the Executive Office in 1939, continue apace. Most recently, the 1978 Civil Service Act and 1980 Paperwork Reduction Act have given Presidents new and important powers over civil-service recruitment and mobility and over OMB's rule-making powers. Given these and other administrative control devices, it is not surprising that Presidents now use them as complementary to legislation, rather than as alternatives following failures in Congress. The transition from Nixon, who favoured the latter course, to Carter and Reagan, who favoured the former, is clear.

Yet as we saw, both with Nixon and Reagan the programmatic consequences of administrative strategies have been relatively small compared with those resulting from legislation. In Nixon's case, a failure to define clearly what his programmatic objectives were probably explains the limited outcome of his strategy. While no such criticism could be levelled at Reagan, in the federalism and welfare areas at least, it was the 1981 Budget Reconciliation Act which resulted in the most critical changes. And although it is too early to judge the full results of his administrative and judicial strategies, they will probably be modest, given bureaucratic resistance, and above all the importance of the much more established rules and procedures which Congress legislates and the courts adjudicate. As Elizabeth Sanders has put it 'Without control of Congress, it [the Reagan administration] was unable to codify its revolution in statutes, and without statutory legitimation even the most powerful administrative strategy will yield only transient changes in the relationship between government and society.'[13]

We can conclude that while sometimes important – perhaps especially so for Presidents on the right who rarely advocate increases in domestic spending – adaptation strategies must take second place to Presidents' legislative agendas.

Leadership, the presidency and the American state

Both the bargaining model of the presidency and more state-centred approaches acknowledge the importance of leadership in any study of the institution. Both are pessimistic about the current prospects for the exercise of presidential leadership, however. In the absence of a new political regime, leadership potential is seriously circumscribed. And successful bargaining is hardly compatible with the implicit chaos of the interest group liberalism and 'democratic distemper' which the bargaining school claim are now the hallmarks of the system. Yet in very different ways Lyndon Johnson and Ronald Reagan exercised effective presidential leadership over the social-policy agenda. Johnson's ideological commitment led to a greatly expanded federal role – albeit largely within the limits set by the New Deal regime. Reagan's ideological commitment to disengage also led to dramatic changes – although these fell short of a dismantling of the New Deal and the Great Society. While Johnson's achievements may, as Skowronek claims, have been greatly aided by a highly amenable regime environment, the same cannot be said for Reagan. Indeed, by some criteria, Reagan modified the agenda virtually through the exercise of ideology and leadership alone – a phenomenon which may apply to any President incumbent during a period of regime fragmentation.

Potentially, a President able to combine leadership, policy coherence and a carefully worked out adaptation strategy should be able to achieve major successes during his first term. Whether a President has a mandate for such a combination seems largely irrelevant. Voters often vote against candidates rather than for the eventual winner (as in 1980 and 1984) and whatever the size of their victories, modern Presidents will face an independent and potentially hostile Congress, whether controlled by their own party or the opposition's. That in such an environment leadership is crucial is axiomatic. Carter was unable to exercise the appropriate leadership, either within the White House, or when dealing with Congress. Nixon's first term was characterized by a much clearer conception of how policy should be formulated within the White House, but he failed to carry his commitments through to Congress and the public. The quality of Reagan's first-term policy-formulation process was relatively high and his subsequent commitment outside the White House unquestioned. Where Reagan failed was on the question of substantive policy content or coherence. His New Federalism proposals made little economic or political sense – a fact that was quickly recognized on the Hill and among state and local leaders.

Naturally leadership involves persuasion and bargaining with Congress, interest groups, the bureaucracy and ultimately with the American people. In this sense the bargaining model of American politics is appropriate to the study of the presidency. But leadership also involves management skills, the ability to order priorities, to grasp the intellectual complexities of substantive policy issues and to present these to the mass of the American people. During the crucial first year of a presidency, it is these skills, not the talents associated with traditional political bargaining, which will be crucial in shaping the policy agenda, not just for that year but for the whole presidency.

In a recent paper Theodore Lowi labelled the American welfare state 'the ethical equivalent of a European state'.[14] So, in the absence of any political authority representing a hierarchy of values above and beyond society, the New Deal social policy measures, which largely displaced private with public responsibility, reflected broad societal preferences at the time. Later, much expanded and modified, these laws came to represent a scale of values based on rights and expressed by public authority.[15] Lowi dislikes the ways in which the welfare state has developed and particularly the tendency towards the provision of benefits according to decentralized discretionary criteria as opposed to the 'rule of law'. He further pleads the case for fundamental reform 'based upon a fundamental analysis with a fundamental critique'.[16] From our earlier analysis it is clear that the only political authority capable of such an analysis, and the translation of ensuing reforms into public policy, is the presidency. In this sense it is the presidency which most closely resembles the state in the United States. The fact that the White House is now more isolated from the pressures of party and has acquired a range of centralist institutional powers to aid the formulation and implementation of policy adds weight to this claim. To be sure it is a highly personalized conception of the state but no other institution in the American system has either the same degree of autonomy or the moral authority to set the agenda and to re-order values and resources in both the public and private realms. The political priorities and ideological preferences of the Johnson, Nixon and Reagan administrations constituted the single most important explanation of the rapid expansion, consolidation and then reduction in federal grants-in-aid to individuals, states and localities in the 1964–87 period. None were able or willing to institute fundamental reform, however. In an era of the regime fragmentation, the opportunity for such a transformation remains. It is one which future Presidents have the responsibility to exploit.

NOTES

1 See Stephen Skowronek, 'Presidential Leadership in Political Time', in Michael Nelson (ed.), *The Presidency and the Political System*, Washington, DC: Congressional Quarterly Press, 2nd edn, 1988, pp. 115–59; also his 'Notes on the Presidency in the Political Order', in Karen Orren and Stephen Skowronek (eds.), *Studies in American Political Development, Vol. 1*, New Haven, CT: Yale University Press, 1986, pp. 286–302.
2 See, for example, Morris P. Fiorina and John A. Ferejohn, 'Incumbency and Re-alignment in Congressional Elections', in John E. Chubb and Paul E. Peterson (eds.), *The New Direction in American Politics*, Washington, DC: The Brookings Institution, 1985, pp. 91–115.
3 Stephen Skowronek, 'Notes on the Presidency in the Political Order', in Orren and Skowronek (eds.), *Studies in American Political Development, Vol. 1*, pp. 294–6.
4 Ibid., pp. 299–301.
5 Ibid., pp. 296–9.
6 On the continuing salience of New Deal issues to voters and the myth of America's turn to the right under Reagan, see Thomas Ferguson and Joel Rogers, *The Decline of the Democrats and the Future of American Politics*, New York: Hill and Wang, chapter 1. Evidence of a shift of public opinion is presented in James R. Kluegel and Eliot R. Smith, *Beliefs about Inequality: America's Views of What Is and What Ought to Be*, New York: Aldine De Gruyter, 1986, chapter 6. One study shows that the public were more liberal on the social issues by 1986 than they were at the end of the Carter years; see Robert Y. Shapiro, Kelly D. Patterson, Judith Russell and John T. Young, 'The Polls: Public Assistance', *Public Opinion Quarterly*, 51 (1987), 118–22.
7 For a discussion of American attitudes to welfare and how enduring they have been, see Hugh Heclo, 'General Welfare and the Two American Political Traditions', *Political Science Quarterly*, 101:2 (1986), 179–96.
8 For a discussion, see Richard P. Nathan, Fred C. Coolitle and Associates, *Reagan and the States*, Princeton, NJ Princeton University Press, 1987, chapters 2 and 3.

9   As suggested by Samuel H. Beer in 'Federalism, Nationalism and Democracy in America', *American Political Science Review*, 72 (1978), 9–21; and by Henry J. Aaron, *Politics and the Professors: The Great Society in Perspective*, Washington, DC: The Brookings Institution, 1978.

10 Studies from the ideologically distinctive Brookings Institution and American Enterprise Institute agree on this conclusion. See Claude E. Barfield, *Rethinking Federalism: Block Grants and Federal State and Local Responsibilities*, Washington, DC: American Enterprise Institute, 1981, chapter 6; Paul E. Peterson and Mark C. Rom, 'Federal Welfare Performance: the Determinants of Interstate Differences in Poverty Rules and Benefit Funds', Paper before the Annual Conference of the American Political Science Association, The Palmer House, Chicago, September 3–6, 1987.

11 See Paul E. Peterson, Barry G. Rabe and Kenneth K. Wong, *When Federalism Works*, Washington, DC: The Brookings Institution, 1986, chapter 9.

12 The bargaining model of American politics implies that most policy areas are characterized by chaos and inefficiency which tends to lead scholars away even from suggesting major reforms. Systematic evidence in support of policy chaos is scant, however. Probably only those policy areas involving moral absolutes, such as abortion and capital punishment, are not amenable to some sort of rational analysis, critique and reform.

13 Elizabeth Sanders, 'The Presidency and the Bureaucratic State', in Nelson (ed.), *The Presidency and the Political System*, pp. 402–3.

14 Theodore J. Lowi, 'The Welfare State: Ethical Foundations and Constitutional Remedies', *Political Science Quarterly*, 101 (1986), 197–220.

15 Ibid., 214–16.

16 Ibid., 220.

Index

For EU product safety concerns, contact us at Calle de José Abascal, 56–1°,
28003 Madrid, Spain or eugpsr@cambridge.org.

www.ingramcontent.com/pod-product-compliance
Ingram Content Group UK Ltd.
Pitfield, Milton Keynes, MK11 3LW, UK
UKHW010043140625
459647UK00012BA/1569